SOWING THE
SEEDS OF VICTORY

SOWING THE SEEDS OF VICTORY

American Gardening Programs of World War I

Rose Hayden-Smith

McFarland & Company, Inc., Publishers
Jefferson, North Carolina

LIBRARY OF CONGRESS CATALOGUING-IN-PUBLICATION DATA

Hayden-Smith, Rose, 1960–
    Sowing the seeds of victory : American gardening programs of World War I / Rose Hayden-Smith.
    p.   cm.
    Includes bibliographical references and index.

    ISBN 978-0-7864-7020-4 (softcover : acid free paper) ∞
    ISBN 978-1-4766-1586-8 (ebook)

    1. Victory gardens—United States—History. 2. Vegetable gardening—United States—History—20th century. 3. National War Garden Commission—History. 4. Women's Land Army (United States)—History. 5. United States. School Garden Army—History. 6. School gardens—United States—History—20th century. 7. World War, 1914–1918—Food supply—United States. I. Title. II. Title: American gardening programs of World War I.
    SB321.H37 2014
    338.1'75—dc23   2014007874

BRITISH LIBRARY CATALOGUING DATA ARE AVAILABLE

© 2014 Rose Hayden-Smith. All rights reserved

No part of this book may be reproduced or transmitted in any form or by any means, electronic or mechanical, including photocopying or recording, or by any information storage and retrieval system, without permission in writing from the publisher.

On the cover: World War I poster "Sow the seeds of victory!"—artist James Montgomery Flagg, ca. 1918 (Library of Congress)

Printed in the United States of America

McFarland & Company, Inc., Publishers
  Box 611, Jefferson, North Carolina 28640
    www.mcfarlandpub.com

For Natalie
Wherever your path leads, your immense talents,
passion and love will surely fill some part
of the world's deep hunger and need.
I love you to the moon and back.

———————————

For Daryl Wagar
Civic horticulturalist,
family man, friend

Table of Contents

Acknowledgments — ix
Preface: Sowing the Seeds of Victory — 1
Introduction: Summary of the National War Gardening Effort — 5

One: The Garden Revolution — 11
Two: In the Furrows of Freedom — 32
Three: The United States School Garden Army — 72
Four: Propaganda, Posters, Promotion and Memory — 98
Five: The Pennsylvania School of Horticulture for Women — 121
Six: "Sisters of the Soil": The Woman's Land Army of America — 143
Seven: Mobilization for Nutritional Defense — 181

Conclusion: Demobilization, the Trajectory of the Programs and Public Policy Implications for Today — 192
Chapter Notes — 215
Bibliography — 234
Index — 247

Acknowledgments

Good soil is the foundation of a good garden, and I owe deepest thanks for improving the foundation of my work to many people.

I am particularly grateful to the faculty at the University of California Santa Barbara History Department, including Dr. Randy Bergstrom, Dr. Lisa Jacobson, Dr. Ann Marie Plane, Dr. Mary Furner, Dr. Laura Kalman, Dr. Patricia Cohen, and Dr. John Majewski. I also offer gratitude to the friends who participated in UCSB's graduate survey course in United States history in 2002–2003 and to my colleagues at the University of California Agriculture and Natural Resources, particularly Dr. Daniel Desmond, who guided me into lines of applied research that have been avocational in nature and rewarding in ways I could not have imagined. Special thanks to my friend and fellow historian Dr. Maeve Devoy, who provided support at key moments and would not let me fail.

I am also extremely grateful to the W.K. Kellogg Foundation, the Thomas Jefferson Institute, and the Institute of Agriculture and Trade Policy for their generous support in the form of a Food and Society Policy Fellowship and the ongoing opportunities they have provided to improve and further my work. Particular thanks are due to Susan Roberts, who challenged me to apply it in new ways and to see the broader public policy implications of my historical research. Deepest appreciation and affection to the Fellows of the W.K. Kellogg Foundation's Food and Society Policy program: your work has inspired my own and you continue to support me in vital ways. You are family to me.

Historians build upon the work of other historians. In the course of a project, we often draw upon the work of many others—both living and dead—to inform our own work. I have had the privilege of meeting or speaking with some of those I most admire; their generosity, enthusiasm, and encouragement have been greatly appreciated. In no particular order, thanks to Dr. David Danbom, Dr. David Kennedy, Dr. David Glassberg, Dr. Amy Bentley, Dr.

Laura Lawson, Dr. Robert Wiebe, Dr. David Potter, Dr. James Machor, Dr. Katherine Jellison, Dr. Stephanie Carpenter (who generously shared materials very early in my project), Dr. William Breen, Dr. Christopher Capozzola, Dr. William Cronon, Dr. William Leuchtenburg, Dr. Eldon Eisenach, Dr. Melanie Simo, Dr. Witold Rybczynski, Dr. Robyn Muncy, Dr. Douglas Sackman, Dr. Robert Cuff, Dr. Harvey Levenstein, Dr. Margaret Rossiter, Dr. Nancy Cott, Valencia Libby, Elaine Weiss, Catherine Kipp, Rae Eighmey, and Martha Nolan.

Gardeners and those who study gardening are the most generous and kind people. To the many librarians, archivists, horticultural experts and gardeners who supported this endeavor: thank you. I am especially indebted to a local institution, the Museum of Ventura County, which works in my community to educate about the importance of agriculture in all our lives. I have visited dozens of gardens (and gardeners) each year, all across the United States: home gardens, gardens small and large, informal and formal, school gardens, botanical gardens, country gardens and city gardens, gardens for children, gardens for seniors, gardens at workplaces, community gardens, gardens that are public-purposed, and farming enterprises that are transforming the food system. Each growing place I visited provided a profoundly moving experience and demonstrated that the Victory Garden model is alive and well.

The roots of this project run deep and are highly personal. My deepest roots are in my family, friends and community. Warmest thanks to my husband, Bill, who mobilized the resources of our family's home front over a period of many years to make this book possible. Our daughter, Natalie, was also helpful and often traveled with me on research trips. She and her peers provided opportunities to share my interests in gardening and food systems education as they were growing up. When I began to study this topic, Natalie was small and stood on a chair to copy pages of books and journal articles for me at UCSB's library. Time marches on; it was she who typed the final citations in my dissertation, which was the genesis of this book.

While those who have worked with me are a critical component of this book and are reflected in it, any errors, omissions or failings are wholly mine.

Preface: Sowing the Seeds of Victory

During World War I, students at the small Ann Street Elementary School in my community of Ventura, California, raised two tons of potatoes in their school garden. Their work, replicated in thousands of schools across the United States, had its roots in a broader national imperative that mobilized citizens of all ages to help boost wartime agricultural production and encourage consumption of local foods. While these national programs encouraging home, school, and community gardening reflected cultural, social, and political conditions specific to the World War I era, they established a public practice that has been revisited during war and other trying times. Today they contribute to national sustainable food systems initiatives.

This book explores the implications of America's national gardening and food production programs during World War I in a historical context. The programs provided models for community food production not only in a later war (World War II), but also in a contemporary setting—today—cast as an analogue of war. Perhaps it is not so remarkable that the histories of these wartime food projects are seriously considered now within the context of creating a more sustainable food system in America. Public commentary, advocacy and scholarship have heightened concern for the public health, environmental, and strategic aspects of food production. Scholars, policy makers and producers recognize that the sustainability of agriculture is a serious challenge not only to our nation's security, but also to the public welfare generally, and not only nationally, but also globally.

Never have food and agricultural policy discussion been so mainstream and never have food and agriculture been connected more explicitly. Early in President Barack Obama's first administration, a department in the USDA was reorganized into the National Institute for Food and Agriculture (NIFA), echoing the organization of the National Institutes of Health. *TIME* devoted an issue to "The Real Cost of Cheap Food" on August 31, 2009. Variations of the phrase "agricultural sustainability and public welfare" garner millions of hits on Internet search engines. The phrase "agricultural sustainability and national security" also nets millions of hits, demonstrating that, on some level, the public does understand that a safe and secure food system is essential to national security.

Popular authors such as Michael Pollan, Raj Patel and Anna Lappe have brought the complex issues surrounding food systems and agricultural sustainability to the general public through books, social media and mainstream television. Pollan appeared on *Oprah* in an episode entitled "Food 101" in 2010. The 2009 Academy Award nominees for best documentary included Robert Kenner's *Food, Inc.*, a film about the industrialized food system in America. In 2011, England's Prince Charles delivered a speech entitled "The Future of Food" in Washington, D.C. It has been reprinted and distributed broadly since as a pamphlet evoking earlier forms of broadly disseminated political commentary (striving to offer "common sense" regarding sustainable food systems, much as Thomas Paine offered *Common Sense* in the early days of the American Revolution). A food revolution is afoot.

Much of the current concern about food relates to the question of where food originates. First Lady Michelle Obama's public work has focused on addressing issues related to food systems as well as to childhood obesity. She recently shared her experiences with the White House kitchen garden in her best-selling first book, *American Grown*, published in 2012.

Today's explosive interest in food and agriculture had a counterpart in the public's enthusiastic embrace of gardening programs in the early twentieth century. If advocates now argue that citizens need education about food systems in order to consider the health, economic, ecological, and social issues involved in food production, processing, distribution, and consumption, advocates one hundred years ago intended their gardening and land army programs to have similar educative effects. The renewed attention to war gardening fits current advocates' sense that history holds lessons, that Americans should understand not only how agriculture shaped our nation's history, but also how it has influenced lives in myriad interconnected ways. That understanding, they argue, can be regained by deliberate reengagement in the process of food production.

Those who encourage participation in the food system today aim to educate, but they are also trying to transform the food system. Food system activists seek to contribute to food sustainability, and, by extension, the sustainability of the cultural, social, and economic life that is tied closely but far too invisibly to food production. They seek to create transparency around the food system, to create a national ethos that supports a sustainable and just food system, and to create alternatives for consumers. The creators of the wartime programs in the last century had comparable intentions: to have all citizens, especially children, recognize the importance of agriculture in their lives; to create better citizen-consumers; to promote good decisions as policy makers; and to encourage Americans to lead a healthy personal and community life that twenty-first century advocates would term "sustainable."

During World War I, agricultural activists, educators, legislators and policymakers made great efforts to assure that these things happened in America. Those efforts are once again informing current public policy in important ways, as today's leaders employ past wartime gardening programs as a roadmap to a more sustainable future.

Introduction: Summary of the National War Gardening Effort

Sometimes, to move forward, we must look back. Our past can inform our present. The period of United States involvement in World War I, from 1917 to 1919, is one of the most relevant to understanding and informing current work on food systems in America. During World War I, the federal government—urged by and in partnership with private organizations and a strong grassroots effort—promoted several national programs related to gardening and agriculture, programs which encouraged Americans to express loyalty and patriotism for the nation through voluntarism in food production and conservation efforts. While many Americans are familiar with the Victory Gardens of World War II, few realize that their origin can be found in the Liberty (and later Victory) Garden program that enjoyed widespread participation during World War I.[1] Educational efforts—some led by American food czar Herbert Hoover—focused on food production and preservation, elevating them to a national priority, with significant effects on American food production, consumption patterns, and cultural life.[2] Possibly more than any other aspect of wartime mobilization, the activities related to food production (including gardening) and distribution touched American lives on a daily basis during World War I.[3]

This book examines two national war gardening and agricultural programs: the National War Garden Commission and the United States School Garden Army. It also discusses a third program, the Woman's Land Army. These programs grew out of opportunities presented by America's war mobilization. The production needs generated by war, the vastness and speed of home front mobilization, the demands placed on state direction, and the move

Helping Hoover in Our U.S. School Garden. American Lithographic Co. (1919). Created for the United States Food Administration. In a more traditional depiction of children with Victorian overtones, young gardeners pledge their support for Herbert Hoover's efforts (Museum of Ventura County, photographer Aysen Tan).

to institutionalize reform efforts under the guise of wartime mobilization all combined to create a sense of urgency. This, in turn, led to the quick development and implementation of wartime gardening programs on a national scale. John Dewey expressed the sense of national import thusly: "The immediate urgency has in a short time brought into existence agencies for executing the supremacy of the public and social interest over the private and possessive interest which might otherwise have taken a long time to construct."[4] (Dewey also believed the war would facilitate a process that would lead to the communal use of scientific knowledge for the advancement of society.) Wartime need trumped all. (A modern analog might be the emergency presented by 9/11, when life on the American home front was quickly adjusted in response to that unprecedented crisis.)

The urgency of wartime mobilization enabled proponents to promote gardening and food production as a vital national security issue. The connection between the nation's food readiness and national security resonated and worked within the context of America's political and cultural life, which was struggling to synthesize urban and rural interests, grappling with the nation's plurality and the challenges and opportunities presented by millions of immigrants, and reconsidering the role of America in the larger world. Linking food security with national security was reinforced by the president's decision to use War Department monies to fund one of the programs, the United States School Garden Army. The recasting in World War I of youth education in food production had lasting effects on agricultural education in the United States, including a sustained federal funding stream to youth programs such as 4-H. Could the same message—that food production is vital to national security—resonate today? Americans have certainly embraced the notion that home and community food production is vital to self-sufficiency and perhaps greater family food security, but the explicit connection between community-based food security and national security should be reflected in public policies that support local and regional food production.

In the shorter term, the complementary nature and interconnectedness of these World War I programs supported the development of a national ethos of gardening, resulting in a vibrant network of gardens—and gardeners—that transformed the American food system for the duration of the war. Though instituted as temporary measures and short-lived in practice, these programs built on previous garden movements and established a longer legacy, resurfacing as models for subsequent mobilization of collective public efforts at food production and conservation in other times of crisis in American life, up to the present day. As in World War I, there is strong evidence that the national surge we have experienced in recent years in school, home, and community gardening efforts is having important effects in communities across America. (Some of these efforts will be explored in later chapters.)

Gardening may seem to be an ordinary topic, too mundane and unchanging to have an impact on history. In this book, I argue that on the American home front during World War I, the call to gardening was new and distinctive, elevated to high public importance. The civic appeal was not just immediate, though, and not presented entirely as modern, however progressive and reformist its underpinnings. In their imagery, the programs invited the nation's citizens to create (or re-create) gardens as a way to recapture an earlier "golden age" in American experience (a golden age that may or may not ever have existed). The imagery was of republican self-sufficiency, mutuality, and civic contribution, in unexamined juxtaposition to the simultaneous celebration of massive corporate production and state direction of other war industries. Gardens became an integral part of American life during the war era as a location of national identification and purpose, of synthesis between competing spheres (urban and rural, domestic and public, consumer and producer, immigrant and native-born) during a period of national transition and transformation.[5] They were also to be a place of redemption from any number of ills that plagued American social and cultural life. They still are.

The act of gardening was appropriated by a dizzying array of groups and organizations with diverse reform agendas, including childhood education, civic beautification, and the assimilation of immigrants; this is the case even today. Gardening presented many groups with an opportunity to explore what John Dewey termed "the social possibilities of war."[6] Those who sought to rally native-born Americans and immigrants to the war effort, those who sought to reform the public educational system, groups advancing the cause of women's rights, proponents of "traditional" producer values, and those who promoted modernity and consumption all embraced the idea of national gardening campaigns. Each group had a notion of how America's rural past (in both real and perceived ways) influenced and ought to influence an increasingly urbanized and industrialized future. While the agendas varied, many of the techniques and methods they utilized were similar, and each national gardening effort bore the imprimaturs of national state-associative purpose and progressive civic intention. These different groups shared something else: they sought to change America, and also to synthesize diverse American experiences through the simple act of gardening. Those who participated in these programs had various agendas of their own, including patriotism and identity formation in addition to horticulture promotion. Through their participation, they shaped program outcomes.

Considered within the context of World War I and the Progressive Era, gardening was anything but ordinary. For those interested in United States history, national gardening programs speak directly to issues of early twentieth century progressivism; wartime as a transformative moment; state building through associational liberalism; citizen identity formation; and public policy. For those engaged in the ongoing challenges faced by America's rural dwellers today, we can derive contemporary ideas of the urban and rural, and understand the tensions inherent in—and the ascendance of—America's consumer-based culture (and how that may inform our globalized food system). The Liberty and Victory gardens of yesteryear also teach us about the history of childhood, education, and their relationship to landscape and the making of place, and provide ideas about how we can more strongly connect today's youth with the land that sustains them. Women's work in wartime gardens (and the case study in this book of a precursor program—the Pennsylvania School of Horticulture for Women) teach us not only about the practice of horticulture, but also about women's history (in the negotiation of citizenship, female activism and civic life, professionalization, every day agency, and intellectual realms). Through the study of wartime gardening posters, we learn about propaganda and visual culture, and perhaps gain insight about how the food movement is using the modern analog to war posters—social media—to great effect in furthering its goals and reach. For those interested in current food systems policy and reform, the historical example of wartime gardening programs can offer suggestions on how we can negotiate our way through the hard times we currently find ourselves in, one garden at a time.

ONE

The Garden Revolution

"A Garden for Everyone. Everyone in a Garden."

This tagline appears on my email signature, in nearly all of my presentations and in my personal and professional work. It summarizes my personal and professional mission: to be an advocate for school, home, and community gardens.

In January 2008, I sat in a conference room at a nondescript hotel off an interstate near St. Louis. It was a bleak day that would entice few gardeners outdoors. As we worked together to prepare an elevator speech about our life's work, my new friend and colleague Alissa Hamilton coined the following term to characterize what I was trying to achieve: "Victory Grower."[1] That night, I sat down and created my initial Victory Grower website and blog posting.

I didn't create the tagline that appears in my work. It was taken and adapted from United States government literature produced during World War I, specifically from a federally promoted educational program called the United States School Garden Army (USSGA), which had as its slogan "A Garden for Every Child. Every Child in a Garden." The USSGA was an effort that provided one of the first nationally promoted curricula, through the Federal Bureau of Education, now the Department of Education. The program and its curriculum were created during a time of national crisis. The War Department (now the Department of Defense) funded the program, which it viewed as vital to securing the home front—and Allied victory—during World War I. It is nearly impossible to imagine that as our nation fights a seemingly endless series of wars in the Mideast, that our leaders would have any serious concerns about the security of the domestic food supply, but that was not the case during World War I.

President Woodrow Wilson himself made the decision to fund an army of school gardeners, affirming that their work in gardens was of great importance to national security. His initial allocation of $50,000 represented 25 percent more than its founders requested. To fund the effort, Wilson used money from the National Security and Defense Fund. Additional funding was provided as the war progressed. A school garden program funded by the War Department? A national gardening curriculum for urban and suburban youth? Why?

Perhaps the better question is: Why not now?

National leaders in World War I understood what our national leadership today fails to fully grasp: when we fail to educate youth about the food system, we do so at our nation's peril. Understanding where our food comes from is essential to making healthy and informed decisions about our diet and our public policies. Educating youth about agriculture is also essential to "growing" the next generation of farmers. Without an understanding of the role farmers play in our national and global economies, how will we encourage youth to consider farming and agriculture as career choices? But these are just some of the lessons we can learn from America's experience with gardens during World War I, which spanned school, home, community, and workplace efforts. There are breathtaking implications for public policy today. We simply need to take the opportunity to recalibrate our thinking.

The modern analog to the USSGA and Liberty and Victory Garden programs of World War I, for example, might be an allocation of Homeland Security funds for school, home, and community gardens. (What a great idea!) Or perhaps for the Department of Education to develop and facilitate the delivery of a national school curriculum focusing on sustainable food systems, healthy lifestyle, and environmental education. Think "Race to the Crop," rather than the current administration's national educational effort, "Race to the Top." Soon, public schools in the United States will embrace the common core curriculum. What if that core curriculum linked every part of the educational experience to some aspect of food systems, human health, and sustainability? Is there anything more fundamental or "core" than food?

Possibly more important for us to consider is why Americans believed that gardening on the home front during World War I was vital to national security. Why did so many national leaders promote the gardening message? Are the goals the nation sought to achieve through gardening then—including improving the health of its citizens—meaningful today? (As we enter the era of a national healthcare system, I argue that prevention through healthy diet is a vital goal, a national necessity, and perhaps even an obligation of citizenship.) When America entered the "War to End All Wars" nearly a hundred years ago, President Woodrow Wilson told the nation, "Food will win the war." Few of us think of food as a national security issue today, even though we are again engaged in wars on foreign soil. But in World War I, home food pro-

Plant a War Garden. Fill the Market Basket!! Food Will Win the War. Patriotic magazine cover from *Youth's Companion Magazine*, spring 1918. Readers of this boy's magazine are encouraged to plant a war garden to help their nation win the war (National World War I Museum, Kansas City, Missouri).

duction was a vital national security interest, a civic virtue, an act of patriotism, and also a means to accomplish a wide range of public-purposed reform goals, including improving American health, engaging and beautifying communities, reconnecting Americans to their food supply, educating youth, reducing the "food mile," and encouraging the local production and consumption of food (a notion we would deem entirely modern in its origin). Americans were called to become "soldiers of the soil." Cultivating the soil to produce food took on a patriotic fervor and provided an opportunity to return to the nation's storied past.

The result? National wartime gardening programs that helped the nation accomplish its wartime goals, develop a gardening ethos, and create a generation of Victory Growers who would be re-engaged in the iconic Victory Garden program of World War II. Why did millions of Americans—young and old, native born and immigrant, male and female, urban and rural, representing all ethnicities—feel compelled to pick up hoes and become "soldiers of the soil," or as I refer to them, "Victory Growers?" Would they do it today?

One could argue that they are already doing it. A recent survey conducted by the National Gardening Association indicates that home food production in America is increasing at a rapid rate. Those who planned to participate in a home gardening effort grew 19 percent between 2008 and 2009.[2] Young people are flocking to urban agriculture, driven by an impulse some refer to as "civic agrarianism." Their motivations to garden and farm in urban and rural settings are driven by a broad impulse that is challenging the widely accepted (and sometimes unquestioned) orthodoxy of the American food system in serious and fundamental ways. They seek not only to produce food, but to transform society. From the White House to my house, Americans are focusing on food and gardening in ways that are significantly influencing American cultural and political life. How does the situation we currently find ourselves in relate to World War I? Does the past have the ability to inform the present?

The answer to these questions is an unqualified "Yes!" This book examines the link between the Victory Gardens and Victory Growers of the past and today's growing (and greening) garden revolution. We are at a unique moment in our national history, and our work in gardens and food systems provides at least part of the solution to many of the most critical problems our nation and world face. This is a teachable moment: the past has the ability to inform the present ... and the future.

What Is a Victory Garden?

What is a Victory Garden? And could the garden movement sweeping the nation help us to meet the monumental challenges we face? Victory Gardens were gardens that sprang up at schools, at home, in communities, and in workplaces on the American home front during World War I and World War II. In both World War I and World War II, earlier programs in the United

Kingdom and Canada served as models for the American program. Gardens were also located at hospitals, on military training bases, and even in rear trenches on the battlefront. They were found on vacant lots and in public spaces, including the National Mall, Boston Common and at the White House. Gardens were ubiquitous. And because of new wartime demands on the food supply, they were seen as a necessity.

World War I: The Abyss

Some today object to the term "Victory Gardens" for contemporary use because of its historical association with the destruction of war. I understand this objection. War is a terrible thing. War changes things. The First World War—also called The Great War—was a cataclysmic series of events that transformed and forever changed the world. It changed borders, destroyed nations, created nations, changed the form and reach of governments, and challenged the idea of "empire." It left in its wake the certainty that an even greater conflagration would occur. World War I killed untold millions. It changed how people thought, felt, and acted. The world stepped into an abyss in 1914, and would never be the same. To understand the modern world and the events of the twentieth century, one must understand what occurred during World War I.[3]

Since the topic of this book is a limited study of the American home front, the causes of World War I and the details of the battlefront are not discussed in great detail. But some background is essential, because the home front and the battlefront represent opposite sides of the same coin; cause and effect come into play. Military needs dictated home front mobilization, and what occurred on the home front affected what could be executed on the battlefront.

World War I brought massive challenges to governments across the world from workers, from women seeking suffrage, and from groups seeking political change, including self-government and some degree of freedom from imperial rule. Dissent on the home front—or the battlefront—was ruthlessly suppressed by nearly all governments. There was extreme violence on the home front as well as on the battlefront: lynching, the coercive "slacker" raids of military-aged men in public places—one of the most shameful episodes of American history—and the execution by the military of some conscientious objectors. Some dissenters were simply thrown into jail, where they languished without charge. Governments co-opted the press and encouraged academics to rewrite history to reflect poorly on the "enemy." Misinformation, propaganda, and manipulation were the order of the day. Propagandists successfully vilified combatant nations, often in overtly racist terms (this was used to great effect again in World War II, against the Japanese). This, in large part, made the conflict impossible to resolve via diplomatic means and ultimately led to a punitive "peace" that was destined to fail.

The pace of global change was stunning. Within a single six-week period, the centuries-old Romanov Empire in Russia collapsed and America entered the war and began mobilizing millions of men to fight on foreign soil. This mass mobilization of Americans for foreign combat was unprecedented. A bias rooted in America's colonial experience with an occupying British Army had kept America from maintaining a strong, centralized military, and the nation scrambled to respond to its new wartime footing.

In World War I, the industrial and economic might of nations turned toward the prosecution of total war. Technological "advancements" compounded the horror and misery. World War I brought the widespread use of machine guns (capable of firing up to six-hundred rounds per minute, with deadly results), the introduction of chemical warfare (chlorine and mustard gas), aerial warfare, flamethrowers, and the tank (which, in fact, proved of limited use in World War I). *Unterseebooten* (U-boats) prowled the seas. Barbed wire, more commonly used in agricultural settings, was used with deadly effect on the battlefield. The war created an international arms race, with the goal to inflict as many casualties as possible.

People weren't the only casualties: the tractor became more commonplace after the war in part due to the massive casualties suffered by draft horses on the battlefront.[4] World War I was simultaneously the last old-fashioned war and the first modern one, pitting troops with bayonets—or mounted on horses—against machine-gun wielding opponents. Artillery ruled. Newly introduced big guns capable of long-range bombing (up to seventy-five miles in the case of the infamous *Kaiser Wilhelm Geschütz*, or Paris Gun) were used in a German assault on Paris; the guns weren't incredibly accurate, but they caused great psychological damage. Trench warfare, shell shock, and gas masks were other iconic horrors of the battlefield.

Never had so many traveled so far to fight and die. Soldiers from French colonies in Africa and British-held India died on the Western Front in Europe, needlessly sacrificed by military leaders who failed to adapt older military strategies to the realities of evolving technologies. Thousands of Anzac soldiers from Australia and New Zealand died on Turkish shores or were thoughtlessly sacrificed on the Western Front, at battles including the Somme. (The Canadian and Anzac forces, led by "colonials" despite the objections of some in the British military, proved to be among the United Kingdom's strongest units and played a pivotal role in many military engagements. Lingering bitterness over the large and needless casualties taken by Canadian and Anzac forces led to a stronger sense of national identity for these countries, and eventually to greater loosening of the ties binding them to the United Kingdom.[5])

Russian soldiers—many fielded without arms—died by the millions, and eventually turned from fighting the Germans to fighting one another as revolution and civil war consumed that nation. German ships were seized in Argentina and Chile. Troops from Japan invaded and occupied German-leased territory that Germany held in China. Millions of young Americans deployed to Europe to fight in the latter part of the war. Some who had been grain farmers in the Midwest died in the wheat fields surrounding Belleau Wood, near the Marne River in France. (A young man from my agricultural community fell within sight of his childhood friend at the battle of Château-Thierry in 1918, one of the first military engagements fought by the American Expeditionary Force under General Pershing. The news appeared in the local newspaper, in the form of a letter written by the survivor, and thrust the community into mourning. Nearly ninety years after his death, I held this young man's picture in my hand, and visited his gravestone at a local cemetery, which lies within sight of the same agricultural fields he likely saw.) Like him, millions of other young men died on foreign shores; many lie in those places still, and each loss still feels acute and personal and needless.

Depleted of a generation of young men, nations expanded military drafts to include younger and older men. In 1916, Germany passed a broad Auxiliary Service Law placing all German males between seventeen and sixty at the government's behest: they could be impressed by the War Ministry into military service or deployed to farms or factories. The policy proved a failure and was soon abandoned. The British eventually drafted men up to the age of fifty: some units were comprised of men mostly older than forty. The mass deployment of men to the battlefront created further hardship on the home front, but also created opportunities for some, including women, who by some reports filled more than one third of industrial jobs in France and Great Britain by the end of the war. Global agricultural production fell sharply during World War I, which provided economic opportunities for American farmers. But with men deployed to the military, in many places, women and children were mobilized to help plant and harvest crops. In the United Kingdom and the United States, a Woman's Land Army movement took hold.

The implications of total war—of entire national economies turned to the destruction of other nations—changed the rules of war, with tremendous consequences for civilian populations. Supplies were redirected to military purposes. While the civilian and military populations of some nations managed fairly well (thanks in part to imports from the United States), the citizens of other nations experienced extreme or utter deprivation. Total war displaced millions upon millions of civilians from their homes, as invading troops (or troops from their own nations) burned farms, bombed cities and destroyed livelihoods. The war inflamed long-standing suspicion between ethnic groups resulting in bloodshed and displacement. In some places, captured civilians (including women and children) were simply shot dead. No quarter was offered or given in some battles; captured enemy combatants were executed on the spot. In blockaded nations, and those destroyed by war, famine reigned. (The blockade of Germany continued even during peace negotiations, assuring the death of probably another 250,000 German citizens, many of whom were children. This, and the hard reparations forced upon Germany by the victors, led to bitterness and enabled a decorated soldier named Adolf Hitler to eventually achieve a role of prominence in that nation's political system.) Millions starved, froze to death, or died of disease. To add to the world's misery, an extremely virulent and deadly influenza pandemic resulted in millions of deaths during World War I, causing even more casualties than the fighting. An inordinate number of its victims were young adults.[6]

Desperate for labor, some nations, including Germany, Russia and Austria-Hungary, forced those they conquered into internment camps and used them for labor. Conquered Belgians were transported to Germany to work in factories. It was a standard practice to use prisoners of war for labor; many nations also used jail prisoners (including conscientious objectors) for labor, some promising to reduce sentences for service rendered. The internment camp model, used by the British during the Boer War, was now used by other nations, presaging its wider use as a tool—concentration camps—for repression and organized killing during World War II.[7] Some nations used the war as an excuse to turn their anger inward; the result was genocide, mass killing and violence against minority groups.

Writer G.J. Meyer describes World War I as "a kind of hole in time, leaving the postwar world permanently disconnected from everything that had come before."[8] In many ways, he is correct. But in a world gone mad, a world "completely undone," people persisted and persevered. They always do. Some did this, in part, through the act of gardening. Even in the direst circumstances, in the rear trenches, within earshot of the battlefield, evidence of gardening was found. Wartime gardening efforts accomplished many goals. Gardening was a practical, purposeful, and healing activity in the face of so much destruction. It also provided a way for people to reconnect to a simpler past.

And the past was important in America. At the outset of World War I, America had a strong proximity and connection to its past. Fifty-four thousand Civil War veterans attended the 50th anniversary gathering of the Battle of Gettysburg, held in 1913. Thousands were living who had been born into slavery. The West was still largely undeveloped: Arizona and New Mexico had only recently achieved statehood. Progressivism was at its height, bringing social reform and economic change to the United States. It was a period of transformation and transition, and the war accelerated these impulses. The nation was shifting from a producer to a consumer ethos. Some recognized the dangers inherent in this, and new consumer advocacy groups (such as the National Consumers' League) arose. One national organization urged Americans to "reunite consumption and production." This became one goal of the Victory Garden program.

America's consumer culture was moving outwards to foreign markets, facilitated by a growing number of government agencies and departments. Challenges to the old order were seen in popular amusements and modern culture. Population demographics were shifting, as well, with more citizens residing in cities, leading to rural labor shortages and urban-rural tensions. Technological and scientific advancement informed the era. President Taft rode to his inauguration in a horse and carriage in 1909; only four years later, Woodrow Wilson became the first president to ride to his inauguration in an automobile. It was a period of reform and transformation.

The nation faced enormous challenges: high infant mortality rates, poverty, slums, class animosity, labor issues, urban-rural issues and immigration. (Many of these tensions have re-emerged today.) An enormous challenge was the nation's division over the war in Europe. Should America join the war or remain neutral? While America's "neutrality" policy was wonderful for American businesses, it was difficult politically. And the investment of American resources in France and Great Britain made it vital that those nations prevail; loss of the war "over there" might lead to economic ruin "over here." There was not only a sense that France and Great Britain held the higher moral ground, but that they shared strong cultural ties. And again, America's financial investment made it ultimately impossible to retain neutrality. America found itself unprepared for war in many ways. The rapid mobilization of school, home, and community gardeners was one of the home front's successes when war was finally declared on Germany. Even after the war ended, the Victory Garden effort continued, but with different goals.

Why Are Victory Gardens Needed Today?

Victory Gardens, then, are both an historical fact and a contemporary impulse. I urge those who object to their very real militarized past and rhetoric to frame the term another way: consider these contemporary Victory Gardens as representing victory over hunger, over complacency, over community blight, over obesity. I've met cancer survivors who have planted "victory" gardens to celebrate the completion of chemotherapy. You choose your own frame. Because whatever you choose to call them, gardens are sorely needed today.

In the next few decades, the United States and international community will face daunting health, food security, and environmental challenges. We're already experiencing them. One challenge is simply to feed the world's growing population, with more than 1 billion people already estimated to be experiencing hunger. In a much-touted October 2009 report, the United Nations indicated that global food production would have to double by 2050 to feed the world's population. This does present a challenge, as agricultural productivity remains relatively flat. Research investment and investment in infrastructure to support food production (especially lacking in developing nations) is declining, in part due to the recession and ongoing global financial crises. In the United States, a persistent anti-science and anti-intellectual thread in our nation's political life has led to a significant decline in public investment in agricultural research.

Global food markets remain extremely volatile, with serious implications for political stability around the globe. Empires rise and fall on food. Riots in Egypt are about democracy, but they are also about the price of bread and basic necessities. In a globalized food system where some nations rely on imports to feed themselves, the implications for political stability are clear.

There are other challenges as we consider global food production. The natural resource base is under threat, water at a premium. Agriculture is the world's largest consumer of water. We will need to look closely at cropping patterns, cultivation practices, and processing to make certain that we're making the right kinds of decisions given the changing resource base and climate. Despite what a fringe minority may say, climate change is an unequivocal reality. There will be winners and losers geographically and in terms of species. We are already experiencing climate disruption and extreme weather events, and all that those things mean in terms of challenges to crop and animal production, plant and animal biodiversity, cultural shifts, and geo-political change.

There is also the issue of oil, a limited resource, but also a significant input in agricultural production, processing, distribution, and waste management (about 20 percent of fossil fuel goes into the food chain). Oil is used to run machines used in agricultural production, processing, distribution, and waste management. Petrochemicals are used in fertilizers, and also to produce herbicides and pesticides. Food is a form of energy; calories are energy units. Energy production and policy and food production and policy are tightly connected. Americans must have serious discussions about energy policy, particularly biofuels. The use of corn for ethanol production at least raises the specter of philosophical questions: grain production for fuel, or for people? (Its American counterpart, corn ethanol, has not replicated Brazil's biofuel success with sugarcane ethanol.) Contributing to the interlinked issues of energy, climate change, and food is the question of meat consumption: is it sustainable at its current levels, especially with an increasing population? As the new economic powerhouses (China and India) become more westernized in terms of dietary practices (especially increased meat consumption), the demand for products (and the demand rising consumption places upon natural resources) is increasing. What effects will those burgeoning economies (and populations) have on food systems and the resources required to feed the world's growing population?

While society and ecosystems can adjust, adapt to, and mitigate some of these factors, it will take time and present enormous challenges. In unpredictable times (just as in the past), gardening and local food production can play an important role in providing fresh, healthy, and safe foods and increasing community-based food security.

And community-based food security is vital to national security. Remember: food is fundamental ... empires rise and fall on food. Adlai E. Stevenson II once said, "A hungry man is not a free man." If one equates national health with national security (and I do), we can help increase national security and begin alleviating hunger *now*, by teaching people how to garden and farm in their communities. I'm not certain that bureaucrats employed by the City of Los Angeles should tell resident Ron Finley that he must tear out a successful community gardening venture that is feeding mouths and feeding souls, growing hope on 1,500 square feet of city-owned median strip between the curb and the sidewalk, at no cost to the city.[9] Should we perhaps, instead, make it easier for people to garden at schools and in their communities? Invest in seeds and tools and education? Real homeland security begins with access to good food. It's that simple.

The USDA is a premiere source for hunger statistics in the United States. Its Economic Research Service (ERS) website provides an amazing amount and array of research. The ERS focuses its research on agriculture, food, the environment, and rural development. It provides research to enhance public and private decision-making.

The ERS site contains reports, graphs, and all sorts of sliced and diced statistical data on animal products; crops; trade and agriculture; diet, health and safety; farm economy; farm practices and management; and food and nutrition assistance, just to list a few. The most popular items (recently) are the USDA's food access research atlas (which provides a spatial overview of low-income neighborhoods with high concentrations of people who have limited access to grocery stores); food availability; and the adoption of genetically engineered crops in the United States. In addition to providing an amazing breadth and depth of information on countless topics, ERS demonstrates the interconnectedness and multiplicity of topics related to the food system.

The USDA conducts a survey and issues an annual report on household food security, assessing that factor, as well as food expenditures and the use of food and nutrition assistance programs. This survey is linked to Labor Department surveys about employment. Near the end of 2009, the ERS published new data on hunger in America; a statistical supplemental was published at the end of 2010.[10] The reports contain shocking statistics about Americans and food security and food insecurity.

The USDA bases its definitions of food security and food insecurity on a core indicators report produced by Life Sciences Research Office.[11] *Food security* is defined as household access by all members at all times to enough food for an active, healthy life. In other words, food security means that there is adequate food. There are minimum indicators of food security, including:

- The ready availability of nutritionally adequate and safe foods; and
- Assured ability to acquire acceptable foods in socially acceptable ways (that is, without resorting to emergency food supplies, scavenging, stealing, or other coping strategies).

Food insecurity is defined as limited, uncertain (and perhaps, variable) availability of nutritionally adequate and safe foods. In other words, food insecurity means that there is not enough food or that there is poor access to food. The definition also includes the notion of a household's or individual's limited or uncertain ability to secure nutritious and safe food in "socially acceptable" ways.

It is no secret that the shaky economy has affected American families. However, the USDA's hunger reports showed how deeply and widely that economic hit was being experienced by the nation: 14.7 percent of surveyed United States households had experienced food insecurity at least once during the year surveyed (2009). A whopping 5.7 percent had experienced significant food insecurity. Twenty-eight percent of those surveyed who received Supplemental Nutrition Assistance Program benefits (SNAP, previously called food stamps) had obtained food from a food pantry. Fifty-four percent of food pantry users and 58 percent of emergency kitchen users had received SNAP benefits in the previous 30 days.[12] (Clearly, governmental food assistance programs fall short of fulfilling impoverished families' needs in today's economy.) Children are inordinately affected by hunger. Many middle class Americans had been pushed down a few rungs on the economic ladder, and—many for the first time—were accessing local food banks.

Food banks typically lack adequate amounts of fresh fruit and vegetables. Some exciting models for providing hungry and low-income food bank clients with fresh fruits and vegetables exist, including one developed by the FoodShare program in my own community, and the Cultivate Iowa model, discussed later in this book. Processed foods are more easily garnered from corporate support of national hunger organizations, such as Feeding America. That group has received millions of dollars of cash and in-kind product support from food giants such as Kraft, ConAgra, Nestle, Kroger, Wal-Mart, General Mills, Kellogg and others. As could be expected from the donor list, much of the in-kind food product received is highly processed, although it should be noted that Kraft has made millions of dollars available to fund a mobile pantry program that is supplementing shelf-stable and processed foods with fruits and vegetables (the company has funded 25 mobile pantries over the course of the last few years). It's not kind to look a gift horse in the mouth, but the fact is that the corporate in-kind donations helping American families bridge the hunger gap aren't generally the healthiest or freshest kinds of foods.

Which leads us again to the issue of food access. Some of the most impoverished in our nation live in areas where access to healthy, affordable food is limited. Areas of limited access can be either in an urban or rural area; however, a common feature is typically the low-socioeconomic status of its residents. Poor access to food in America inordinately affects communities of color, creating health and learning disparities over the long term. For example, an urban neighborhood might have a corner market or bodega (with limited food options), rather than a retail supermarket. Lack of access to healthy foods will certainly bring attendant health problems, such as Type II diabetes and childhood obesity. Hunger and poverty and health are inextricably linked. Having ready access to good food is fundamental to good health, and can also be a predictor of educational and economic success.

When one considers the employment situation in our nation, the rapidly increasing poverty rate in America, the growing gap in wealth, *and* hunger, it doesn't take a rocket scientist to understand that we're sitting on a social, economic, and political time bomb. Childhood hunger, in particular, has effects on development, education, and our future economic health. Hunger in our nation, with its abundance of food wealth (much of it exported), simply cannot be tolerated. It is one of the great moral issues of our time. *"A hungry man is not a free man."*

We were (mostly) a nation of farmers at origin: we are still a nation of farmers at heart. There are strong connections between the cultivation of land and notions of liberty, national security, and national identity. A nation that cannot feed its people or regulate its food supply is a nation at risk. The globalized food system relies upon some nations being net importers of food, and others net exporters. But there must be resiliency built into food systems that encourages and supports production and processing capacity at the local level, creating a web of different-scale food systems that will prove enduring even in the case of disruption or failure in another part of the system. School, home and community gardens can play an important role in creating the kinds of smaller-scale models that are essential in creating a more resilient and sustainable food system.

Presidents Eat, Too

The public policy framing our current food system can be traced through our presidents; some had an enormous influence on the food system and the ideas about agriculture we have today. George Washington, a farmer who led other farmer-soldiers in the American Revolution, was greatly concerned with fair trade and scientific knowledge. (And very concerned with details about his personal agricultural enterprise at Mount Vernon, which is the subject of numerous longing letters he wrote home during the war.) Thomas Jefferson was a citizen scientist who saw the importance and value of farmers in American civic life (and his little purchase from the French enabled Americans—many of them farmers—to push westward). Abraham Lincoln signed into law legislation creating land grant universities (the primary place where American agricultural research and education occurs and which was the genesis of the nation's public system of higher education). Lincoln also signed the Homestead Act and Railroad Act, which had enormous implications for American agriculture. He did all of these things within a few months. Lincoln also created the USDA, making it a cabinet-level position. (Today, the USDA secretary is included in the presidential succession, oversees more than 100,000 employees working in 17 agencies, and manages an annual budget of $95B. The position is arguably one of the most overlooked—but most important—positions in the president's cabinet.)

Theodore Roosevelt grappled with difficult issues created by urban-rural tensions during the Progressive Era; he created the Country Life Commission, which sought to synthesize the best of the American urban and rural experience. He also signed into law the Pure Food and Drug Act in 1906, which provided the first federal oversight of food and drug safety (this legislation was signed the same day as the Federal Meat Inspection Act). Franklin Delano Roosevelt's secretary of agriculture, Henry Aagard Wallace, redrew major portions of the food system with New Deal policies and programs that still shape America's agricultural and food system. Harry Truman signed legislation creating the national school lunch program, which allocated part of the nation's food to public schools. Dwight Eisenhower signed the National Interstate and Defense Highways Act in 1956, which created the vast and amazing infrastructure of roads and highways that has made it easier for Americans to ship food long distances, an average of 1,500 miles per food item.[13] This federal legislation, passed before I was born, is one reason that my East Coast friends can eat strawberries grown in my community while their states remain locked in the grip of winter. Lyndon Johnson signed landmark legislation promoting childhood nutrition as part of America's Great Society legislative movement, legislation that still shapes USDA feeding programs (which are under increasing attack politically). These are just a few examples. The point is, agricultural policy is fundamental to our national life and our legislative and executive branches spend a great deal of time formulating it, sometimes with lasting effects.

The nation's first ladies have also had an influence on the national landscape and food system. To do her bit on the home front, Edith Wilson grazed sheep on the White House lawn during World War I: wool from the sheep was spun into yarn, which she knitted to raise funds for the war effort. Eleanor Roosevelt oversaw the creation of a small Victory Garden during World War II. Jackie Kennedy and Lady Bird Johnson both oversaw gardening projects and campaigns that sought to beautify and improve American communities. Since entering the White House in 2009, First Lady Michelle Obama has encouraged the creation of a vegetable garden on the South Lawn of the White House, as well as a series of initiatives focusing on childhood nutrition.

While each president has something to recommend him on the food and agriculture front, Abraham Lincoln is one of my favorites. Lincoln offered an address at the Wisconsin State Fair in Milwaukee in 1859, when he was stumping for president of the United States. (It should be noted that the votes of Midwest farmers still remain important to presidential candidates.) Lincoln's words and legislative acts are vital to understanding American agriculture both today and within an historical context. Again, it was under his presidency that the federal government enacted the Morrill Act (framing the system of public higher education and land grant institutions that have helped United States' agriculture become a globally dominant force); he also created the USDA. The USDA's top administrators are housed in the Whitten Building, which borders the National Mall. The USDA's presence on the National Mall says a great deal about the importance of agriculture in American life and the national psyche.

The USDA's People's Garden, founded in 2009 on the biennial of Lincoln's birth, is an organic garden located on a corner outside the Whitten Building. Secretary Tom Vilsack and Michelle Obama stood together to break ground on the garden. There, USDA staff and community members volunteer their time to raise food for the hungry in our nation's capital, cultivating food on land we hold sacred, in the midst of one of our greatest cities, in the heart of our nation's republic. Every time I visit this garden, I am deeply moved. The People's Garden and the White House kitchen garden affirm everything I believe to be good about gardens, the American character, and this nation.

Lincoln had the vision to elevate agriculture to a cabinet level position, and to create, through the establishment of land grant universities, a mechanism that would insure that the pursuit of agricultural science was a national priority. That Lincoln pursued this course of action when the nation was ripped apart by the Civil War shows incredible optimism and enormous foresight ... and tells us something about the importance of agriculture to national security.

On the day Lincoln spoke in Wisconsin in 1859, his audience probably consisted largely of farmers. Lincoln viewed the pursuit of agriculture as an opportunity for "cultivated thought." (This was a nice pun, and probably unintended.) He shared this idea with his audience. But he also shared important ideas about the link between agricultural literacy—knowing how to produce food—and the nature of liberty, saying,

> And thorough work, again, renders sufficient, the smallest quantity of ground to each man. And this again, conforms to what must occur in a world less inclined to wars, and more devoted to the arts of peace, than heretofore. Population must increase rapidly—more rapidly than in former times—and ere long the most valuable of all arts, will be the art of deriving a comfortable subsistence from the smallest area of soil. No community whose every member possesses this art, can ever be the victim of oppression of any of its forms. Such community will be alike independent of crowned-kings, money-kings, and land-kings.[14]

This is pretty heady stuff, radical even, a strongly pluralistic message about land. While Lincoln's feeling that the nation might be more devoted to peace hasn't exactly panned out, I think the rest still resonates. I read it to mean that as long as every American knows how to cultivate land, we will be free from oppression. Oppression from all sorts of kings, but perhaps also free from the oppression presented by hunger, obesity, and lack of community engagement. Knowing how to cultivate land is an essential ingredient of independence (on all sorts of levels). It is an art. It is a science. It is essential to survival. When I read these words more than 150 years after they were spoken, the clarity and strength and truth of them compels me to state again: "A Garden for Everyone. Everyone in a Garden."

Our relationship to the land links us. Even when we don't have direct contact with it, land sustains us. Those who worked on national gardening efforts during World War I understood the connection between rural and urban. They envisioned a "nation of garden cities" ... and all that the term promised. Beautiful, vibrant, healthy cities. After the Armistice was signed in 1919, one national leader expressed his feeling that the war gardening effort was "a forge that is daily strengthening the links in our chain of democracy.... Link by link the chain of our democracy has grown stronger."

Can the act of gardening really strengthen democracy? I believe the answer is "yes."

Linking the Past and Present: Sustainable Food Systems and Public Policy

"Food systems" is a term that we hear a lot, but that we seldom take time to unpack and truly understand. It considers all aspects of food production, processing, distribution, consumption, and waste management, with a strong focus on environmental sustainability. Food systems education is also sometimes referred to as agricultural literacy. Within the larger field of food systems education are smaller disciplines, including garden-based learning (GBL), also referred to as garden-based education or plant-based education. The term "sustainable" in relation to "food systems" stirs up debate. Some farmers might argue for "sustainability" relating to economics, and they would be right. Others interpret the term "sustainable food system" to mean a "good food" system that ensures economic and social justice, food access, and protections for the environment; they would also be right. Some define "sustainable" as organic (not correct, in my opinion). One meaning of the word "sustain" is to maintain. I would argue for that meaning, with the corollary: without significant inputs. Agricultural inputs that must be considered when evaluating agricultural productivity and sustainability include pesticides, fertilizer, labor, energy, durable goods (including equipment), land and water. Even if we don't know precisely what it is, most of us agree that sustainability is a positive goal and attribute.

The University of California Sustainable Agriculture Research and Education Program suggests that a sustainable "community" food system "is a collaborative network that integrates food production, processing, distribution, consumption and waste management in ways that enhance and support the environmental, economic, physical and social health of a particular place."[15] Organizations such as the W.K. Kellogg Foundation (WKKF) support sustainable food systems and their relationship to healthy children and communities in a larger sense. WKKF seeks to address the root causes of health inequities, to transform the school food system, to increase community access to healthy foods and encourage physical activity, and to catalyze national movements in this area. That focus resonates in a social sense, and includes the notion of grower and worker equity (fair food) and a food system that improves the health of families and the wealth of communities.[16] To me a sustainable food system and a good food system—one that includes school, home and community gardens—is

- healthy, because food is fresh, nutritious, and minimally processed.
- green, because it is produced and distributed in a way that supports a healthy and sustainable environment not only now, but into the future.
- fair, because it generates an equitable wage for those producing and selling it.
- affordable and accessible for everyone. Access to good food should be a right, not a privilege.
- a system that invites participation, collaboration and shared decision-making.
- reflective of community and cultural needs, norms, practices and traditions.

Whatever the definition, food systems are all about relationships and networks of relationships: relationships between producers, processors and distributors, retailers, and consumers. Everyone who eats participates in the food system; everyone is a stakeholder. Our active participation—or our failure to act in intentional and thoughtful ways—either supports existing food systems or helps create models we deem more sustainable. We vote with our forks. Food issues are political, economic, cultural, and social.

Within America today, there are multiple and myriad food systems, many local and alternative in nature. Most citizens participate in several food systems simultaneously. However, the majority of Americans procure a good portion of their food from a national (and globalized) food system that is generally pretty large, consolidated, corporate, and anonymous, a system in which the average food product travels many miles to market, and in which the foods we eat are often highly processed. There is pushback against what some perceive as a meta-food system; local and regional food enterprises are increasing at a rapid rate in response to the growing interest in what we eat and where it comes from. For example, a recent *New York Times* article reported that there were 7,175 farmers markets in the United States as of August 5, 2011. Of those, 1,043 were established in the first half of that year. USDA statistics indicate that in 2005, there were around 4,000 farmers markets across the nation. Today, there is a farmers market within sight of the White House.

Portland, Oregon's Bureau of Planning and Sustainability recently revised its city codes to more closely reflect the growing importance of and interest in local foods. That city, long a national leader in the local foods movement, adopted Ordinance 18412 in June 2012. The ordinance clarifies policies on a range of local food issues, including urban chickens, backyard bees, and urban agriculture (including micro-farms). It encourages neighborhood-scale community gardens, market gardens, farmers markets, food buying clubs and CSAs, among other things. Portland's hard and innovative work in this area, conducted by the city's Bureau of Planning and Sustainability, could provide a blueprint for other urban areas to advance the good food movement. These are just some examples of the tremendous growth in aspects of local and regional food systems. One thing is clear: there will be no going back, and the local and regional food movement is revitalizing the food system in many ways.

The term "food mile" has become part of the discussion in food systems in recent years, but really originates as a concept during World War I, when citizens were exhorted to grow their own food or purchase locally. In World War I, reducing the food mile would save railroad resources for the transport of troops and materiel. The seminal contemporary report on the food mile was a case study of Iowa produced in 2003 by the Leopold Institute at the University of Iowa, although previous studies garnering nearly identical results predate that. While some contest the figures, the statistics are calculated with figures provided by the USDA.

The current food system is in many ways an outgrowth of federal farm and economic policies and agricultural production practices developed during the Progressive Era and Great Depression. It is largely oriented to big producers, i.e., agri-business, and to centralized (aggregated) processing functions dominated by conglomerate (read: multi-national) food processors. It is a system that is extremely dependent upon fossil fuels for production, processing and distribution processes and largely emphasizes a model in which consumers have little connection to the food they buy and eat.

The disconnection between producer and consumer in the dominant food system raises philosophical concerns about national security. But there are also practical problems when we are disconnected from our food supply. As American farmers age, the art of farming is quickly being lost. The United States government conducts a population census every ten years; it conducts a census of agriculture every five. Per the 2007 USDA Census of Agriculture, the average age of the American farmer is 57 years, up from 50 years of age in 1978. The fastest growing group of farm operators in that census were those 64 years of age or older.[17] This is a frightening statistic, and a real threat to national security. In March 2010, Drake University's School of Law (located in America's agricultural heartland, Iowa) convened a national forum on "America's New Farmers: Policy Innovations and Opportunities." The forum was held in Washington, D.C., and concluded: "It is a vital national interest to identify America's next generation of farmers." While some states, such as California, are seeing more new farmers (many of whom are younger, female, and people of color), most Americans simply no longer possess the basic skills required to cultivate food. According to the USDA, fewer than two percent of Americans currently farm; only about ten percent of Americans are classified as rural dwellers. The shift from rural to urban dwelling that began well over a century ago has been fully realized, and we are now a nation of urban and suburban dwellers who are only marginally connected to the food system that sustains us.

While many millions of Americans do enjoy gardening as a pastime, a relative few of those gardeners would be able to translate that hobby into a meaningful contribution to their family's table in the event of a crisis in the food system. The federal government in America tackled this issue head-on during World War I, imploring its citizens to garden, and providing networks of support to facilitate those efforts. How might that work help Americans become more food secure in an era that seems to feature unending global crises?

There is a growing recognition that a healthy and sustainable food system is vital to the health and well being of youth, families, communities, and the nation as a whole. This might please the organizers of the World War I programs. There are increased demands for alternative food sources and systems as awareness of local, organic and artisan possibilities grow; increasingly, Americans want to know more about their food, and the people who raise it. Consider the USDA's Know Your Farmer, Know Your Food program, launched in the fall of 2009, which seeks to increase economic opportunities by connecting consumers to local producers. In 2012, the USDA enhanced the program to offer a compass to help effectively enable consumers to navigate local and regional food systems.

Farming is once again becoming a valued profession, which creates both challenges and opportunities for our nation vis-à-vis training and supporting the next generation of farmers, many of whom are not from rural backgrounds. The 2008 Farm Bill provided provisions to support and train new farmers. The USDA has provided funding through its Community Food Security Grant program to support local food projects, including urban agriculture, a growing trend in the United States. More is needed, including education among school-aged children about the "growing" opportunities available in agriculture. Funding to land grant universities—where much of the nation's agricultural research and knowledge is centered—is being drastically cut in many states, which seems counterintuitive given the many challenges facing national and global food systems. The nation ought to be investing more in agricultural and food systems education at all levels. Research about food systems issues ought to be a national priority as well; unfortunately, public research dollars to agriculture—which truly serve a public good—have declined in recent years.

This is just a brief summary of some of the issues facing the food system in America today. There are many others. My greatest hope for this book—this historical view of World War I gardening programs and policies, ideas that are nearly one hundred years old—is that it may be used as a lens through which to view our current situation. The past can inform the present. We were a nation of farmers at origin (at least that's the myth). We are still a nation of farmers of heart. Perhaps it is time for a new American revolution: one that encourages a garden in every school, every home, and every community in our nation.

TWO

In the Furrows of Freedom

"A Call to the Hoe"

"The men of America will die fighting, and in the name of humanity let us not let them die starving," admonished Charles Lathrop Pack, president of the National War Garden Commission (NWGC), which spearheaded the Liberty/Victory Garden Program during World War I.¹ Others shared his sense of collective responsibility and feeling of urgency; the message was also echoed in the press and popular media. "Let us … try to realize the grave fact that upon *each of one of us with a plot of land at his disposal* rests the responsibility of helping," wrote journalist Louise B. Wilder in *Good Housekeeping Magazine*.² Wartime gardens were pitched as a way to help American soldiers: a popular gardening magazine entitled *The Patriotic Garden* exhorted, "He also Fights who helps a Fighter Fight."³ The fighters themselves even grew some of the military's food supply via gardens at military camps, and in the rear of the trenches. An entire chapter of Pack's book *War Gardens Victorious* was devoted to military war gardening, with a special case study—including photographs—of young soldiers gardening at Camp Dix, New Jersey.⁴

Wartime gardening was not only an obligation to the nation, but to the world. One of the primary rationales for the program was to enable more farm-raised food to be sent to allies abroad. "The world looks to the United States for food" became a shared national understanding, and a shared national obligation.⁵ Even President Woodrow Wilson elevated the importance of wartime gardening to the international realm by telling American citizens, "Everyone who creates or cultivates a garden helps greatly to solve the problem of feeding the nations."⁶

Out of this seed of self-concept—America as Columbia, as savior—exceptional because of her ability to produce food during a period when global food production was in disarray due to disruptions created by nature and war, grew

The Spirit of '18, The World Cry / Food / Keep the Home Garden going. Artist: William McKee. United States Food Administration, Boston (1918). This is a poster variation of the famous painting *The Spirit of '76.* American patriots keep the home garden going, bearing implements of food production rather than guns (Museum of Ventura County, photographer Aysen Tan).

A young man kneels at an offering of fruits and vegetables, with soldiers behind him. Patriotic magazine cover from *Youth's Companion Magazine*. The image evokes an altar, and plays into wartime themes of food as a sacrifice those on the home front could make (National World War I Museum, Kansas City, Missouri).

an American identity that framed in important ways how the nation would be perceived by—and would perceive—the world during the twentieth century. As well-provisioned American troops poured into France during the latter part of World War I, they appeared to war weary Europeans to be strong and well fed, almost larger than life; this also fed the image of America as a cradle of plenty. Many lessons were learned from World War I and its tragic aftermath. One lesson was that rebuilding defeated nations was an important strategy to ensure the future military and economic security of the victors.

For example, the post–World War II Marshall Plan created new and captive markets for all kinds of American products, including food. Prior to American victory in World War II, though, as American GIs reclaimed areas of Europe long held under enemy rule, they brought in their packs food to share with foreign civilians. The image of the American GI sharing a Hershey bar with a European child not only evoked strong emotional responses, but also contributed to the idea of America as a powerhouse in food production and a nation of food abundance. During World War II, Coca Cola built bottling plants specifically targeted to serving active military; they, in kind, shared products with European civilians (consumers). This type of activity helped to create brand recognition for American food products during the post-war Era. The Berlin Airlift (1948–1949), which was a response to one of the first crises in the post-war Cold War Era, enabled America to deliver food and other "essential" supplies (including candy) to blockaded civilians.

While Americans remember the Victory Garden effort of World War II with deep affection, the World War I Liberty Gardening program has faded into obscurity. Yet, it was as pervasive as its World War II counterpart, and driven more by real needs on the home front (the need to secure the food supply). From 1917 to 1919, gardening was promoted and understood as a way to express patriotism and solidarity and a means to offer service to the nation. Americans were even willing to challenge deeply-held beliefs to engage in wartime gardening; very public debates on the appropriateness of gardening on Sunday and the appropriateness of women laboring in agriculture occurred in American parlors, communities and newspapers.[7] The nation engaged the service of children to help produce food via gardening during World War I and developed a national curriculum focusing on wartime gardening that was distributed through the Bureau of Education (BOE), gathering at least two million enlistees. College-educated, urban women left their studies to help the nation produce and harvest food. Wartime gardening not only was designed to serve practical purposes (increased food production), but also was a vital contribution to—and even an obligation of—American citizenship.[8] What would our nation look like today if Americans and policy creators viewed work in school, home and community gardens as a contribution to the community's good, an expression of patriotism, an obligation of citizenship, and an act of national (and global) service?

This chapter is about the work of the National War Garden Commission (NWGC), which created the Liberty/Victory Garden program that operated between 1917 and 1919.[9] The NWGC provides a powerful example of the kind of private-public enterprise that arose to meet home front mobilization needs of the war era.

The narrative is simple but compelling: prominent urban Progressives, led by a wealthy forester, made local food production via school, home, community and workplace gardens a national imperative. Representing a private, "grassroots" effort, the NWGC found where its leaders' reform interests intersected with national security concerns: the nation's food system. The NWGC loosely partnered with the federal government to support home front mobilization, forming a private-public effort that translated into one of the most iconic programs of either world war. (And Victory Garden programs were among the largest and most successful home front mobilization efforts in both wars. During World War I, the NWGC claimed its efforts resulted in 3 million uncultivated lots into production during 1917; 5,285,000 war gardens were "conservatively estimated" to be in production in 1918.[10]) Much of the program propaganda drew from Progressive and largely urban understandings and perceptions of an idealized sense of American rural life. The perceived best values of rural life—including the identity of producer—fused with modern cultivation, marketing, educational and propaganda techniques, providing a synthesis of urban-rural interests during a period when tensions between the two ran high. It has been argued by historian David Danbom that urban agrarians looked to rural America because it "symbolized what America has been and was an antidote for what it was becoming."[11]

The national Liberty/Victory Garden wasn't only about local food production. The program was used for the purposes of state building, to create national unity during a time of great trial, and to enable Progressive reformers to coerce their fellow citizens into adopting particular practices and behaviors for the "common" good. The leaders of the NWGC believed that encouraging home food production was vital to national security. Like other wartime gardening programs, the NWGC was really a new-fashioned old idea (and ideal) promoting self-sufficiency, citizenship and service under the guise of a new national collectivism.

The NWGC, like other wartime gardening programs, provides a powerful example of influences that were quite populist in origin because of their ideals and their appeal to "every man" (and woman and child). They idealized America's past, hearkening back to the idea of the nation as the New Jerusalem, a nation of "garden cities," an exceptional place populated by an exceptional citizenry. The NWGC's chair, Charles Lathrop Pack, wrote of a goal that fed into this ethos: "Making a Nation of Garden Cities" that would unite "cities and towns" and enable "big business" to align itself with common Americans.[12] Gardens could bridge all gaps in American society and merge even opposite interests. Gardens could help the nation mediate and synthesize diverse interests during a time of national crisis; gardening together could unify the home front. "Keep the Home Soil Turning" paraphrased not only the best practices of soil keeping, but also the lyrics of "Keep the Home Fires Burning," a popular World War I tune.

A key aspect of "winning" the war at home during World War I relied on the extensive use of public education and public persuasion by the national government and private interests, delivered through a number of newly created government agencies and departments as well as through existing civic organizations. Using the infant industries of mass media and advertising, the federal government and organizations such as the NWGC partnered to quickly create a broad public information mechanism and campaign that was highly effective in shaping public opinion and behavior on the American home front in a wide range of areas (war gardens, food and energy consumption, bond efforts, military enlistment, public health, etc.). The newly created Food Administration provides some of the best examples of these governmental efforts; the work of the Creel Commission is also highly instructive.

Progressive Era influences shaped the philosophy behind these efforts, not only in terms of formation, but also in modes of delivery and in content. Gardening was promoted through posters, magazine articles, public rallies, community-based demonstration garden efforts, pageants, parades and even Victory Garden Days. The World War I public education and public persuasion campaigns had an influence on American life that endures to this day through public institutions and practice, such as Extension education and even through public-minded campaigns discouraging or encouraging a range of behaviors (smoking, physical activity, etc.).

Some of these efforts utilized fear and no small degree of coercion. For example, one NWGC bulletin told Americans "Help Uncle Sam Fill the Ships with Food by Feeding Yourself. If We Do Not Feed Ourselves We Will Have Food Cards Decorated With a German Eagle at the Top That Will Tell Us What We Can Eat." (That tension exists even today, as Americans concerned with maintaining their freedom to choose squabble over the role of government in the nation's dietary choices. The controversy over soda taxes and GMO labeling are just two examples.) Americans were told to "Spade for Your Life and Liberty." According to estimates during World War I, perhaps 5,000,000 Americans did garden, although these numbers are merely estimates and cannot be verified with real accuracy.[13]

The work of the NWGC during World War I represents a natural progression in a tradition of centrally driven collective or community gardening efforts in the United States. Earlier efforts, local in scope, had focused on poverty or food relief, social reform or change and education. The NWGC did all of these things, and more. The local model was adapted for national use through organizational impulses generated during the Progressive Era. Practical gardening information from a variety of sources, including agricultural research stations (created as a result of the 1887 Hatch Act), land-grant universities, and private gardening organizations exploded onto the public stage. Sources of information also included the NWGC, the Food Administration, the United States Department of Agriculture, magazines, newspapers and commercially produced gardening guides. Gardening was promoted nearly everywhere, and in nearly every way. In this way, the NWGC responded to President Wilson's challenge to train the nation.

The Need

A driving force behind the work of the NWGC was the fear that America's food system was tenuous on the eve of the nation's entry into World War I. There was also a need to help feed the nation's European allies. By 1917, nearly every able-bodied male ally had mobilized to soldiering. Europe faced a third consecutive year of very limited agricultural production, cause by acute labor shortages and the total devastation wrought by war on vast swaths of agricultural land. Ships carrying much-needed American food supplies to Europe fell prey to German U-boat attacks, further aggravating the situation. The combination of plunging European agricultural production and reduced American imports fueled the crisis. Disruptions in distribution due to the war produced severe food shortages in Europe (and contributed to the success of the revolution overthrowing the Russian monarchy). Millions of Europeans faced starvation. The need of Europeans, particularly Belgians, was well documented in the American press; this helped to build sympathy and support for America's entry into the war. Prior to his appointment as the nation's food administrator, Herbert Hoover was active in relief efforts on behalf of Belgians, and his work brought national attention to the horrific situation in Europe. His advocacy for food relief made him a natural choice to become the nation's first food administrator when America entered the war. Through first-hand reports from Europe, then, Americans were exposed to the issues around food access and agricultural production, functions that were made complicated by the war. And fear about the food system on the part of American leaders was not unfounded, but rather, had some basis in fact. For agriculture in the United States faced difficulties in any number of areas, including production, yield, labor sources and distribution. (There was also concern about unifying farmers behind the war effort, as many were somewhat opposed to America's participation in the war.[14]) Again, even prior to the war, the nation faced real problems that justified the need to increase agricultural production on the home front.

America's food pledge. United States Food Administration (1917). This poster announces a pledge of 20 million tons of food for hungry and starving Europeans, something that will require sacrifice and food savings on the part of Americans. Many Americans signed food pledges (Library of Congress).

Simultaneously, America's food system was in a state of transition to a more modern age. This was being facilitated by market forces; cultural changes; the political sense that an inexpensive, secure, and ordered food supply was essential for civil order and national progress; and the federal government's efforts through land-grant institutions, agricultural experiment stations, and the USDA's newly launched Cooperative Extension Service (created by the passage of the Smith-Lever Act in 1914).

All of these things became driving forces behind the stepped-up movement towards scientific agriculture and a more coherent approach towards policies and practices to organize the nation's food system, especially with the possibility of war at least on the horizon. (Some historians, including David Danbom, argue that while parts of the United States Department of Agriculture were ill prepared for war, the Cooperative Extension System was working well. Extension was able to quickly increase the size and capacity of its corps of Agents when America entered the war, which had positive effects on home front gardening and food preservation efforts.[15])

Despite issues with the food system, successful industrial models that might have improved the situation had not yet been fully applied to the agricultural sector.[16] Between 1890 and 1911 there were periods of overproduction and underproduction; in general, the yield per acre tended to fall on the low side. There was near national consensus that agriculture needed to be "revolutionized" or rationalized in the way that industrial life had been organized and made more efficient in the nation. There is general consensus among historians about key trends in agriculture during the pre-war era, including the flat and/or declining productivity of agriculture per acre; the rising cost of food staples; and the changing patterns of imports and exports. Imports steadily increased during the pre-war years.[17] What is remarkable is that those historical trends represent current concerns about today's food system.

Without the full benefit of the tools coming into use in modern agriculture—tractors were just in their infancy and crop treatment options were limited—American farmers (in general), cultivated large acreages with only modest efficiency. Agricultural production increased largely because more acreage came into cultivation. For the most part, this method had served the nation's interests, because there was a large (seemingly endless) supply of arable land. But America was past its expansion days.[18] While the pre-war years were part of the "Golden Age" in America for some farmers due to relatively good prices and returns, rural life and production agriculture were not ordered in the same way that industrial life was.[19] The government felt a pressing need to improve the situation, because food shortages and price increases in urban areas had historically led to civic unrest and violence. (There have been a number of food and alcohol riots in the nation's history. Major food riots occurred in urban areas during 1837, 1863 and 1893. The Panic of 1893 led Detroit mayor Hazen Pingree to create "the Detroit Experiment," also called "Potato Patch Farms" in 1894.[20]) Dual needs informed government policy makers: the need to increase agricultural output and the need to reduce consumption. These needs generated a variety of wartime initiatives and programs, including the NWGC.

There were not only economic imperatives to synthesize rural and urban life: there were also cultural ones. In the view of certain Progressives, America's entry into World War I demanded that citizens subsume individual interests and play a greater role in the nation's collective wartime life. Progress required a more ordered and collective existence.[21] "Pioneer life ... stimulated independence and called for individual effort ... it fostered the spirit of self-reliance ... the most characteristic features of the American people.... But increase in population and wealth, scientific knowledge and modern methods of industry ... demand organization and cooperation and turn individualism from strength to weakness."[22] Interestingly, Americans still struggle with the idea of maintaining the sense of the individual versus the sense of collective. The challenge for those leading the wartime gardening programs was to evoke individual effort and the "spirit of self-reliance" while yoking American citizens to larger and more modern ideas of collective service to nation.[23] Again, it is a struggle America still faces and that we can see in our work in gardens today: gardening in a contemporary sense meets a deep desire for self-sufficiency in American life, but also the desire we have to be in community with one another, and to use our collective work to make our communities better places to live.

Roots: Myth and Practice

To flourish, seeds require fertile soil, water and warmth. The national call to garden during World War I fell onto particularly fertile soil. What about the nation's gardening history prepared the nation's psyche to capitalize on this imperative? The answer lies in both myth and practice. The influence of myth was powerful; the practice included the streams of other gardening movements (school, vacant lot cultivation, Garden Cities, and others) that became a national confluence during World War I.

Americans are often presented (and frequently still view themselves) as an agricultural people who have never entirely forgotten the Jeffersonian agrarian ideal and our nation's rural roots.[24] To this day, we celebrate agriculture and the American farmer; images of "amber waves of grain" and "fruited plains" are part of our nation's cultural heritage.[25] Few of us practice agriculture today, but nearly all of us perpetuate the myth of farming and the importance of the farmer in American life (even if we don't know one, although new programs such as the USDA's Know Your Farmer, Know Your Food are encouraging consumers to learn more about those who produce the food we eat).

Gardening links the myth and practice of agriculture. In practice, gardening is agriculture on a personal scale; it represents an individual's relationship to a specific piece of land. In World War I, gardening also sought to link the individual and cultivated land to the nation as an expression of patriotism and service, by evoking a connection to the myth of an agrarian nation. Historian Thomas Bassett argues that the vacant lot garden was made into a "symbolic space where the quarter-acre plot was equated with homesteads and gardeners with yeomen."[26] This notion reinforces the Jeffersonian agrarian model of citizenship—agricultural production as civic virtue—ideas that were reemphasized at the beginning of the 20th century in the work of Liberty Hyde Bailey and others involved in the Country Life Movement.

Even today, gardening still links rural and urban interests, not only experientially, but also through the shared language that frames the planting, tending and harvesting of food. In today's city, large-scale gardening becomes "urban agriculture," a part of the agricultural ethos that can be experienced by even a city dweller. Gardening is a democratizing experience; the intent, experiences, and best practices of gardening are largely undifferentiated by class, economic, and gender differences. Gardening builds bridges and calms troubled waters.

In contemporary America home gardening is not typically essential to survival. It is an enjoyable activity with physical markers of productivity, but it is not generally an important part of a family's economic base. In terms of survival and economic advancement, gardening was much more critical to American families in the past. In colonial times, kitchen gardens were central to the household economy. A good household garden could provide much of a family's food and was an important hedge against a bad field harvest or difficult economic times. Gardens were useful in any number of ways, including as a source of medicinal herbs and plants that could cure disease and illness, and as dye for coloring clothing. A household garden also provided a way for women to participate in the economy by marketing surplus product through barter and trade. Gardening skills were valued and passed from generation to generation (along with seeds). Values of thrift and a work ethic could be instilled through gardening. Gardening could be a collective activity as well; some communities developed large-scale plots that were commonly tended. American rituals of unity and celebration focusing on the harvest could be replicated in small but important ways in home and community gardens. American home gardens may also have served an important psychological purpose: American soil not yet overworked and depleted provided security and contrast to the overworked soil and deprivation common in parts of Europe.[27]

Gardens also provided—and still do—an important link for Americans to understand, at least conceptually, larger-scale agricultural operations. As smaller scale, more diversified agriculture was giving way to larger operations emphasizing single crop production, gardens may have provided a way for Americans to understand a simpler and more sustainable past, when their food system was more regionally and locally based, and those who produced the food interacted more directly with those who consumed it.

In practice, gardening has been a persistent and organized civic activity in urban areas for well over a century. The Panic of 1893, an economic downturn that brought distress to both urban and rural populations, was particularly difficult on Americans; there were few social safety nets for the poor and destitute. Programs we view as commonplace today, such as unemployment insurance, food stamp benefits (now called the "supplemental nutritional assistance program") and subsidized healthcare were non-existent. Ironically, the Panic of 1893 and its strains of income disparity and corporate greed have been echoed in the most recent American downturn, and once again, urban gardening programs have come to the fore as a form a relief. And as in that earlier time, some politicians and political parties carry forth an argument that government subsidy and relief programs should be cut and replaced by private, voluntary assistance programs through churches and other non-profit organizations.

The Panic of 1893 created a dangerous social climate in America, particularly in urban areas teeming with under- and unemployed factory workers. The recent Occupy movement, which began in 2011, is a mild reminder of the power that large groups of protesters can wield in urban areas. Recent political and social movements in other parts of the globe (such as the 2011 Arab Spring) have turned violent and have overthrown governments and paralyzed major urban areas (consider the riots in London in the summer of 2011). The crisis wrought by the Panic of 1893 brought to the fore a model of relief gardening that quickly took hold across the United States, and which could inform today's urban experience. The "Potato Patch Farms" model, also called the "Detroit Experiment," emerged under the leadership of Detroit's mayor, Hazen Pingree.[28]

Pingree's model connected hundreds of acres of vacant land in Detroit with unemployed workers and their families, who were provided with the materials, tools, and education to garden the unused land.[29] Pingree's idea of ethical relief was met with strong resistance from many who believed that the unemployed—many of them immigrants—were too lazy to work.[30] (A similar sentiment was expressed more than a century later by 2012 Republican presidential candidate Newt Gingrich, who shared his opinion that "really poor children in really poor neighborhoods have no habits of working.") The idea of ethical relief was simple: to provide temporary assistance while maintaining "good" work habits in the recipients.

The United States was not the first nation to connect unused land and needy populations; there were historical precedents in England, France, and Sweden. More than a century later, urban agriculture in Detroit continues to make news, as a crisis created by depopulation, unemployment, and poverty has led to the development of a number of successful models in urban agriculture. And more than one hundred years after Hazen Pingree introduced the potato patch model to Detroit, a new generation of residents is seeking to transform and revitalize the city through a network of innovative gardening and urban agricultural work. D-Town Farm, operated by the Detroit Black Community Food Security Network (DBCFSN), has helped the Detroit community strategize about food security and food justice. The Farm serves as a regional training center for a new generation of urban farmers, in partnership with Growing Power, another successful urban model fashioned by MacArthur genius grant recipient Will Allen (Growing Power is based in Milwaukee, but operates in other urban areas). The D-Town Farm has expanded from two to seven acres, and also has served as a point of innovation for a variety of other programs and projects, including a food buying cooperative and a lecture series. The non-profit DBCFSN has successfully addressed food justice issues in Detroit and improved food access and food security in its community, much as the Potato Patch Farms helped Detroit residents more than a century ago.

Hantz Farms, a business enterprise, seeks to convert vacant land in Detroit into agricultural production. In December 2012, a major controversy erupted in the City of Detroit, when, in a 5–4 vote, the city council decided to sell 140 acres of city-owned land on the east side to Hantz Woodlands, at a cost of 8 cents per square foot. Hantz has agreed to tackle urban blight by clearing debris, demolishing vacant structures and planting 15,000 trees on the acreage. Detroit's urban agriculture and community activists have resisted the project, citing the city's resistance to selling land to citizen farmers at the same price, calling it a "corporate land grab." As interest in urban agriculture grows, there will be more disputes over land access and zoning. Land is wealth, even in what might be considered blighted urban areas. How we move forward in finding ways to distribute (really, redistribute) productive land in an equitable fashion will determine how well we deal with the challenges facing us on the food front, and in other areas of social concern. Despite the successful efforts in many urban areas, much work remains to be done.

Detroit's Georgia Community Garden (now the Georgia Street Community Collective), featured in *TIME* magazine in 2009, is another example of a successful urban gardening program. Mark Covington began his work as a garden activist by clearing a debris-filled vacant lot near his home after he lost his job. He started gardening. Now there is a greenhouse, chickens, and a goat, and the gardening project has expanded to other community self-help projects, including an informal after-school program for youth. The collective's theme is "One House, One Block, One Neighborhood at a Time." The North Cass Community Garden, operated in midtown Detroit by the University Cultural Center Association, is yet another model that is working in Detroit.

Located on the site of a former gas station, it provided the kind of environmental mitigation challenges commonly found in urban areas. (Lead contamination of urban soil is a key concern, and is an obstacle to some community-based gardening projects.)

In 1893, as at present, skeptics were wrong about the appetite for work among impoverished and immigrant residents: 3,000 families applied for the 975 allotments available the first year of the Potato Patch program (1894).[31] The program grew during the next two seasons (1,546 families participated in 1895, 1,701 families gardened in 1896).[32] The city's agricultural committee kept records of the investments made in the program and the value of crops harvested. In 1896, the value of food produced in Detroit's potato patches was greater than the money provided to needy citizens by the "poor commission." The idea quickly spread to other urban areas: New York City, Buffalo, Philadelphia, Boston, and Seattle were among nineteen cities sponsoring vacant lot projects on some scale, according to an 1898 report.[33] The model Pingree developed in Detroit was particularly innovative and visionary for its time; it clearly provided a rationale for the cultivation of vacant lots during the NWGC's effort in World War I.

The Garden City Movement influenced the work of the NWGC (and was also claimed by that organization). The focus of the NWGC was on food production, although the program drew from the Garden City movement, which, like the NWGC, represented a variety of reform impulses. Progressive reformers may have been dissatisfied with rural life, but they felt discontent with urban life as well. The Garden City movement was a response to that discontent. The Garden City movement was a civic impulse that sought to provide "moral uplift" through city beautification and greening, and also to create landscapes that blended the best aspects of urban and rural experience.[34] Its original attempt was to provide something closer to a utopian community than either rural or urban life alone could provide. In some ways, the Garden City movement anticipated the development of the ultimate American middle landscape: the suburb.

The word "garden" is laden with meaning as both physical and spiritual space; the Garden City movement combined both meanings. It not only represented the New Jerusalem of the American Puritan dream in a spiritual sense, but also echoed its intent as a social construct that would determine how cities were viewed and developed.[35] Clearly, the NWGC sought to develop a new kind of American city through wartime work, to transform the country into "A Nation of Garden Cities."[36]

The Garden City movement is not easy to classify or characterize: like the NWGC, it contained many Progressive impulses and agendas. Some efforts were simultaneously "charitable and civic."[37] City beautification didn't limit the focus to ornamental horticulture; it also included food production. The movement carried forth qualities and benefits that were both "material and spiritual" in nature; this was certainly a theme evoked by the NWGC in its work during World War I. In essence, the Garden City movement gathered many threads of social reform agendas and combined them with different models of gardening in America, reweaving them into a civic fabric that could shelter the interests of many.[38] Distinct gardening movements served multiple purposes: civic gardening programs incorporated many elements, including nature study, the Americanization of immigrants and recreation, rejuvenation, and respite from the challenges of a highly industrialized urban existence.

In addition to attempting to reform urban life, the Garden City experience in America hewed strongly to the concept of rational and aesthetic planning (the movement coincided with the growing trend to professional specialization in many fields). In many ways, this was represented in the life of Frederick Law Olmsted, who considered the social gospel an essential component of successful planning, and who believed that social benefits would accrue from the city beautiful implementation.[39] Olmsted believed that the cultivation of the physical aesthetic also cultivated the intellectual and civic life of an individual—and by extension the community—and could reform social ills. Olmsted was an early urban agrarian and reformer who valued rural life, as he believed that it could renew the challenged spirits of urban dwellers. His efforts at rural-urban synthesis—and his attempts to achieve some degree of "urban pastoralism"—were evident in his promotion of natural, open cities that featured parks and green spaces, including gardens.[40]

The Garden City movement in America assured that the notion of vacant lot cultivation persisted in the years prior to the war, and also generally kept alive in the minds of Progressive reformers the potential of urban gardens to accomplish many reform goals. Civic gardening assured that urban gardening in a wide range of forms remained a persistent—and even pervasive, in some areas—activity. In this way, the movement helped keep the soil fertile and receptive for the national gardening movement that was to follow.

Forests and Gardens

Charles Lathrop Pack organized the NWGC in March 1917, just prior to America's entry into World War I; he served as its president until the program was decommissioned in June 1919.[41] The NWGC was not a governmental agency, but rather a private-public partnership that loosely aligned with the government to accomplish national gardening goals. Organizationally, the NWGC found a home in the American Forestry Association (AFA) Conservation Department. The AFA was created to "promote public understanding and support of sound national, state, and private forest policies."[42] The AFA was a powerful advocacy force for public policies that benefitted the timber industry; however, the organization also provided national leadership for conservation and natural resource education efforts. An example of this kind of dual work conducted by the AFA was the McNary-Woodruff Act, which provided federal funds to purchase forests for national use—mixed commercial and recreation.

Thus, the organizational location of the NWGC's work came about as a practical matter, via a personal and professional association. Percival S. Risdale was the executive secretary of the AFA; he worked with Pack while the latter was the AFA president. This offers an explanation of how a national garden campaign became linked with the seemingly disparate issue of forest conservation (through the AFA's Conservation Division), as opposed to the USDA.[43] It was through the AFA organization that Pack met P.S. Risdale, who served as AFA's publicist, writer, and editor of the AFA's magazine, *American Forestry*. (Forest and garden became inextricably linked, and more information about this is provided in Chapter Five, which presents a discussion about the Pennsylvania School of Horticulture for Women.)

Professionally trained in forestry and other aspects of plant science, Pack held deep concerns about American agricultural production even before the war. He was a serious and avid proponent of forest conservation, and during World War I, added the topics of home gardening and agricultural education to his advocacy work. He was also a successful business magnate with strong organizational and media skills, specific ideas about professional practice, and an ardent desire to aid his nation.

There are conflicting stories about how the NWGC came into existence, and cloudiness around its relationship with the federal government. Certainly, the federal government had a more limited role in civic life at the outset of World War I than it does today (opinion varies on the reach of the state during the era).[44] The government was not fully prepared to tackle by itself the mobilization of the nation for the war effort; it relied upon the voluntarism of American citizens and partnerships with private organizations to achieve wartime goals. The notion of voluntarism was a strong part of the philosophy underpinning many home front mobilization efforts. The government did play an important role in gardening and food conservation efforts, but many of Pack's contemporaries felt he was the primary mover behind the NWGC. He was a founder, served as its president and provided much of the operational funding.[45] And operational funding was key: Pack personally contributed $375,739 to the NWGC, in addition to raising funds for its wartime gardening work. To appreciate the extent of Pack's largesse, one can note that this amount is more than the administration of Woodrow Wilson provided to the USSGA.

In his own book, *The War Garden Victorious*, there is no mention of government's involvement in the founding of the NWGC. Rather, Pack describes vigilant citizens who saw an unmet need and devised a solution. "Keen-eyed Americans who saw the situation as it really was, decided that if the mountain would not go to Mahomet, they would see that Mahomet went to the mountain.... These men, with that vision without which the people would perish, possessed imagination."[46] Another contemporary report of the NWGC's work, appearing in *Country Gentleman* magazine, was even more dismissive of the government, reporting that "for a number of reasons—or no reason at all—our Federal overseer of husbandry was asleep at the switch when the call for action came.... It took a private citizen ... and has caused most people to think that the United States Government was doing it."[47] Later in the piece, the government's response was described as "pathetic."[48]

But the NWGC *did* maintain relationships with the federal government. In several of its gardening and food preservation guides, it includes letters from Newton Baker, secretary of war and a representative from the newly formed federal Food Administration.[49] The NWGC had a particularly friendly relationship with the Bureau of Education's USSGA program and assisted that organization by providing posters and gardening curriculum.

Charles Lathrop Pack remains somewhat of an enigma. He was a wealthy timber man and civic leader.[50] Loosely reputed to be one of the five wealthiest Americans in the pre-war years, Pack lent his name and considerable resources to the NWGC.[51] Much of the NWGC's success is directly attributable to the resources and connections Pack was able to provide. Pack was passionate about wartime gardening and able to persuade others to join the cause, although how he came to the cause himself remains somewhat obscure. The character and motives of Charles Lathrop Pack remain obscure. Pack is a complex character; some have accused him of self-aggrandizement and great hypocrisy. His professional and philanthropic contributions to the field of forest conservation and forestry education, however, were critical in the development of these sciences. Professionally, Pack's credentials (if not his application of them in his own work) were respected and remain so. His books on forestry are included in the American Core Historical Literature of Agriculture.[52] Pack was not a gardener or farmer per se; he is best known for his work in the emerging conservation effort of the early 20th century, and specifically for his contributions to the fields of forest conservation and forestry education.[53]

Pack was apparently greatly influenced by his participation in President Theodore Roosevelt's Conference of Governors, which was held in May 1908 at the White House. This was one of the first national-level conversations about natural resource conservation in the United States, and participants emphasized the importance of using renewable resources. Roosevelt delivered the opening address, which was entitled "Conservation as a National Duty."[54] Gifford Pinchot, the nation's forester, played a key role in organizing the conference. The Pinchot family was wealthy and endowed the School of Forestry at Yale University (still in existence). In 1898 Gifford Pinchot became chief of the Division of Forestry (later the U.S. Forest Service). Pinchot and Pack became close friends and collaborators on conservation advocacy and education. (The Pack family fortune, ironically, was in part made by clear-cut timber harvesting in the American South and British Columbia; Pack may have touted the replanting of cut trees and reforestation efforts, but did not always practice sustainable forest management techniques.) Pack was generous with his resources, however: numerous forestry research stations, experimental forests, and endowed chairs still bear his family's name. Washington State and the State University of New York system were two of the many beneficiaries of Pack's largesse. Whatever his motivations, his work was of great significance.

Pack was an extraordinarily ambitious man with big ideas. He saw the work of the NWGC as a national crusade that required the "systematic" education of "100 million people" through "persistent publicity" and "continual preachment."[55] In this work, Pack was joined by a distinguished group of Progressive leaders. Pack's goals for the NWGC clearly described the nation's need:

> War conditions made it essential that food should be raised where it had not been produced in peace times, with labor not engaged in agricultural work and not taken from any other industry, and in places where it made no demand upon the railroads already overwhelmed with transportation burdens.[56]

Pack was incorrect in his assessment that food had not been produced in urban areas during peacetime, but the other issues he raised warrant attention. Other NWGC members were equally prominent. Careful examination of the NWGC's board reveals that it was rich in the kinds of personal and professional associations that proved fundamental to its success as a proponent of national gardening.[57]

Among the members were scientist Luther Burbank, noted plant breeder and cousin to the heirs of the Burpee seed dynasty. In his lifetime, Luther Burbank developed more than 800 varieties of fruits, vegetables, grain crops, and ornamentals. His work in developing pest and disease resistant varieties (including the Burbank potato, which would end fears of potato blight) revolutionized agriculture.[58] Burbank's feelings were obvious. On behalf of the NWGC, he offered the following statement sharing his view that agricultural education had been neglected in America: "Agriculture and horticulture had not generally been taught in the schools; the old hit-or-miss plan of farming was all too common; the home garden was neglected and the school garden a novelty."[59] Like others associated with the NWGC, he saw the education of youth through the school system as vital to the nation's future; this belief had a strong influence on programs such as the USSGA.

P.P. Claxton, U.S. commissioner of education (1911–1921), headed the agency (the BOE) that oversaw the USSGA; he was also a member of the NWGC. Again, in typical Progressive fashion, through networks of association and professional interest, the NWGC linked with other wartime efforts, and in the process, amplified its message. Other members of the NWGC board included representatives from higher education, among them Dr. Charles Eliot, former president of Harvard (and an important Progressive thinker); Dr. Irving Fisher, president of Yale University; and John Hibben, a pastor who succeeded Woodrow Wilson as president of Princeton. Inventor and wealthy philanthropist John Hays Hammond was among the NWGC's most brilliant and interesting members. Myron Herrick, former ambassador to France, was also a member. In organizing the NWGC, Pack saw the importance and value of including agricultural interests: Carl Vrooman, assistant secretary of agriculture, served on the board.[60] Vital to the success of wartime mobilization efforts on the home front were women's civic groups. Realizing this, the NWGC's membership included one woman: Mrs. John Dickenson Sherman, chairman of the Conservation Department of the General Federation of Women's Clubs. (The General Federation of Women's Clubs, a national organization of women's groups, focused on reform and civic service, and played an important role in mobilizing women and children to participate in the war garden effort.)

The membership of the NWGC represented well-connected Progressive thinkers with personal and professional ties to numerous national associations and organizations. Their associations greatly aided the proliferation of the war gardening message. For example, NWGC member P.P. Claxton, who also served as the United States education commissioner, helped the NWGC gain entrée to public schools through a targeted campaign creating the USSGA, which marked one of the first federal efforts to influence the curriculum and activities of American school children on a national basis.

The Location of Wartime Gardening

The NWGC aggressively promoted wartime gardening on the home front. It targeted Americans of all ages and stripes, including children, women and immigrants. It also sought to encourage gardening in a variety of spaces: schools, homes, community areas, vacant lots, on industrial easements, in workplaces, at military bases and nearly anywhere else that people gathered. The

NWGC encouraged gardens of all shapes and sizes, from multi-acre workplace gardens to modest window gardens for urban dwellers. A number of publications published tables providing detailed garden plans for spaces ranging from 15 by 20 feet (labeled a city garden) to 40 by 40 feet (a suburban garden).[61] Gardening linked urban, suburban, and rural interests in service to the nation and the land.

American experience with—and reliance upon—the "commons" had diminished over time, as private life and enterprise gained prominence and Americans became disconnected from their rural roots. Gardening programs during World War I brought back from our English and colonial roots the example—and power—of places such as Boston Common, and the idea of the use of public land for the common or collective good. For example, portions of Boston Common were turned into a massive community garden cultivated by various civic, community, and youth groups.[62] Public parks around the nation provided space for demonstration gardens and for war gardening efforts. Lands previously given over for the beautification of cities or for recreational potential were given a new purpose—creating a unified home front and building morale— and transformed into productive urban agricultural use. The land near San Francisco's Civic Center was turned into a garden; a War Garden Day celebration in the city drew thousands of citizens. (In a commentary on the similarities between challenges facing America's food system during World War I and today San Francisco has once again planted a Victory Garden at its Civic Center, more than ninety years after the outset of World War I. The city has also started a new Victory Garden Program that is attempting to increase community-based food security by teaching low-income families how to grow their own food.[63]) Potomac Park, near the Washington Monument, served as a site for Liberty/Victory Gardens tended by citizens.[64]

The NWGC created a demonstration garden near New York's Union Square, in the heart of the city.[65] The Union Square demonstration garden, created by Park Commissioner Cabot Ward in response to the Mayor's call for "soldiers of the soil," was particularly evocative because of its location next to another recruiting station: this one for the United States Navy, which consisted of a huge model of a battleship, featuring guns and demonstrations of military drills by sailors. Historic sites were also considered suitable for war gardens: Grover Cleveland's birthplace provided a home for a garden tilled by Boy Scouts.[66] No space in American public life was too sacred or grand for the humble act of food production. In fact, gardening reinforced the importance of American soil (in the most literal sense) and agricultural productivity as not only vital to the nation's success in wartime and the salvation of starving nations abroad, but as an integral—almost sacred—part of American identity.

And the production of food was viewed as vital to liberty. From his post at the International Institute of Agriculture in Rome, agriculturalist David Lubin wrote to NWGC secretary P. S. Risdale, "Food for the Allies is the price, the price we are to pay for liberty; we cannot obtain liberty if we have not that price; and without liberty we shall have slavery, and a full measure of it.... Food production is, therefore, at the present, no more secular labor; it is even more sacred at this time in the world's history than praying in a church."[67] (Lubin's words echoed the sentiments expressed by Abraham Lincoln in 1859, linking food production with liberty.)

In addition to reclaiming public space for wartime gardening, Americans renegotiated their understanding of private property to make room for gardens there. The use of both private and public land for vacant lot cultivation was already a successful model in the preceding three decades as a coping strategy for cities dealing with underemployment and unemployment created by the Panic of 1893 and other economic downturns.[68] But it gained new life during World War I. Gardens were presented as "community assets" that could enhance vacant and unproductive city lots and transform them into places of higher service to the nation and the world.[69] It was not only cities that might claim unused private property for communal gardening use; individual citizens also were encouraged to participate in vacant lot cultivation, "to arouse the patriots of America to the importance of putting all idle land to work."[70] Even school children used vacant lots in their neighborhoods to cultivate war gardens.[71]

Perhaps because of his business background, Charles Lathrop Pack particularly encouraged gardening in the workplace. Numerous corporations provided space and resources for workplace gardens.[72] At least sixty acres of land were set aside for employee gardens at the General Electric Company in Schenectady, New York.[73] Not surprisingly, the Country Life Press in New York turned its grounds into potato fields cultivated by employees.[74] Companies such as Eastman Kodak and Carnegie Steel provided space for wartime gardens. Some anecdotal reports from the period indicate that workplace gardens improved relations between employees and employers, improved morale, and may have even reduced turnover, in part simply because employees valued their investment in wartime gardening efforts and were reluctant to leave established gardens behind.[75] There is evidence from both World War programs that gardening mediated differences between groups, smoothing over class, social, economic, and even, in some cases, racial differences.[76]

Private property owned by railroads became prime gardening land, as those companies provided easements to employees, communities, and other groups seeking to cultivate wartime gardens.[77] Wartime gardens also demonstrated democracy at its most successful, easing class, socioeconomic, and ethnic distinctions, which also became a claim of the Woman's Land Army of America, where college coeds and factory "girls" worked together as manual laborers, or in the case of a workplace garden where immigrants from many different nations worked together to cultivate food for the war effort. In some ways, then, wartime gardening provided a way for Americans to accommodate the nation's inherent pluralism, especially in community settings and places of work.

Wartime gardening efforts also helped Americans reclaim private spaces. The home would be, as Laura Lawson terms it, "the point of intervention."[78] Home gardening was declining in importance in early twentieth-century American life, but World War I renewed extant gardens and introduced gardens to households that had not cultivated them previously. Even the USSGA program, which was school-based, termed its work "a school-supervised home gardening effort."[79] While gardening activity took place in many different public and private spheres, much of the effort focused on the importance of home gardens to the success of the nation's wartime gardening efforts. Women were critical to that "point of intervention." Mrs. John Dickinson Sherman, the sole female on the NWGC's board, said of the opportunity to produce food in wartime, "American women are confronted by a condition and a responsibility and opportunity without parallel in the history of the world."[80] Thus, garden promoters helped to extend the public sphere (and purpose) into private space, expanding government's presence into the back lots and side yards of countless private homes.

The emergency of wartime also enabled the NWGC to redefine space as it related to understandings of individual property rights, which were relaxed to enable the cultivation of "slacker" land. NWGC leaders co-opted the concept of the "private sphere" and used it to expand the reach of the federal government. Had this not been a time of national emergency, such an intrusion into private rights would have been much more controversial. In large part, however, dissent was quelled by calls to patriotism, by evoking America's agrarian myth, by the real need to address issues in the nation's food system, and possibly by the fact that gardening seemed like such an ordinary, wholesome and unifying activity. Thus, a school student named Harriet in Long Beach, California, felt empowered to cultivate bean plants on a vacant lot owned by her neighbor, Mrs. Charles Bate, in response to the call to serve her nation.

Food Conservation

Americans met wartime food goals not only through increased food production, but also through food conservation efforts. While this book is not about food conservation, a topic that has been covered superbly by other historians, some of the bounty harvested from America's Liberty/Victory Gardens was conserved. And the fruits and vegetables produced in gardens made it possible to reduce the consumption of staple foods and ship more to America's allies, helping the nation achieve food conservation goals. The methods and messages encouraging gardening and food conservation were inextricably intertwined. Food conservation, after all, is the flip side of food production. It deserves some discussion.

America's entry into World War I required an enormous shift in the nation's resources. By the war's end, America had exported 23 million metric tons of food to Europe, an astounding amount of food. Historian Rae Eighmey argues that wartime food conservation was "the first large-scale, social-networking enterprise of the twentieth century."[81] Eighmey makes a wonderful point. Along with its companion programs in gardening and home front food production, food conservation did represent an unprecedented mobilization of American citizens, and it did take advantage of the social and community networks that were not only local, but that were national in scope and characteristic of the Progressive Era.

Eighmey's point is particularly resonant when considered within the context of today's food movement and its effective use of social technologies, such as Twitter, Facebook and Instagram, among others. Some food enterprises are now using crowd-sourcing models to fund their work, including Kickstarter. While those seeking to mobilize support during World War I used pledge cards, posters, four-minute talks and other means to convince their friends and neighbors to join in the efforts—all socially-oriented communication forms of the Progressive Era—today's food activists use new forms of social technology to communicate their messages and mobilize support around their agendas. Social technology, which research indicates is being used increasingly by younger audiences and those of color, levels the playing field in terms of message and advertising. It is free, it is adaptable, and it is fast. In many cases, food activists are using social technologies to "speak truth to power" and are taking on major corporations and institutions they regard as being part of the "food problem" in the United States. Witness the use of social technologies in the recent mobilization of America's fast food workers nationwide, who are staging strikes to protest low wages and poor working conditions.

Realizing the value of social technologies in advocating for the transformation of the food system, some foundations are offering fellowships to food activists, fellowships that focus on developing the capacity of young people to use social technologies to persuade, influence and ultimately change the food system. Smart phone applications that provide ways for those interested in transforming the food system to find resources or connect with like-minded individuals are common. One can certainly draw many similarities to how Americans influenced their peers to garden and conserve food nearly 100 years ago to how Americans are using social media to engage and build movements on line today.

When America entered the war in April 1917, efforts were immediately undertaken to reduce food consumption and food waste. Those efforts might be extraordinarily useful in addressing today's national (and global) crisis involving food waste. Once again, food waste in America is gaining attention, as we seek not only to address limited space in landfills, but also to address the moral and ethical issues related to hunger, food access, and the careless disposal of food that is entirely usable. The problem is intractable and counterintuitive. On the one hand, we are a nation of incredible food abundance, but on the other, we have millions of people who are food insecure in our nation. We are a hungry nation, but we throw away a shocking amount of food. It is estimated by the U.S. government that between 30 and 40 percent of our nation's food supply is thrown away annually, representing an average of $390 per year, per consumer. (This figure represents a month's worth of food for many.) In June 2013, the USDA and the Environmental Protection Agency (EPA) launched a U.S. Food Waste Challenge. The Challenge focuses on reducing food waste and on what it terms "food recovery." It includes reducing waste in the federal school nutrition program, and educating consumers about food waste and food storage (and conservation). The USDA will also work with industry to streamline administrative procedures for donating misbranded food products. As part of the challenge, the USDA will test a meat-composting program to reduce the amount of meat being sent to landfills (as part of the food inspection process). All of these things are vital, because in addition to the ethical issues involved, food waste has significant environmental effects, not only on the consumption of freshwater and fossil fuels, but also because the methane and CO_2 emissions from decomposing foods may be contributing to climate change. A recent study indicates that food waste in the U.S. has sharply increased since 1974, and currently represents 1400 kcals per day, per person.[82] There are wonderful lessons to be garnered from past, and imperative reasons to reconsider the food conservation policies developed during World War I.

World War I food conservation efforts gained steam on June 5, 1917, when the draft began, registering men between the ages of 21 and 30. The scope of the mobilization effort of American men into what became known as the American Expeditionary Force was unprecedented, as millions of young men began moving into training camps to prepare for deployment overseas. America had always believed in a small standing army, and the sheer number of men called up to service—ultimately, nearly four million—was staggering. These young men needed to be housed, to be trained to fight the Hun ... and to be fed. Two themes, then, began to drive the food conservation and home front food production efforts: feeding American soldiers, and feeding starving European allies.

University-trained home economists helped to devise menus for soldiers

Keep it Coming. Artist: George Illian (1894–1932). United States Food Administration (1917). Food trucks make their way across snow-covered roads behind the lines in this poster reminding Americans to waste nothing, as food is vital to feed soldiers and European civilians alike (Museum of Ventura County, photographer Aysen Tan).

in training, and also turned to helping homemakers cope with wheatless and meatless days, and less sugar. And in fact, wartime food conservation efforts provided a wonderful opportunity to educate the American public about nutrition, a relatively new area of scientific practice, and professionals in the area seized upon it as an opportunity to improve the nation's overall health. Home economists were employed by—or volunteered for service with—the Food

Administration and the USDA. These women churned out recipes and menus that provided for reduced use of sugar, butter, wheat and meat. They created educational materials, curriculum, courses, and a variety of outreach materials to educate Americans about nutrition and the best practices of food preparation and conservation. The USDA used the opportunity presented by war time to conduct national research on the food habits in hundreds of American homes, providing vital baseline information that could be combined with information gathered from the male draft to gain information about the health and dietary practices of the nation's citizens. The USDA and Food Administration cross-referenced one another in their work and collaborated on the national effort.

Proponents of the "New Nutrition," the USDA and the Food Administration emphasized substitution of often used food items such as meat, white flour, butter, and sugar. For example, protein from beans could be substituted for meat. Instead of relying on white flour, consumers could find carbohydrates from corn meal and oats (instead of wheat). Recipes offering reduced use of fats and sugars were quickly produced, and were shared throughout the nation, scribbled on paper and handed to a next door neighbor, or reprinted in newspapers and shared nationwide. It is estimated that during this effort, Americans reduced their meat consumption by about half. (And certain Americans—the middle class—consumed more fresh fruits and vegetables and milk.[83])

The daily average calorie allocation for soldiers in training was approximately 4,000 calories. Many draftees from less affluent settings had never been

Sugar—Save It. United States Food Administration (1918). This poster lists a number of ways in which Americans could save sugar, from using less in coffee and tea to using other sweeteners altogether. This advice could improve America's health today (Library of Congress).

... Eat more fish. Artist: Charles Livingston Bull (1874-1932). United States Food Administration (1917). By eating more fish, the public could conserve "the products of the Land" (Museum of Ventura County, photographer Aysen Tan).

as well fed as they were during their military service; weight gain was common during training. The quality and quality of food was a topic that often appeared in letters written home by draftees, who described large and varied meals. The daily average calorie allocation for civilians on the home front who voluntarily followed the recommended food consumption patterns was approximately 2,000 calories per day.[84] It would be remarked upon in the 1930s by those who had participated in the food conservation and Victory Garden programs of World War I that the period marked a "watershed" in America's attitudes toward food; people realized that they could get by with less food, although the positive effects appeared primarily in the middle and upper middle class.[85]

Corn—The Food of the Nation. Artist: Lloyd Harrison. United States Food Administration (1918). Corn is served in a variety of forms including grits, muffins, and hominy, in this poster highlighting the importance of corn, which was preferred as a more economical choice over wheat during the war years (Museum of Ventura County, photographer Aysen Tan).

A coherent national plan featuring a variety of policies and recommendations for different groups was needed to guide the home front. Herbert Hoover proved to be the single most influential American in that regard, creating a "food front" that supported the nation's military goals. Before America entered the war, Hoover had worked as a private citizen in relief efforts, first organizing assistance for American expatriates trapped in the war zone in Europe, and then extending his efforts to organize relief for Belgian civilians affected by the German invasion. Hoover's efforts on behalf of Belgium demonstrated his prowess in encouraging broad and massive voluntary participation in such programs, while keeping administration to a minimum through the strategic and effective use of volunteers. Hoover was also a master at publicity, and his work not only elevated the needs of suffering non-combatants in Europe, but also his own profile. He was held in great esteem by the American public, well known to the Wilson's administration, and would be ideally positioned to become America's "food czar" when it entered the war.

As early as March 1917, before war was declared on Germany, Wilson's administration conceptualized legislation that would enable the federal government to enact controls over various aspects of the food system. America's painful experiences with food riots in urban areas, food shortages, and rampant inflation fueled concerns about civil stability, hoarding, price gouging, food access and distribution in the case of a national emergency. The idea of more coherently organizing and managing the food system found life in legislation proposed by U.S. Representative A.F. Lever of South Carolina (who had partnered with Senator Hoke Smith on the 1914 Smith-Lever legislation that created the Cooperative Extension Service). Lever's legislation called for a new federal agency—the Food Administration—which would be given broad powers to regulate the food supply. (And this notion of more direct federal oversight of the nation's food system strongly influenced the larger ideas of regulating, organizing and rationalizing the food system that appeared post–World War I, during the New Deal.) If the legislation was passed, the new food agency would be empowered to enter the market (purchasing and distributing food), to license food producers (and distributors), to regulate food production and distribution, to fix farm prices (if needed), and to impose rationing.[86] The legislation provided for oversight and influence of both public and private practice, and at all locations in the food system: production, distribution, and consumption. The Food Administration could exercise some degree of authority and influence over some of the nation's largest corporations, as well as individual citizens.

Congress was in a fractious mood, and the legislation creating the Food Administration was not passed until August 1917. But Hoover used the several months prior to the legislation's passage to great effect. He worked closely with the USDA to develop materials for distribution to consumers. During that period, it was imprinted on the American mind that the nation's food conservation and home front food production efforts would rely, in large part, upon the voluntary participation of Americans. Hoover truly embraced this philosophy, refusing to accept a salary for his service as the nation's food administrator. Eventually, more than 750,000 Americans volunteered for the Food Administration, and millions more would voluntarily adopt food rationing and conservation measures as a demonstration of patriotism and commitment to the nation's wartime goals.

She is doing her part to help win the war. **Artist: Howard Chandler Christy (1873–1952). (1918). A young woman cooks using rolled oats, barley, and corn. Wartime necessity restricted the use of wheat for civilians (Library of Congress).**

Hoover identified a handful of conservation measures, which later appeared on a variety of posters. Eating local food was identified as a key strategy, because that would save transportation resources for the shipment of materiel and men. Consuming more fruits and vegetables (and other perishable items) was also encouraged, as that might save shelf-stable staples to be used to feed troops or to be shipped abroad to America's allies. Hoover also focused on eliminating waste in the food system. Prices on food items such as sugar

Blood or Bread. Artist: Henry Raleigh (1880–1945). United States Food Administration (1917). Conserving food was as important as the blood sacrifice of soldiers, according to the message of this poster (Museum of Ventura County, photographer Aysen Tan).

and wheat had been driven up by European demand and crop failures in 1916, and the new focus on reducing the consumption of key items—coupled with increased home food production—also aimed to help families financially. There was an emphasis on family food self-sufficiency, an impulse that is reemerging today. It was simultaneously a collective expression—doing something for the national good—and also an expression of individualism—the spirit of the American pioneer self-sufficiency reborn.

The element of sacrifice was also emphasized. The Food Administration and USDA (and various wartime committees) printed elaborate food schedules. Each meal represented an opportunity to sacrifice, reduce or substitute a scarce food item for something more readily secured. The suggested schedule of restrictions and substitutions became stricter over time; by February 1918, of the 21 weekly meals outlined, only 3 offered no restrictions.[87] Households were asked to sign a "Food Pledge." A neighbor might ask another neighbor to sign the pledge, or a school child might knock on the door and ask a neighbor to sign. Community-wide events were held to secure support for food conservation efforts. While participation was touted as being voluntary, there was extraordinary pressure to participate. Like other home front mobilization efforts, there was a coercive feel to some of the methods used to secure participation.

Those on the home front were reminded that their food sacrifices were vital to the nation's military success. The notion of the blood sacrifice of American soldiers was inextricably linked with the sacrifice of bread (produced with white flour). There was something almost religious in some of the calls to food conservation and home food production, something that elevated the ordinary work of the home front to the sacred work on the battle front: assuring that the light of liberty and freedom would burn brightly and prevail over evil.

Media and Message

Wartime gardening efforts claimed public and private spaces, many of those spaces with great cultural meaning. It also took on increasing importance in the collective American consciousness; this was largely due to the precedence the topic of gardening was given in American media. In addition to the patriotic appeal of wartime gardening work, there was nearly always a reform angle, whether it be community beautification, the value of hard work, or improved nutrition. Media and community messages about this topic, like other home front mobilization efforts, were ubiquitous, relentless, and often coercive in their effort to get all Americans gardening.

The NWGC used a variety of mass media to spread the gardening gospel, including poster art, print media, and speakers bureaus. All forms of publicity—articles, speeches, and posters—incorporated a war-flavored rhetoric. The mass media message systematically linked gardening with the war effort. This message was pervasive. Part of the NWGC's stated mission was "spreading the idea of militant war gardens."[88] The NWGC gardens became "munitions plants."[89]

In particular, posters boasted distinctive looks and themes, and targeted different audiences. The poster series created for the NWGC by children's illustrator Maginel Wright Barney, for example, employed illustrations, colors, and themes that appealed to children. The most popular war gardening image of the day incorporated Lady Liberty and was created by noted artist James Montgomery Flagg. This image showed Lady Liberty (Columbia) dressed in a flag, sowing seed. Various slogans were used with this image throughout the war. To celebrate the arrival of peace, the slogan "Victory Gardens" was incorporated. Poster art was made widely available for home use as well. "Registered War Garden" posters enabled gardeners to proudly display their belief in the gardening gospel on a front door, on a garden fence, or in the window of a school or business.[90] Some cities printed their own war garden registration posters.

Not all exhortations were positive calls to service. NWGC's Charles Lathrop Pack referred to vacant lots as "slacker land," a shockingly provocative term considering the armed raids coercing military service that occurred in some United States cities. The "slacker raids" mark a dark chapter in U.S. history. "Slacker" was the extremely pejorative term given to those avoiding (or appearing to avoid) military service. During one three-day period in New York and New Jersey, armed U.S. sailors and soldiers rounded up thousands of military-aged men at restaurants, ball games and other public places in an effort to conscript them. Many U.S. cities and communities experienced violence associated with slacker raids.[91] Other phrases generated by the NWGC were equally charged. "Hohenrakes versus Hohenzollerns" evoked the Hohenzollern family, which represented Germany and Prussia's dynasty, and the enemy. This play on words reminded American gardeners that all things German were the enemy. Americans were exhorted to "Get into the Garden Trenches," were told "The Hoe is the Machine Gun of the Garden" and "Food Must Follow the Flag."[92]

Public speaking engagements were critical to spreading the gardening gospel, and the NWGC and its local affiliates developed speakers bureaus, identifying community leaders and gardening experts to encourage gardening efforts. Some of the famous "four-minute" men who pitched war bonds at movie theatres also spoke about the importance of war gardens. Lou Henry Hoover, wife of Food Administration head Herbert Hoover, gave the war gardening effort a big boost when she delivered an inspirational speech from the steps of the Washington, D.C., Public Library in April 1918, in which she exhorted her fellow citizens to garden. Hoover also facilitated the effort of the Girl Scout organization to plant war gardens, and even wrote a piece on food conservation for that organization's magazine, *The Rally*.[93]

Members of the NWGC authored articles for a wide variety of high-circulation popular magazines and trade journals, targeting various audiences dividing among gender, age, class, and interest. For example, articles appeared in women's and gardening magazines, as well as in magazines targeted to male audiences, including *Illustrated World* (later absorbed by *Popular Mechanics*) and *Country Gentleman*.[94] Other articles appeared in leading Progressive journals, such as *The Touchstone*.[95] Articles also appeared in both *Country Life* and *American City*, another indication that gardening was linking rural and urban interests. These articles appeared frequently, sometimes monthly. Women's magazines and journals offered regular war gardening articles; some appeared as regular monthly reports or series from war gardeners, or served as "almanac" articles to guide work in the garden.[96]

NWGC leaders and other gardening experts made themselves available for newspaper interviews. At the height of American involvement in the war, between April 1917 and April 1919, the *New York Times* ran a number of pieces pertaining to the work of the NWGC and war gardens in general. Gardening articles were frequent, appearing at least on a weekly basis. Some articles provided technical and practical information, some provided recipes, others simply offered encouragement. Opinion editorial pieces exhorted citizens to "pick up the hoe" for Uncle Sam. Information about the NWGC and war gardening appeared in articles on other subjects as well, including daylight savings time (introduced during the war), agricultural production, education, public policy, weather reports, and even social register articles.

In addition to generating its own forms of publicity, the NWGC utilized other agencies and organizations to encourage gardening and implement educational and community gardening programs, serving as a clearinghouse of information. The work of the NWGC echoed the Food Administration's messages and themes; the Food Administration in turn advertised the availability of NWGC publications. The NWGC cooperated with the Massachusetts Agriculture College at Amherst to provide instructional Victory Garden motion pictures for viewing throughout Massachusetts and New England.[97] Facilitating this effort was well-known landscape architect, Grace Tabor, who campaigned for war gardens through speaking engagements at women's clubs and chambers of commerce.[98] In Ohio, the Red Cross was the NWGC's lead agency, and in some parts of Kansas, the Y.M.C.A. took charge of local war gardening efforts. Every community was encouraged to develop a food committee, and many cities adopted formal efforts to spread the cause of war gardening.

Audiences

The NWGC made a concerted effort to involve a wide range of Americans by encouraging many "genres" of gardening efforts. In a series of cleverly conceived cartoons, the NWGC identified numerous prospective gardeners and gardening sites, including home gardens, school gardens, workplace gardens, vacant lot gardens, community gardens, church gardens, club gardens, and window box gardens. One cartoon shows a garden box perched near the top of a flagpole, being eagerly watered by a happy young gardener. The NWGC encouraged both individual plots (also called "the allotment plan") and undivided, large-tract gardens (also called the "industrial plan"). Scale (size) and location were an important consideration in classifying plots. Home gardens would be considered part of an allotment plan. An industrial plan garden would be demonstrated by the use of Boston Common, or railroad easements given over to the cultivation of potato patches. The NWGC published and distributed information instructing local communities on survey, mapping, information gathering, and planning techniques to encourage industrial and community gardening efforts. Some communities did mapping surveys of vacant lots as part of the vacant lot cultivation movement. (Mapping the food shed using social technologies and GIS is occurring more frequently in today's food movement.) The press cooperated by publishing gardening information that the NWGC provided. Publications emphasized the fact that planning was essential to a successful gardening effort, and often published gardening series to enable gardeners to build their skills incrementally.[99] Gardening received a great deal of print: a single issue of *The Touchstone* published in August 1917 contained three articles providing practical gardening advice totaling nearly fifteen pages, or nearly fourteen percent of the publication. Due in no small part to the work of the NWGC, a significant amount of American print space was devoted to providing instruction to the public about efficient gardening practices. In this and other ways, the NWGC reflected Progressive impulses.

In photographs and cartoons the NWGC showed men, women and children of all ages either engaged in gardening or holding the fruits of their efforts. One of the oldest gardeners pictured was eighty-one-year-old Lewis Hunt of Pearl River, New York, who worked a half-acre plot by himself.[100] Depictions of gardening as a group activity (such as soldiers at Fort Dix, workplace gardens, canning clubs, or young women at a summer resort) also promoted the effort.[101] In an effort to show that immigrants were encouraged to join in this effort, that participating in the war effort was an act of assimilation and loyalty, and indeed, vital to its success, the NWGC published a photograph of a group of male employees at the Inspiration Consolidated Copper Company of Arizona; this group represented twelve different nationalities and many different languages. Employees of the company reportedly cultivated 217 acres of wartime gardens.[102] While the picture of the employees is grainy and difficult to decipher, some of the men appear to be non-white, perhaps Asian, Mexican, or Native American. The NWGC also produced something akin to a modern publicity package through its "War Garden Guyed," a lighthearted look at the national pastime, which provided short stories, gardening jokes, clip-art cartoons and other pieces that could be used by media to promote war gardening in filler space.

While all groups were targeted, women were particularly important to the success of wartime gardening efforts because of their role in the home and in civic efforts on the home front. The NWGC linked with several State Councils of Defense to implement war gardening programs.[103] The Council of National Defense, State Councils Section was charged with coordinating the activities of the individual State Councils of Defense. The Council of National Defense had no authority, and relied on cooperation to achieve its goals. State Councils of Defense undertook responsibility for a wide range of home front and military front mobilization activities during World War I, including war garden efforts in some states. Several State Councils of Defense created woman's land armies, loosely aligned with the NWGC and the Food Administration, to encourage women to garden. State Councils were particularly effective in targeting women for war gardening efforts, which was vital, since women were estimated to control ninety percent of a family's food consumption.[104]

A number of women's organizations, including the National Women's Farm and Garden Association, instituted "agricultural divisions" in an effort to increase women's knowledge of agriculture and encourage home gardening.[105] Women responded in great numbers to the call to cultivate war gardens. This is not surprising: in a not so distant past, women had borne primary responsibility for the cultivation of a family's kitchen garden. Ornamental gardening was also a popular pastime with many middle and upper class women. In addition, wartime mobilization efforts focused strongly on the need for women to provide the extra help needed in countless areas on the home front, as the number of male draftees rose into the millions.

Women's work in home front gardening efforts was notable. Wartime gardening and concurrent food conservation activities created what historian Amy Bentley refers to as "the politics of domesticity": to successfully mobilize the home front, the government had to secure the commitment of American women on the "food front."[106] Since American women managed the family's food supply and consumption, their cooperation was vital to the nation's Liberty/Victory Garden program. While Bentley writes within the context of World War II, much of what she argues also applies to the American home front during World War I. She argues, as do other historians, that while wartime needs have provided opportunities for American women to transcend their traditional roles (and this was certainly true in World War I), wartime also intensifies the need for women to maintain their "traditional role as keepers of civic virtue."[107] By providing service to the nation as gardeners on the home front, women maintained civic virtue and emphasized the importance of the domestic sphere to winning the war.[108] Eve may have led to Adam's banishment from the Garden of Eden, but her work on the home front enabled America to reenter the garden on a massive scale during World War I.

Bentley also emphasizes the "communal nature" of wartime food programs, and in this, her research about World War II also rings true for World War I. Women were bombarded with messages about gardening and food conservation during World War I. Popular magazines were full of articles and advertisements about the importance of the home garden, newspapers featured articles and recipes about the topic, and posters were displayed in many public spaces. There was tremendous pressure on American women to produce food in home gardens, not only as an expression of patriotism and as their concrete contribution to helping America win the war, but as an expression of their role as women. While wartime gardening at home was a private activity, the emphasis on the national need moved gardening into the public realm. Gardening claimed important space in magazines and advertisements targeted to women, and on the American home front during World War I. Messages about food conservation—and the signing of food pledges—placed additional pressure on women to comply on the food front. Within that context, some women may have felt that other women were judging their performance in this area.

Children represented approximately one-third of the American population, and their contribution was important to the success of the NWGC's campaign for several reasons. Not only could children provide necessary labor to cultivate war gardens, but their participation also provided an opportunity to educate them about the importance of agriculture, traditional values of thrift and hard work, and their responsibility as citizens. School-based and other children's war gardening efforts proved particularly successful, not only by inculcating values of service, but by providing experiential learning in agriculture through the act of gardening.

The Harvest

In the wartime months of 1917, there were reported to be approximately 3.5 million home food-producing lots in the United States, with a product valuation of $350 million. Due to the lack of statistics about home gardening prior to this date, this figure was used as the baseline number upon which the NWGC gauged the success of war gardening efforts in the subsequent year. Estimates of home gardens reached 5.3 million in 1918, with a product valuation of $525 million. The 1918 food valuation figure indicates more producing lots, but also perhaps more intensive cultivation and/or higher yields. NWGC chair Pack attributed the increase in part to the adoption of daylight savings time, which ostensibly provided more hours of light in which to work the

War Gardens Victorious. Artist: Maginel Wright Barney (1877–1966). National War Garden Commission (1918). A young farm boy bearing a hoe leads flag-bearing vegetables in a victorious march, embodying the message that every garden planted in war time was a "peace plant" (Library of Congress).

land. The difficulty with any of these statistical figures is their lack of reliability. Their source is *The War Garden Victorious*, a recap of the NWGC's work written by Pack, immediately at the conclusion of World War I. (Even today, home and community food production is notoriously difficult to assess.)

However, even anecdotal evidence, and certainly the pervasiveness of war gardening as a topic in popular media, indicates gardening efforts were prevalent during wartime. Considering the United States population in 1917 (around one hundred million), the statistics presented by the NWGC might be interpreted to suggest that a statistically significant percentage of the home front population—possibly ten to twenty percent—was participating in some sort of war gardening effort. It will likely be difficult ever to devise a method to reliably gauge citizen participation, but even if the NWGC's figures are exaggerated, the participation rate was significant in the amount of food produced and conserved. Equally importantly, the perception of participation created a sense of national unity.

War Gardens Victorious and Beyond

After the November 1918 Armistice, the NWGC began using the terminology "victory gardens" and "war gardens victorious" to refer to the war gardening effort. It continued to produce and distribute posters and publications, which were updated to "victory editions." One of the NWGC's key promotion taglines, "Every Garden a Munitions Plant," was replaced by the more promising phrase, "Every Garden a Peace Plant." Charles Pack and others saw a real need to keep citizens gardening as the world sought to rebuild from the vast devastation wrought by a lengthy war. They lent this new effort their support. There was a systematic effort to keep the momentum of agricultural education going; part of this was carried forward through voluntary associations and federal agencies such as the USDA via the United States Cooperative Extension Service and the Food Administration. The NWGC's focus on food preservation also provided an additional rationalization and momentum for the professionalization of the home economics profession. While the NWGC was decommissioned, its legacy continued.

Most importantly, perhaps, the NWGC created a lasting and ongoing culture of service and civic participation around gardening that has had lasting outcomes evident in the voluntary forms and associations of the gardening world. Today this can be seen in some USDA volunteer programs, which would eventually arise as the "private" interest in the public work of that agency, meeting many of the needs identified by the NWGC, including encouraging, educating, and supporting urban and suburban gardeners through the USDA's Master Gardener Program, which operates through each state's land grant institution's Cooperative Extension Service. (The Master Gardener Program was created in 1972 in Washington state, in part as a response to the environmental movement. It is now found in all fifty states, and maintains strong programmatic links with the USDA.) These governmental volunteers also serve as a key link of information transfer and practice between agricultural experts from the land-grant university system and consumer audiences, adapting technical information to lay audiences, and providing feedback to the universities about community concerns and findings.

Following the 1941 bombing of Pearl Harbor, the NWGC was re-established, but in a more official government capacity. Marketing techniques had been refined, but the general focus remained voluntary citizen cooperation. The gardens of this era were never called "war gardens": from the outset, they were referred to as "victory gardens." By World War II, the sense of public-private partnership had been largely replaced by less permeable bureaucratic forms. "City farmers" were apparently not needed to secure the nation's food supply, and a part of the rural-urban synthesis was lost as Victory Garden programs of World War II were strongly promoted to rural residents.[109]

While not entirely attributable to the work of the NWGC, but in part because of its efforts, the war itself elevated the issue of agricultural production, education, and literacy to one of critical national importance and security. There was simply no turning back on this point. This served to affirm that the work of the NWGC was critical. During the World War I era, the United States developed strategies and Progressive-influenced institutions that focused on an issue that the NWGC had in part espoused: the need to systematically educate the American public about food production.

This significant movement has been largely forgotten, but it left an important mark on certain aspects of twentieth-century American agricultural and educational policy and practice. Influenced by the great Progressive thinkers such as John Dewey and nature study and Extension guru Liberty Hyde Bailey, the shape of these and other educational programs, such as 4-H, focused on experiential learning and non-formal education. These organizations also emulated models from other Progressive-era institutions, particularly the Children's Bureau "Little Mothers Clubs" to form agricultural and food preservation "clubs" that educated reluctant adults in best practices through the organized club work of their children.[110] National models, goals, and policies developed during this era still exist.

Charles Lathrop Pack spoke of the real value he perceived from wartime gardening efforts after the Armistice was signed. "If the democracy of a nation depends upon the democracy of the individuals who compose the nation, then assuredly the war garden is a forge that is daily strengthening the links in our chain of democracy.... Link by link the chain of our democracy has grown stronger."[111]

What Pack stated then about the ability of gardens to strengthen democracy holds true today. Citizens are actively engaging in national discussion and action about food policy, part of a growing national food movement that is broad, but that has at its core values of transparency, a sense of activism, self-reliance, the ability to produce or procure food locally, and a thirst for connection to the land. Young people today play a vital role in that burgeoning food movement. In World War I, young people also engaged their nation and the food system by gardening in schools, at home, and in their communities. The USSGA, then, presages modern efforts, such as the Food Corps.

THREE

The United States School Garden Army

It was summer, 1917, in Los Angeles, California. The world was at war, and newspaper headlines screamed about labor strikes, the "I.W.W. Menace," the Russian offensive, and "Turmoil in China."[1] It had been somewhat dry throughout the southwest.[2] Despite the uncertainty surrounding her, in the quiet Los Angeles suburb of Long Beach, an elementary student named Harriet Johns harvested "exactly 1,769 beans from four stalks, raised from as many seeds," growing them on a vacant lot owned by her neighbor, Mrs. Charles Bate.[3] That summer, Harriet joined millions of American boys and girls who became "Soldiers of the Soil" during the course of World War I, cultivating war gardens for Uncle Sam through their participation in the United States School Garden Army (USSGA).

From Portland, Oregon, to Portland, Maine, children gardened. The *Los Angeles Times* reported that 14,000 students worked 13,000 gardens and field sites in Los Angeles schools (some of them were undoubtedly schoolmates of Harriet's).[4] What was so extraordinary about Harriet's gardening experience was that on the American home front during World War I, it wasn't extraordinary at all, but rather an activity in which millions of American youth were routinely engaged at home, at school, and in their communities. Harriet's effort amounted to much more than a hill of beans grown in a Los Angeles suburb: it signified a successful public quest by progressive activists, enabled by wartime urgency, to foster traditional producer values in an urban populace through the most modern of means, the associative state and public media. While school gardens and nature study had gained traction in some parts of the United States, the national gardening effort during World War I elevated the importance of the work. The imperatives of wartime enabled the proponents of youth gardening and agricultural education to move their agenda forward in an ambitious fashion that would have national implications far beyond the war years. Among other things, they sought to challenge urban ascendancy by reinvigorating traditional producer values among the nation's urban children.

Building on the previous work in school gardens and nature study promoted by Extension educator Liberty Hyde Bailey, the USSGA made horticulture modern, educative, purposeful, and civic in nature. It engaged the imagination and energy of millions of American children. Nearly one hundred years after the USSGA made its debut, gardens are once again springing up in many American schools, and increasingly are institutionalized as part of farm-to-school programs linking the cafeteria with the curriculum through gardening and nutrition education.

The USSGA translated a long strain of scientific agricultural and horticultural education advocacy, through Progressivism, toward a hoped-for synthesis of urban and rural experiences in American life. The USSGA also reflected American life on the home front, in sometimes unique, sometimes more broadly experienced ways. In all of this lie its significance and its connections to other Progressive Era and wartime horticultural and popular agricultural programs.

"The school garden has come to stay"

In 1909, Ventura, California, schoolteacher Zilda M. Rogers wrote to the Agricultural Experiment Station at the University of California, Berkeley, then the flagship agricultural campus for California's land grant institution, and a primary proponent and provider of garden education resources for schoolteachers in the Golden State. Rogers wrote in some detail about how her school garden work had progressed, what the successes and failures were. She shared how the children were responding to the opportunity to garden, how her relationship with the children had changed as a result of the garden work, and what she saw as potential for the future. "With the love of the school garden has grown the desire for a home garden and some of their plots at home are very good.... Since commencing the garden work the children have become better companions and friends ... and to feel that there is a right way of doing everything ... it is *our* garden.... We try to carry that spirit into our schoolroom."[5]

Her words were later included in a publication produced by the University of California Agricultural Experiment Station, entitled "Suggestions for Garden Work in California Schools."[6] One of the most important primary source documents about the school garden movement in the pre-war era, this publication was also known as Circular No. 46. More than a hundred years after Rogers wrote those words, school gardens have continued to be cherished in the public school system in which she worked, Ventura Unified School District (VUSD). The district has developed a nationally recognized Healthy Schools Project that links school gardens, nutrition education, and a farm-to-school lunch program featuring locally sourced fruits and vegetables for its 17,000 public school students. In its schools, VUSD has provided hands-on experiences, standards-based classroom lessons, a Harvest of the Month program, farmer visits, and physical activity programs. The goals outlined by VUSD's program in the 21st might be considered part of the Rogers' educational legacy, and confirm the value of gardens as part of VUSD's educational mission for more than a century.

In addition to offering information about how to build a school garden program, Circular No. 46 was also an excellent recruiting tool (much of its content is relevant today). Gardening was to be no one-time accessory, but an integral part of primary schooling. Further, Circular No. 46 was intended to provide information about how adults might prepare themselves to teach elementary agriculture (including gardening).[7] As the circular declared, "*The school garden has come to stay.*"[8]

The author of the circular—Ernest Brown Babcock (1877–1954)—was a University of California educator and nationally known author and advocate of agricultural education. Babcock was a noted plant biologist and geneticist, who enjoyed a long and illustrious career. A gardener from childhood, Babcock's first career was as a teacher. Eventually, he joined the University of California as a scientist, and in the early years of his career there produced work at the Agricultural Research Station, and a body of work that supported gardening and agricultural education in schools. In some of this work, he collaborated with Cyril Stebbins, another noted agricultural educator, who wrote much of the curriculum used by the USSGA. Stebbins' son, G. Leydard Stebbins, authored a memoir of Babcock's life for the National Academy of Sciences. Babcock's contribution to the early national literature about agricultural and gardening education was notable.[9]

During this period, the University of California, in collaboration with the Berkeley School District, offered a California Junior Gardener Program. In addition, gardening and agricultural education programs were present in some of the California Normal Schools, which provided teacher education during the period. (Some California Normal Schools—which were teaching colleges—evolved into campuses affiliated with the current California State University system.) Thus, nearly a decade before the creation of the USSGA, school gardens were regarded, at least by some, as a permanent and highly desirable feature of the educational landscape.

School gardens were used in parts of Europe as early as 1811, and mention of their value preceded that by nearly two centuries.[10] Philosophers and educational reformers such as John Amos Comenius (1592–1670) and Jean-Jacques Rousseau discussed the importance of nature in the education of children. Comenius specifically cited the value of using gardens in school settings, saying, "A school garden should be connected with every school, where children can have the opportunity for leisurely gazing upon trees, flowers and herbs, and are taught to appreciate them."[11] The use and purpose of school gardens was multifold; gardens provided a place where youth could learn natural sciences (including agriculture) and also acquire vocational skills.

Indeed, the very multiplicity of uses and purposes for gardens made it difficult for gardening proponents to firmly anchor gardening in the educational framework and a school's curriculum; it still does. The founder of the kindergarten movement, Friedrich Froebel, used gardens as an educational tool.[12] Froebel was influenced by Swiss educational reformer Johann Pestalozzi, who saw a need for balance in education, a balance that incorporated "hands, heart, and head," words and ideas that would be incorporated nearly two centuries later into the goal of the USDA's 4-H youth development program: "head, heart, hands and health." Gardens required all three of these things; for this and other reasons, Froebel advocated for school gardens during the course of his life.

Late 19th century educators such as Maria Montessori and John Dewey built upon educational theories espoused by these earlier philosophers and reformers. Both Montessori and Dewey spoke specifically about gardening and agricultural education for youth.[13] They both saw the acquisition of practical (i.e., vocational) skills as only part of the value of gardening experiences. Dewey, in particular, like other Progressive leaders, sought the reorganization of rural schools to include more gardening and nature-study opportunities. Many educators of the time, including the USSGA's Cyril Stebbins and the author of Circular No. 46, Charles Babcock, saw gardens in schools as providing an opportunity for developing a sense of responsibility to others:

> When he [student] knows that the life of the plants that have been sown depends upon his care in watering them ... without which the little plant dries up ... the child becomes vigilant, as one who is beginning to feel a mission in life.[14]

This rationale supported the movement for the years to follow. It was expressed, albeit in different language, in the USSGA materials in 1918, many of which stressed the mission-driven nature of the gardening work.

The USSGA was not the first school garden program in either the United States or in Europe, where the school garden movement gained traction earlier. In 1869, a royal edict in Austria mandated that each school must provide a garden for its students; similar movements supporting school gardens in Germany, Belgium, France, Russia, and England followed.[15] The primary goal of the French movement was to "inspire a love of country." It is interesting that the Americans and the French, who shared so many cultural and political ideas of revolution and equality, should promote nationalism through gardens. The USSGA certainly sought to encourage youth to express their love of country and commitment to the nation's wartime goals through gardening, service, and civic engagement.

Probably one of the earliest school garden programs in the United States was developed in 1891, at the George Putnam School in Roxbury, Massachusetts.[16] Like others interested in gardening, Henry Lincoln Clapp, who was affiliated with the George Putnam School, traveled to Europe for inspiration. After traveling to Europe and visiting school gardens there, he partnered with the Massachusetts Horticultural Society to create the garden at Putnam; the model was replicated around the state. (Today, Massachusetts provides a national model to engage youth in gardening and agriculture via commercial enterprises through the Food Project. Founded in 1991, the Food Project is a community-based organization that includes a variety of commercial agricultural and gardening enterprises operated by youth, including stands at farmers' markets, a community supported agriculture model, hunger relief and advocacy for improved school lunch programs.[17]) The garden at Putnam was an instant success and was followed in relatively short order by other efforts, including a well-known garden program in New York City, the DeWitt Clinton Farm School.[18]

School gardens in America were a natural outgrowth of earlier community garden efforts, as well as civic and philanthropic work, much of which was conducted by women in urban settings. The civic and philanthropic bent of these gardening efforts was typically progressive in tone: reformers sought to correct a wide range of perceived social, moral, and educational agendas, and advocated associative means. School gardens were one part of the broader nature-study movement. Interestingly, even home gardens worked by children of the household were considered school gardens; the term "school" took on a broader, Progressive meaning that defined "school" as any setting where youth learned through working.[19] Historian Laura Lawson lists the various names included under the umbrella of the movement: "school gardens, school home gardens, children's gardens, school farms, farm schools, garden cities, and others."[20] In *Among School Gardens*, Louise Greene speaks not only of where gardens could be located, but also how they might be characterized: "gardens may be collective or individual or both."[21]

Gardening became nearly a national craze during the Gilded Age and Progressive Era; "school" gardens enjoyed immense popularity. The USDA estimated that there were more than 75,000 school gardens by 1906.[22] As their popularity soared, advocates busily supplied a body of literature about school gardening and agricultural education. Women, reflecting the traditional location of gardening within the domestic sphere of reform work, authored some pieces. Louise Klein Miller's *Children's Gardens for School and Home, a Manual of Cooperative Learning* appeared in 1904, as the school garden movement was gaining momentum in the United States.[23] Miller described two primary purposes of children's gardens: civic beautification and nature study, with the goal of instilling a love and appreciation of nature in youth (which would ultimately influence their civic character and "the public good").[24] But Miller clearly saw other, more formal educational purposes for children's gardens; in her acknowledgements, she thanks for his contributions Dr. William T. Harris, then the Federal Bureau of Education commissioner.

Miller argued that school gardens were not a "new phase of education," but rather, an "old one" that was gaining merit for its ability to fulfill a wide variety of needs. (This idea also supports the argument that the USSGA and other wartime gardens were really an old fashioned idea reworked to include modern themes.) Miller also argued for the importance of gardening education and nature study for *both* urban and rural youth, for "sociological and economic" reasons. She further contended that one important reason to garden with urban youth was to teach "children to become producers as well as consumers," and for the possibility "of turning the tide of population toward the country, thus relieving the crowded conditions of the city." Other reformers echoed this idea, including Jacob Riis, who said, "The children as well as the grown people were 'inspired to greater industry and self-dependence.' They faced about and looked away from the slum toward the country."[25] These purposes were echoed in the literature of the USSGA, in nearly identical terms, more than a decade later.

Greene's *Among School Gardens* also became a standard in the literature; it addressed the purposes of school gardens; gave information about the best school gardens and model programs; provided detailed and practical how-to information; and shared information about the quickly growing school garden movement in the United States.[26] Greene relates the intense period of growth of the school garden movement between 1900 and 1910, describing the "chain of gardens, as it were, from the Atlantic to the Pacific."[27] Later, the USSGA built upon existing networks of school gardens (which represented both formal and informal efforts). However, the USSGA had an unprecedented opportunity to institutionalize its message and goals because the strength and influence of the federal government was behind the initiative. Wartime helped to create a sense of common purpose around gardening.

Greene's book provides an interesting glimpse into the developing school garden movement's Progressive reform purposes. Civic beautification, an important Progressive theme, was mentioned in Greene's work several times, with references to "decorative planting."[28] One illustration employs the caption, "Boys should be Formed not Reformed," to provide information about the National Cash Register Company garden.[29] Greene writes that the "underlying purpose of the teaching is threefold, educational, industrial and social— or moral."[30] The founder of the children's school farm at DeWitt Clinton Park in the Hell's Kitchen neighborhood of New York was quoted in Greene's book, saying:

> I did not start a garden to grow a few vegetables and flowers. The garden was used as a means to ... teach them in their work some necessary civic virtues, private care of public property, economy, honesty, application, concentration, self-government, civic pride, justice, the dignity of labor, and the love of nature.[31]

The creators of the USSGA articulated many of those goals, in addition to wartime food production.

Agricultural Education and Links to Gardening

As social scientists and reformers studied rural life and sought ways to reform and recast its social structures using "modern" methods, a parallel movement, already underway, sought to improve cultivation practices through the application of scientific agriculture. (The Hatch Act of 1887 used the term "scientific agriculture" in its legislative mission. The Hatch Act provided money to states to develop agricultural experiment stations, which were usually affiliated with the land grant institutions created by the Morrill Act of 1862. These agricultural experiment and research stations became the basis for many Cooperative Extension Service operations after the passage of the Smith-Lever Act in 1914.[32])

As a result of the growing interest in scientific agriculture, and in nature study, a number of influential books on agricultural education were published in the early twentieth century. These books sought to promote the value of agricultural education for all elementary school students, and in so doing, grafted agricultural education to the school gardening movement. Among the most influential books was *Elementary School Agriculture: A Teacher's Manual to Accompany Hilgard and Osterhout's Agriculture for Schools of the Pacific Slope,"* written by Cyril A. Stebbins and Ernest B. Babcock.[33] (Stebbins, an influential agricultural professor, later authored the USSGA's manual for the Western United States.) Another important book, *The Principles of Agriculture through the School and Home Garden,* was authored by Stebbins in 1913; it clearly linked school and home gardening.³⁴ Gardening and agricultural education were cross-referenced in many publications produced during this period.

Among gardening proponents' concerns was linking urban and rural experience, which could be achieved through nature study and gardening. Liberty Hyde Bailey (who published the third edition in six years of his book on nature study in 1909, and in the same year published a book on the training of farmers) certainly sought to do this through gardening.³⁵ Interestingly, although he sought to reach rural youth through Extension education, it was urban educators who most eagerly seized on the nature-study idea; that is where the school garden movement founds its greatest strength during the pre-war years. Although California's agricultural educator Babcock and other agricultural educational advocates still saw a need for additional school garden efforts in urban and suburban America, they were perhaps more concerned with the apparent reluctance of rural communities to undertake this kind of work. In the University of California's Circular No. 46, Babcock openly argued against perceived rural reluctance to adopt school gardens (and agricultural education) by quoting extensively from a National Bureau of Education Report written by James Ralph Jewell.³⁶

The American nature-study and rural education movements led by Extension pioneer Liberty Hyde Bailey had profound and long-term effects on urban and rural education and school gardens, effects that carry forward to the current day. Nature study, agricultural education and school gardens became inextricably linked—they still are—which created both challenges and opportunities for wartime programs such as the USSGA. Wartime gardening programs carefully incorporated many elements of Progressive impulses, including nature study, vocational arts, experiential learning, teaching thrift, and civic beautification.

Bailey, the founder of the Agricultural College at Cornell University in New York, espoused an educational philosophy that emphasized hands-on or experiential learning. (Bailey is also considered the father of the agricultural Extension movement that is today found in the land grant institutions created by the Morrill Land Grant Act during Lincoln's first term.) Educational activities incorporating nature and the garden lent themselves admirably to this philosophy. "There seems to be little personal life-motive in our education. The process produces passive or static results. The solution is to outgrow the sit-still and keep-still method of schoolwork ... to put children to work with tools and soils and plants and problems," Bailey said in his book *The State and The Farmer*, first published in 1908.³⁷

In the first decade of the twentieth century, Cornell University, under the leadership of Bailey, issued a series of publications (books, articles, and leaflets) promoting nature study as an essential part of the public school curriculum, particularly at the elementary level. (Cornell also published a Reading Course series for farmers' wives that included numerous bulletins on the "farmhouse and garden.") The nature study idea encompassed many ideals, and gardening fit well into its framework. Bailey's work at Cornell was influenced by his work on the Country Life Commission (CLM), created by President Theodore Roosevelt in 1907 (it was officially launched in 1908).[38]

The creation of the CLM expressed Roosevelt's concern about rural conditions that he believed "not only held back life in the country, but also lowered the efficiency of the whole nation ... the strengthening of country life ... is the strengthening of the whole nation." At the same time he launched the CLM, Roosevelt also started a National Conservation Commission. Roosevelt strongly connected conservation and rural life, writing, "Conservation and rural-life policies are really two sides of the same policy."

But Roosevelt was also concerned about feeding a growing population, and keeping food cheap and plentiful for urban residents, making agriculture an issue of national security. (It still is.)

The CLM had important effects on public policy. Composed of leaders from the newly emerging middle class (nearly all of them urban), the CLM represented different threads of progressive thought. Some members of the Commission loved the rural, while others criticized the rural experience roundly. But the CLM's membership also included a third group, urban agrarians such as Liberty Hyde Bailey and Kenyon Butterfield, who believed that while rural life needed to be reformed and aligned with America's industrial future, it offered much that could help to salvage America's urban life.[39] The CLM looked at all aspects of rural life, but particularly focused on change in three institutions of primary importance in rural life: the home (and farm), the church, and the school.

Rural homes (and farms), churches, and schools—in fact, the entirety of rural communities—were targets of Progressive reform efforts. Bailey's work with the CLM led him, along with other Progressive leaders, to encourage the reorganization of rural schools. The reorganization of rural schools was but one of their goals; they also sought to reorganize and restructure rural life. This included more gardening and nature-study opportunities for rural youth, as well as educational opportunities for them that might aid Progressive efforts in reaching rural parents in an effort to improve agricultural production and home culture techniques. The land grant institutions created by the passage of the Morrill Act in 1862 were also advancing these goals. The Smith-Lever Act of 1914 gave additional federal impetus to "rationalize" rural life. This advocacy by cosmopolitan leaders to transform rural America both reflected and created tensions. But throughout the nation, leaders and social reformers sought to create urban-rural links; these links created tensions that remained evident within World War I mobilization programs such as the USSGA.

In his Federal Bureau of Education Report, Jewell had provided examples of the success of school gardens in rural Europe and Canada, and termed it "strange" that "other countries think gardens especially fitted for rural schools, while we think them better for city schools."[40] This rural-urban divide persisted, and is clearly seen in the USSGA's programmatic thrust, which targeted urban and suburban school youth and schools.[41] The educational needs of the rural youth population vis-à-vis gardening was picked up by agricultural clubs and the emerging 4-H organization, which emphasized teaching rural youth the latest scientific techniques designed to improve production agriculture and home culture techniques. The Federal Bureau of Education was also involved in some efforts.

Associations and networks of individuals and groups arose around gardening, and national organizations were formed. The School Garden Association and the International Children's School Farm League were both founded in 1910.[42] During this period, educational advocates in government, including the Bureau of Education's Philander P. Claxton (under whose auspices the USSGA operated during World War I), sought to make gardening a universal part of public school offerings. In an annual report published by the School Garden Association in 1916, one year before the creation of the USSGA, Claxton wrote, "I look forward to the time when school gardening and home gardening under the direction of the school may become an integral part of the work of all the schools."[43] (It is interesting to note that some today advocate for the same public policies.)

In 1914, the federal Bureau of Education created its Office of School and Home Gardening.[44] Between 1915 and 1917, the Bureau of Education published at least seventeen "circulars" relating to school and home gardening.[45] As was the case during World War I, the Bureau of Education had limited authority over state and local educational efforts; its work was primarily limited to producing publications for school garden efforts.[46] But this early experience prepared the Bureau of Education for the USSGA program, by providing some infrastructure and resources in advance of that wartime effort. The USDA supported the work by providing materials and pamphlets supporting school gardening. During 1914 and 1915, the Bureau of Education conducted a survey of school superintendents, which made the agency even better positioned by 1917 to provide leadership for the USSGA. In 1916, the results of the survey data were published as "Gardening in Elementary City Schools."[47] The location of work specified in that title—"City Schools"—carried over to the USSGA work. The "Gardening in Elementary Schools" survey detailed reasons to garden, many of which later appeared in the USSGA materials.[48]

School gardens were a valuable tool for Progressive reformers. Their ability to teach youth across the curriculum presented both opportunities and challenges to their formal adoption as part of the national course of study in public schools. A growing middle-class bias against vocational education forced school garden proponents to walk a fine line. Although there was a need for vocational education programs to provide training, strengthened child labor laws had limited the opportunity for on-the-job training and employment internships for youth.[49] But these very factors, when added to Progressive concerns about the increasing disconnection between youth and their food sources and agrarian roots, led to the creation of school gardening programs and fueled government initiatives and programs such as the Country Life Commission.

Advocacy of urban programs to redirect youth were at least as long lived, however, attracting reformers' attention and a multitude of initiatives. The USSGA represented a shift in federal policy by joining the agricultural initiative to the urban "problem," strongly targeting urban and suburban youth. Using patriotic appeals (and no small degree of coercion), the government sought to enlist the aid of its youth to raise food for America.

Home front mobilization efforts such as the USSGA, the Liberty/Victory Garden program of the NWGC and the Woman's Land Army did not simply emerge from the sociocultural landscape of World War I. Each program built upon earlier impulses and movements, all with strongly Progressive themes, and in many ways, building upon the emerging associative state. Each program made horticulture modern, educative, and public-purposed. The rootstock provided by ongoing Extension education programs (and the influence upon them of the Chautauqua movement, which sought to educate the middle class and inculcate certain reform messages while building community), the nature-study movement fostered by agrarianism leaders including Liberty Hyde Bailey, and other Progressive Era efforts had established a system that enabled wartime gardening programs to quickly gain strength and spread.[50] The USSGA, then, owed its existence to decades of advocates' creativity, pilot programs, and other initiatives. Wartime enabled the proponents of youth gardening and agricultural education to advance their agenda of teaching this topic—which they viewed as vital to America's national security—through the nation's schools. Like the rural programs during the period that sought to reach and teach parents through project work with their children, the USSGA also sought to spread the idea of gardens to "city" homes through work with urban school children.[51] Many of the individuals who helped compile this particular curriculum were women.

"Production is the first principle in education"

"Every boy and every girl ... should be a producer.... Production is the first principle in education. The growing of plants and animals should therefore become an integral part of the school program. Such is the aim of the U.S. School Garden Army."[52] With these words, the Federal Bureau of Education launched the USSGA during World War I. The USSGA represented an unprecedented governmental effort to make agricultural education a formal (and informal) part of the public school curriculum—and home life of students—throughout the United States.

The exigencies of wartime enable certain groups to forward their agendas. World War I was no different. In fact, the unprecedented mobilization created a sort of institutional frenzy in the United States that intensified this impulse.[53] Building on a small but persistently supported federal policy thrust in agricultural education, nationally known school gardening proponents such as Luther Burbank, P.P. Claxton, Charles Pack and Cyril Stebbins saw an opportunity to nationalize the teaching of agriculture in the nation's public schools, provide a standardized curriculum for its teaching and promote a philosophy that articulated a particular view of the rural-urban synthesis. (Stebbins even helped write the USSGA's curriculum.) Its founders hoped that the effort would continue after Victory was achieved "over there."

The USSGA was developed by the Federal Bureau of Education, which was housed under the United States Department of the Interior. While the Bureau of Education previously had offered some form of agricultural education to urban and suburban youth through its Division of School and Home Gardening, its early efforts had been limited and nominally successful due to inadequate staffing and the inability to mandate school gardens.[54] As America mobilized for the war, Federal Education Commissioner P.P. Claxton, a strong proponent of agricultural education and war gardening, saw an opportunity for the Bureau of Education to further its agenda and get children—and their families—growing. Claxton served on the board of the influential NWGC, where he was surrounded by individuals passionately dedicated to the concept of war gardening, among them noted plant scientist Luther Burbank, wealthy industrialist and forestry expert Charles Lathrop Pack, and other leading progressive thinkers, including the assistant secretary of agriculture, Carl Vrooman.[55] Claxton hired J.H. Francis to serve as director of the newly developed USSGA. Francis, the former Los Angeles school superintendent, proved to be the right person for the job and quickly organized the program.[56]

The USSGA taught urban and suburban youth traditional rural skills of cultivation—gardening, agriculture on a small, urban scale—and the importance of the producer ethic in American life. A traditional message of producing took form in a modern mode of advertising more oriented to a consumer society. While it emphasized the value of skills more often found in rural life, the USSGA's curriculum relied not on folkways or the "moon farming" techniques still used in parts of rural America, but on the newer theories arising from the growing field of scientific agriculture. (Moon farming refers to the traditional practice of allocating farm tasks according to the phase of the moon. For example, some tasks, such as preparing the soil and planting crops that grow above the ground, were often done when the moon provided light. Other tasks, such as cultivating, planting root crops, and digging postholes, were relegated to the moon's dark phases. Today, some suggest that the biodynamic model of farming closely follows traditional moon farming practices.)

USSGA programs were taught by trained "experts" (teachers or garden organizers) in a school setting, rather than through the traditional rural educational mode of instruction by the parent in the home. Again, the USSGA strongly encouraged home gardening as an extension of school work in gardening: one photo caption (showing four African-American students and their white gardening teacher) reads: "Children who are taught how to make and manage hotbeds and cold frames at the school will also make and use them at their homes."[57]

The USSGA's curriculum gave a nod to the individual by setting production goals for each child, but at the same time, it attempted to somewhat universalize the program for all youth in the target population. Parts of the USSGA curriculum were modified to reflect different climates and growing conditions, and appeared under separate cover for different regions of the United States. However, it was clearly a nationally conceptualized curriculum. Regional differences were balanced by a standard, highly ordered organizational format and a "branded" insignia that identified the program as national in purpose and scope. (Per historian O.L. Davis, "Privates wore a bronze service bar on which 'U.S.S.G.' was stamped. Officers wore a similar bronze bar, but had one star on the border; bars for first lieutenants had two stars, and those of captains had three stars."[58])

The military feel of the program must have been appealing to many children as the nation mobilized for war. The national purpose and scope of the program—as reflected in items such as the insignia—sought to create from many, one, and also to assure a degree of uniformity of purpose and production. The program materials conveyed other important messages for a nation mobilizing its citizens and its food system, such as:

- "Both the educational and cultural values should be brought out in the teaching of gardening";

- "To teach gardening efficiently in the classroom the teacher should have a garden of her own"; and
- "The surplus garden space should be used to grow crops for the market."[59]

Two statements that frequently framed the USSGA's work were "he who produces is a patriot—a good citizen" and "A Garden for Every Child. Every Child in a Garden."[60] These statements demonstrate an attempt to synthesize different American values. Producer values (in both a rural and urban sense) represented a more traditional American past and inform the first statement. The Progressive focus on nature study as a means of reform and enlightenment informs the second. The USSGA incorporated both.

As testament to the notion that food was vital to America's national security during World War I and that children were vital to the production of that food, President Woodrow Wilson decided to fund the USSGA program with funds taken from the national defense budget.[61] Imagine if today, Pentagon or Homeland Security funds were used to fund school gardens. Clearly, this public policy example has important implications for today's school garden advocates, and for those in the federal government tasked with ensuring the security of the nation's food system.

Gaining Traction

Other factors enabled the USSGA to gain traction. Well before America's entry into World War I, as a result of various pieces of federal legislation, probably most notably the Hatch Act, government agencies issued a number of publications discussing agricultural education. The progressive Bureau of Education provided information demonstrating how agriculture and domestic arts could be integrated across the curriculum to teach language (possibly to immigrants; teaching immigrants English as part of the "Americanization" process was important to many Progressives).[62] National associations promoting nature study, school gardening, and agricultural education provided additional materials and impetus. By 1915, Franklin Lane, head of the Department of Interior (which housed the Bureau of Education), was able to report that twenty-one states, including California, required agricultural and domestic arts instruction in rural schools. Lane also reported that a growing number of states—perhaps as many as half of all states—required some agricultural education or nature study in urban schools as well.

While agricultural education may have been encouraged in a growing number of American schools, the USSGA provided the first national curriculum for the teaching of agriculture and gardening. The philosophy of experiential education promoted by educators such as Maria Montessori and Liberty Hyde Bailey certainly informed the USSGA (and other agricultural and nature study curricula). "Do something" was the underlying spirit of the curriculum. Later, "learn by doing" (by providing hands-on, experiential learning) became the primary instructional philosophy and model informing programs such as 4-H and Future Farmers of America. While Babcock and Stebbins' book provides classroom activities, in the note to teachers, they indicate that the hands-on component is the essence of the work, saying, *"Sacrifice the schoolroom work in this subject for the gardening if the gardens need attention."*[63]

Babcock and Stebbins, among others, saw agricultural study as a way to revitalize the "old subjects in the curriculum," including geography, hygiene, arithmetic, manual training, and art.[64] It is significant that Stebbins, a University of California agricultural professor who later served as director of Rural Extension Education for Chico Normal School (now California State University at Chico), did not view agricultural education as oriented to California's Junior Gardener Program (which eventually spun off to management at Chico Normal School, which had established a large garden in 1902).[65] The Junior Gardener Program, which began as a collaboration between the University of California and the Berkeley public school system, targeted urban youth. Eventually, the Junior Gardener Program evolved into a Garden City for Berkeley youth that included elected officers, a bank, and a weekly farmer's market. The program spread to other places in California, and was supported by a University-published newsletter, *The Junior Agriculturist*. This program, with local clubs and chapters, undoubtedly provided a model for organizing the national USSGA effort during World War I, and also may have aided the spread of 4-H work, which was affiliated with the USDA and the land grant institutions in each state. Stebbins was quoted as saying, "We grow flowers, vegetables and children in California gardens."[66]

Other educational and political leaders in California expressed the importance of this work in public policy enacted nearly 100 years later, in the 1990s and early 2000s (through a State Department of Education initiative under Superintendent Delaine Eastin, and, later, by California Assembly Bill 1535, which provided funding for gardens in public schools). Today, like its predecessor, the Junior Gardener Program in California, the 4-H Junior Master Gardener Program, developed by Texas A&M and sponsored by the USDA and 4-H at the national and state levels, annually teaches thousands of youth about gardening, nutrition, and science.

In the introduction of their book on agricultural education in elementary schools, Babcock and Stebbins offered a scathing criticism of America's educational system, criticism that many might consider relevant today. "The mechanics of the school work adapts him [the student] in time to textbook situations, but does not make him easily adjustable to the shifting circumstances of life outside of the school."[67] In agricultural education, they saw the possibility for the teaching of life skills, not vocational arts (although that might be a benefit of such programs), but skills of problem solving and reasoning that would be useful in later life.

"It is a short step from the class process to the business man's process, to the work of the world," they wrote.[68] Gardening would not only prepare students for the work of the business world, but could serve as a tool of civic engagement. America could "use the garden, not for the sake of the garden itself, but that it may lead the children into the life of the state."[69] This profoundly expressed concept of civic engagement and the ideal of larger community informed agricultural education in the period immediately prior to, and during, World War I. The concept strongly influenced efforts such as the USSGA, and could inform current efforts. While gardens can be individual efforts, collective efforts, such as school and community gardens, can build up individuals, families and communities.

Like the Bureau of Education, the USDA used wartime as a means to accelerate the pace of development of its Cooperative Extension Service, part of which focused on youth work (this later became the 4-H Youth Development Program, which still educates millions of American youth each year, many of them in gardening and agriculture). USDA youth programs, such as pig, corn and canning clubs—later to evolve into 4-H club work—stressed educating rural youth on topics in agriculture and home arts. During World War I, largely as a result of the national policy thrust in food production and conservation, the number of rural youth involved in agricultural and domestic arts clubs more than doubled to more than 100,000. And the USDA did field an "army" of agents to accomplish this work: between June 1917 and June 1918, the number of Extension workers more than doubled, increasing from slightly more than 2,200 agents to nearly 6,000, serving nearly 2,500 counties. Many of the new workers aided the USDA's food production and conservation campaign during World War I, either through home demonstration work or through a rapidly growing youth education effort that fielded more than 900 agents who led "boys' and girls' club work."

Soldiers of the Soil

The USSGA program was highly influential during wartime, although the effort was demobilized after Armistice. The USSGA appealed to America's youth: by the end of World War I, the USSGA's leadership estimated that several million American youth had "enlisted" as "soldiers of the soil."[70] Enrollment figures compiled by field organizers working for the Bureau of Education at the close of the program's first year in operation reported some interesting statistics. With 2,125 cities reporting, 1,815,552 student soldiers were registered; 409 cities had not yet reported their numbers.[71] With the addition of the islands in the possession of the United States, and the territory of Alaska, enrollment figures swelled to 1,927,886.[72] More than 50,000 teachers received the USSGA curriculum. Thousands more community volunteers participated by leading or assisting with youth gardening projects.

Youth participants, these soldiers of the soil, were not just abstractions engaged in a rote activity. They were American children who answered their nation's call to service. Their fingers dug into living soil, planted seeds and harvested. Knowing that many American children had relatives serving in France, organizers suggested that children might name their garden after a soldier serving there as a demonstration of patriotism and solidarity. Undoubtedly, some children did this. Motives and feelings are difficult to quantify, but newspapers from the period are replete with reports of youth gardening activity. Again, perhaps the best narrative of the work is the public one that appeared in newspapers and magazines across the nation.[73]

Not everyone agreed that the USSGA was needed, and there was resistance. Some believed that the reaction to the food crisis and the idea of mobilizing children were overdrawn. Former Harvard president Charles W. Eliot "decried the school garden movement as building on hysteria and gross exaggeration."[74] (This opinion did not keep Eliot from serving on the board of the National War Garden Commission, where he was a national advocate for Liberty and Victory Gardens. And again, the Progressive connections to horticulture were significant: the son of Charles W. Eliot, Charles Eliot, was a partner of Frederick Law Olmsted, Jr.) Perhaps the need was over-exaggerated, but the program proved enormously popular. The Bureau of Education claimed that 25,000 acres of previously uncultivated and unproductive land was put to use by youth gardeners.[75]

The USSGA did not simply seek to increase food production, although that was a primary goal. It also sought to educate, reform, and shape cultural values and practices. Per the Bureau of Education, the USSGA would train "school children in thrift, industry, service, patriotism, and responsibility, and giving them such first-hand knowledge of ... plant and animal life as city children can not otherwise get."[76] "Citizenship through Service" became the Bureau of Education's motto after the war, but the concept of practical civics drove USSGA efforts during the war. A *New York Times* article reported:

The idea and the impulse behind the idea are an inheritance from the war. In that time—which, as one looks back upon it, seems so much happier than the peace we were fighting for—there were the School Garden Army ... and other outlets for the patriotism of service.... The material returns ran into the hundreds of millions of dollars; and there was a by-product, possibly more valuable, of character formation.[77]

The USSGA set a goal to use "idle" youth and uncultivated land for a positive national purpose.[78] "One and one-half million children were given something to do last summer; something that helped to carry the burden of their country in the struggle for freedom, something that helped them to build character, and something that appealed to and developed their patriotism," wrote USGGA irector J.H. Francis.[79] The government defined national standards of youth citizenship and education through shared goals and a common curriculum. Just as the factory model could standardize production of material goods, perhaps a national curriculum could standardize the production of citizenship. In the USSGA model, the government served as arbiter of values, reformer, educator, and interested party in the economic production of the nation's children.

The government emphasized the vital contribution that youth's war gardening efforts made to America and the world. It was important work, vital to the nation's economy, its national security; it might even save lives. The United States commissioner of education, P.P. Claxton, addressed this issue directly with youth in the USSGA manual, writing that without food (and presumably their efforts), "men, women, and children will die."[80] Children also received letters from President Wilson and Food Administrator Herbert Hoover. Letters from dignitaries (and sometimes several) appeared in each USSGA publication. Hoover's letter appears on page three of the USSGA's Spring Manual, replacing Woodrow Wilson's greeting, which appeared in the fall manual. This must have represented an empowering message for youth.

And their work was economically valuable: in a government bulletin published in 1919, Francis estimated that "this army of boys and girls may easily produce $250,000,000 worth of food, which will reach the consumer in perfect condition without cost for transportation or handling and without loss through deterioration of the markets."[81] Not only were they saving lives, providing food for their fellow Americans, and freeing up food supplies for starving Europeans, but in the minds of proponents American youth who gardened might even help realign food markets, thus bringing the agricultural sector into closer alignment with the more predictable and ordered industrial sector, a primary objective of certain progressives. In the government's view, the USSGA could play an important role in accomplishing the nation's food production and conservation goals that advocates had identified for decades prior to the war, but that became all the more pressing in mobilizing the national economy for war.

Examples such as this demonstrate that an ongoing Progressive interest in the relationship between urban and rural values clearly guided the USSGA's work. At the outset of World War I, America was engaged in a process of profound and rapid transformation. Rural influence in American life had diminished, and with that came the attendant loss of a fundamental form of American identity, that of the producer. Many Progressives viewed city life as encouraging youth to indulge in vices such as popular amusements and excessive consumption of consumer goods. In those reformers' eyes, urban youth were at high risk of falling prey to the evils of urban life. The USSGA provided an opportunity to instill a traditional American "producer" ethic in an urban population that was increasingly influenced by mass culture and consumerism and increasingly removed from its food system.

Significantly, the three federal programs promoting food production among youth were housed in separate departments. Some evidence points to a power struggle between the more socially progressive Bureau of Education, and the more traditional USDA.[82] The differences between their respective programs reflected the nation's growing rural-urban divide. The USSGA made some effort to position its program as "complementary" to the work of rural youth by discussing—and affirming—the nature and value of production farming.[83] While a Progressive impulse informed the underlying philosophies of both Bureau of Education and USDA programs, the content, delivery and promotion—particularly the imagery—of the youth programs reflected differences between urban and rural interests, values and perceptions. In its methods and delivery, the USSGA exemplifies how Americans mediated competing urban and rural values during a period of national transformation. Through the USSGA, positive values attributed to America's rural past were recast and articulated in a largely urban milieu of gardening. Gardening itself offered a new synthesis of the rural and urban, producer and consumer, scientific methods and folkways.

While the USSGA stressed "traditional" values, the methods used to promote the USSGA were entirely modern. The striking visual imagery and rhetoric associated with the program played into larger iconographic themes stressing the nature of American freedom, citizenship, and patriotism, as well as the nation's changing view of the meaning of abundance. The work of the USSGA also provides a different understanding of how Americans negotiated and defined childhood at a time when the ideal of sheltered childhood (primarily an urban and middle class construct) was becoming more ascendant. All of these themes played out in an era increasingly marked by the ordering of society along industrial lines, and the professionalization of many of the fields involved in the USSGA's work, including education, science, advertising, and social work.

The nature of the war and the swift and radical changes required by mobilization transformed American society in fundamental ways. In *The Search for Order 1877–1920*, historian Robert Wiebe characterizes wartime mobilization as a culmination of a longer process of the bureaucraticization and (re)ordering of American society.[84] Wiebe argues that America's wartime fervor "derived from the familiar."[85] Anxieties about the process of transformation from an agrarian-producer to an urban-consumer society led some groups to hold on more tightly to traditional American values.[86] Yet, beneath the sense of urgency and rapid transformation "lay a deep-flowing current" that provided a sense of coherency and continuity.[87] The USSGA proves the truth of Wiebe's statements. While its work with urban and suburban youth represented a transformation of previous government efforts targeting rural youth, the USSGA retained a strong focus on the traditional American producer ethic. The method that the federal government chose to nationalize—and rationalize—agricultural education represented a modern means to achieve traditional ends. The method was transformational—through a soft mandate and a standardized curriculum—but it also represented a broader interpretation of a previous trend.

Because of its association with the land, Progressive reformers saw the USSGA as a desirable, even necessary, antidote to the disastrous social consequences of excessive urbanization. The spread of consumer culture, mass communication, and popular recreation was threatening to many reformers. American cities teemed with immigrants living in appalling conditions: disease, death, and hunger stalked city streets. Noise and filth characterized the physical landscape. Vices such as drink, prostitution and child labor, in reformers' eyes, diminished the promise of the nation.

Progressive reformers holding an idealized view of rural life saw its potential for healing urban ills. Some aspects of the USSGA—including the focus on producing—seemed designed to salvage, not recast, traditional values. The USSGA enabled reform-minded individuals to incorporate the beauty and uplifting influence of nature into urban settings, and to create new urban landscapes more strongly influenced by things pastoral. In fact, USSGA materials list as a benefit of the children's work the ability to beautify schools and homes.

The USSGA's curriculum spoke of the farmer and his vital role in American life. "He who produces is a patriot—a good citizen," one USSGA publication stated, in a section entitled "Home Gardening Catechism."[88] (The term "catechism" is another indication that its creators viewed the USSGA's work as vital, even sacred.) The program spoke to the city's need for reform, saying "it brings country values to the city."⁸⁹ And it might bring city farmers to the country, reversing the tide of rural to urban migration that was threatening the integrity of the nation's food system. For the USSGA's promotional materials also reflected—and tried to assuage—American anxiety about the tide of rural migration to urban centers, promising that the "farmers of to-morrow may be recruited to-day from the towns and cities."⁹⁰

The USSGA sought to synthesize the structure and order of urban life with practical rural skills and emphasized the value of production, thrift, and hard work. The structure and order are apparent in an organized and somewhat standardized curriculum that reflected contemporary educational theories. The focus on production as a form of patriotism and civic participation are stated as clear goals of the program. The USSGA, then, sought to synthesize the best of rural and urban values. With each USSGA garden that was tilled, its founders sought to demonstrate the interconnectedness of rural and urban experience in American life.

"Education through production"

The content of the USSGA's curriculum, its organizational structure and its goals and objectives spoke to scientific knowledge, efficiency, and ordered life. The USSGA sought to uplift the moral character of youth by instilling traditional values of hard work and thrift. Anxiety about urban culture and mass consumerism had left some Progressive reformers concerned that America's youth would not fully understand or embrace traditional values. Broader USSGA goals, which fell outside of increased food production, attempted to address these concerns. The desire to reform America's youth was clear: "the aim of the USSGA" is "to strengthen boys and girls mentally, physically, morally, spiritually ... education through production."⁹¹ The USSGA's founders were also concerned about thrift, honesty, and proper business practices. A section of the USSGA manual, devoted to marketing surplus product, conveyed the idea that while a "neat profit" is desirable, it would "be a fine idea to invest your vegetable profits in War Savings Stamps."⁹² The manual exhorts USSGA members to engage in a practice that "encourages thrift and business system."⁹³ "Build up a reputation for yourself for honesty and fair dealing," the manual urged, while also suggesting modern ways to increase sales.⁹⁴ Suggested modes of marketing included older methods such as cooperative models and modern methods such as parcel post.

The USSGA also sought to educate youth and reform previous practice by replacing traditional gardening practices with the latest techniques from the fields of scientific agriculture and home economics. Like other national institutions of the period (such as the Children's Bureau), the USSGA replaced folkways with scientific knowledge presented by government "experts." Extensive directions for teachers sought to develop their expertise as "garden educators."[95] Extension agents, university personnel and USSGA organizers traveled to communities and offered demonstrations featuring "best practices." Today's analog is found in the work of Extension agents, and also in programs such as Food Corps, which provides AmeriCorps volunteers to support youth gardening efforts in communities across the United States.

Wartime provided an opportunity for the Bureau of Education, which had little real authority over America's public schools, to flex its muscle and attempt to coerce the adoption of a national agricultural education curriculum in urban and suburban schools, through the USSGA. While dangerous "alien" forms of education such as German language were removed from public schools, traditional "American" forms, namely agricultural education, were inserted. The USSGA's work represents, if not the first, certainly one of the earliest federal efforts at standardizing a curriculum across the nation. As early as 1914, the Bureau of Education attempted to develop "a plan of school-directed home gardening in cities, towns, villages, and suburban communities," although the Bureau of Education's efforts were not branded with the USSGA name until 1918.[96] The Bureau of Education's early efforts were limited by funding constraints.

The exigencies of wartime provided an opportunity for the Bureau of Education. Stressing the state of national and international emergency and the impending worldwide food crisis, USSGA Director J.H. Francis wrote to Education Commissioner P.P. Claxton that the nationalization of the program was immediately needed, saying, "I feel it to be almost imperative that it be put into operation at once in all parts of the country."[97] A budget request of $35,800 was included. Claxton forwarded the communication to Secretary of the Interior Franklin Lane, who in turn shared the information with President Woodrow Wilson. Wilson's concerns about the security of America's food system led him to allocate funds from the National Security and Defense Fund.[98] The administration's initial appropriation of $50,000 exceeded the USSGA's request by about 25 percent. In fact, in a period of less than eighteen months, total federal funding for the USSGA effort reached a whopping $250,000.[99] Again, the notion that food security is essential to national security has important implications for today's advocates of gardening, urban agriculture, and local food systems. The foundation of national security is community-based food security, where large-scale gardening efforts have proven valuable in increasing community food supply.

Interestingly, USSGA Director J.H. Francis wrote that the intent of the USSGA program was to encourage *home* gardening. He used the term "school-supervised" instead of "school-based" to describe the location of work. "The work of the children is to be done after school hours and on Saturdays and vacation days, so that no time is taken from school," he wrote in an official USSGA bulletin.¹⁰⁰ Some USSGA publications suggested that the school was the site of instruction only because of the economy of reaching all students at one time. Perhaps fearing that agricultural education, with its association with manual arts, would face difficulty being accepted as a part of the formal curriculum—especially with urban and suburban audiences—Francis used the pressing wartime need to find a place for the course of study.

"School-supervised" may have been a safer term than "school-based," but the USSGA was clearly designed to be both. In the curriculum's "Suggestions to Organizations" section, which provides information about organizing USSGA programs, the goal is clear: "The aim of this army is to nationalize and unify the great work in gardening now being carried on and *to make it a permanent part of the course of study in all the schools of America.*"¹⁰¹ There was no hidden agenda here.

By encouraging children to engage in physical labor, the USSGA challenged some standard Progressive Era reform themes, among them concern about child labor. It is possible that the creators of the USSGA deliberately sought to allay Progressive Era anxiety about the evils of childhood labor by including larger reform goals in the program's agenda. These reform goals included character education, improved dietary practices, increased physical activity, expanded educational opportunities, and an effort to exert greater control over family life by linking school and home activities. The benefits of physical labor were emphasized, and the manual tasks of gardening were minimized or were construed in different frameworks. Under the cover of patriotism and by introducing the program and its attendant legislative alterations as a wartime (i.e., temporary) measure (this strategy also was used to renegotiate the understanding of female citizenship during wartime mobilization efforts), the USSGA's leaders sought to minimize resistance and advance their agenda. While there was some resistance to the USSGA program, the nature of information suppression and the quelling of dissent that characterized the American home front in World War I make this difficult to fully quantify.

The USSGA curriculum was designed to be delivered by teachers in schools as a formal part of the course of study, integrating agricultural education across the curriculum, the equivalent of modern-day standards-based efforts. Entire sections of the curriculum were directed to teachers. The curriculum was developed under new theories of scientific curriculum development, by committees of educators in consultation with agriculturalists from state colleges of agriculture, the Cooperative Extension Service and industry representatives.[102] While they may have said otherwise, the USSGA's leaders fully intended the program to be a permanent and formal part of the educational system. This was not meant to be a temporary wartime measure.

The USSGA also extended the government's reach into America's urban homes by linking school-supervised gardening work to home-based efforts. The Bureau of Education encouraged schoolteachers to conduct home visits in order to evaluate gardening efforts, to make school gardening and canning equipment available to families for home use and also to provide detailed educational literature about gardening to parents. USSGA Director J.H. Francis advocated a model used by the Children's Bureau and other Progressive Era institutions, including the USDA's Cooperative Extension Service, which provided staff members to engage in home visits. This was intended not only to gauge the success of the instruction, but also to enable the program to reach (and teach) adults. Home visits would presumably enable teachers to learn more about their students' family life, thus aiding their effectiveness in the program. The USSGA hoped that "official" visits might encourage community participation in gardening activities. It is unclear if this element of the USSGA program was widely adopted. There was little concern expressed about how home visits may have felt to some participants: intrusive, perhaps, or prescriptive and patronizing.

The extensive formal mechanisms developed by federal, state and local government to encourage and regulate youth war gardening through the USSGA included supporting legislation in education (i.e., changes in educational codes to permit and mandate youth work in gardening and agriculture); government-funded "field organizers"; food production goals for youth (in volume and dollar value); and school-based cultivation of war gardens.[103] California Governor William Dennison Stephens mandated each Monday as "Conservation Day" in the state's public schools; a prescribed amount of time was dedicated to instructing youth on food production and food conservation. Stephens hoped that California would be the first state to include food conservation in the curriculum. Not surprisingly, the USSGA enjoyed a strong presence in California.

Outcomes

The USSGA exemplifies how Americans mediated competing urban and rural values during a period of rapid change and national transformation. Through the USSGA, positive values attributed to America's rural past were recast and articulated in the largely urban milieu of gardening. It offered a new synthesis of the urban and rural, as new techniques and methods pioneered by urban-led scientific agriculture blended with traditional rural folkways. The USSGA's curriculum reflected new educational philosophies that schooled urban youth in tasks traditionally associated with rural life. The program signified a public quest by Progressive activists, empowered by wartime urgency, to foster traditional producer values in an urban populace through modern means: the emerging associative state and the growing influence of public media. In some ways, gardens enabled urban and suburban youth to create and experience agriculture, albeit on a small scale.

The USSGA cultivated fertile ground of scientific horticultural and Progressive thought to make an old ideal of production modern, educational, and more civically oriented. Advocates used the opportunity of war to make it patriotic and attractive to the imaginations of millions of American children on the home front, and in doing so advanced their vision of synthesizing urban and rural in American life through the associative state. In that, the USSGA ultimately yielded more, promoting producer values in an urban populace through the most modern of means, the associative state and public media.

After Armistice was signed in November of 1918, the USSGA published "victory" editions of its manuals, revised posters to reflect Allied victory, and encouraged Americans to continue gardening to ensure the peace. Gardening was needed to rebuild the world. However, despite these efforts, the USSGA was dismantled soon after Armistice was signed.

It is difficult to know for certain why the USSGA was discontinued. It is possible that in the war's aftermath, as Americans turned their back on the horrors of that period and embraced modernity, they simply lost interest in anything associated with the war. The USSGA's program was framed entirely in military terms, and it is likely that in the rush to forget and in the climate of pacifism that characterized the 1920s, anything so openly militaristic was unappealing. Disillusionment with the government and the war's cost certainly tainted the appeal of voluntarism for some Americans. Certainly, cultural aspects of the 1920s favored individual pleasure over collective sacrifice. And there may have been other reasons, including funding. After the war, military expenditures dropped. The USSGA was funded with defense spending, and its leaders had not developed alternate sources of funding for the program during its tenure.

While food as an issue of national security was less of a visible concern, the need to improve production agriculture and feed America's burgeoning urban population enabled the USDA, in conjunction with land grant universities, to justify and invest in educational programs such as 4-H. Interest in vocational education and continuing interest in rural life supported the development of new programs such as Future Farmers of America (FFA, founded in 1928) and Future Homemakers of America (FHA), which found a permanent location in rural (and some urban) schools.[104] FFA and FHA used 4-H and other Progressive Era youth organizations as models, developing local, state and national organizations to support their work and receiving some government funding.

FOUR

Propaganda, Posters, Promotion and Memory

> "To articulate the past historically does not mean to recognize it 'the way it really was'.... It means to seize hold of a memory as it flashes up at a moment of danger"—Walter Benjamin

The imagery and rhetoric used by the USSGA and other wartime programs provide clues about gender roles, conceptions of childhood, and how Americans struggled to reclaim older producer virtues as the nation developed into a modern consumer society. The USSGA used a variety of recruitment methods, including film. The Bureau of Education created several films to promote the USSGA. The Mary Hemingway School garden in Boston; a school garden parade in Lexington, Kentucky; and a school garden program in Redlands, California were all film topics. The USSGA also filmed a series of instructional pieces on gardening. The Bureau of Education claimed that 300,000 Americans saw these films.[1]

Like the curriculum, and the films, the posters produced by the USSGA and other wartime mobilization efforts used modern means—the associative state and public media—to foster traditional producer values, primarily in the urban populace. USSGA materials also provide hints about how the United States viewed itself in a rapidly changing world order. Columbia was featured. America was portrayed as a strong female presence centered on the nation's belief, in part, that its exceptionalism was based on the bounty of its land.

This striking visual imagery and rhetoric play into larger themes stressing the nature of American freedom, citizenship, and patriotism. Despite the extreme xenophobia of the era, government materials did in part reflect the multiculturalism of American life, appearing in a variety of languages. One of the period's most widely produced posters, "Food Will Win the War," was published in English, Yiddish, Hungarian, Italian, and Spanish.[2] Like other wartime mobilization programs, the USSGA employed advertising and promotion techniques more frequently used by ventures designed to capture consumer audiences. Articles in newsletters and popular magazines, advertisements and posters created by the Committee on Public Information and its Division of Pictorial Publicity (DPP), all popularized war gardens. (The Committee on Public Information was created to mobilize public opinion domestically and abroad to support American wartime efforts. It was also called the Creel Committee, after its director, George Creel.)[3] Professionals used to selling things to the American public produced these items. The "mad men" of advertising (a later generation is featured in a contemporary, award-winning television show) held strategy meetings every Friday night at an office on Fifth Avenue in New York, their "clients" bureaucrats from Washington, D.C.[4] During World War I, a time of national and international crisis, these professionals turned their hand to selling wartime mobilization efforts, including gardening.

President Woodrow Wilson created the Committee on Public Information (CPI) in April 1917, via Executive Order 2594, only a week after declaring war with Germany. The Committee's goal was to mobilize public opinion in support of the war. Journalist George Creel, who was appointed CPI's director, had unerring instincts about how to harness most effectively the expertise of an emerging advertising profession. The CPI engaged the services of hundreds of writers, artists, speakers, and scholars to promote the war effort and to tightly curtail messaging around the war effort. This work aspired to help mobilize a nation, to link the military effort with the home front, to boost production at home and at work, and to unite the power of art with the modern science of advertising. While it had its dark side, the effort was remarkably successful in promoting the notion of school, home, and community gardening.

Shortly after its creation, the CPI formed the DPP under the direction of famed artist Charles Dana Gibson in New York. Branch offices quickly sprang up in Chicago, Boston, and San Francisco, but Washington, D.C., approved all designs. The DPP worked with hundreds of America's most talented artists and writers—most donating their time—to produce posters and other materials promoting government programs and goals. Government agencies became the "clients" of leading advertisers and commercial artists who produced compelling messages that influenced Americans' opinions and behavior.

The imagery and rhetoric of the posters emphasized that the United States was at war. Military terms and images infused USSGA posters, curriculum and publications, as well as organizational structures. The artwork was designed to appeal to youth. The rhetoric was designed to reinforce a sense of urgency and military purpose. USSGA service badges were referred to as "insignia," and its members were "officers and privates."[5] Groups were "enlisted" in "companies" and "regiments." Youth gardeners were recast as "soldiers of the soil," and no plot was left uncultivated, lest it be considered "slacker" land. Gardens were "munitions plants," garden furrows became "trenches," and food was referred to as "ammunition."

The message was explicit: America's citizens, including its youth, must produce. In addition to demonstrating how the United States was synthesizing rural and urban values during a period of rapid transformation, the posters also emphasized the strong ties to a symbolic American landscape that were central to the nation's self-identity, a sort of invented memory. For example, in many of the posters encouraging gardening, the landscape itself is featured as an American flag. Some of the posters recalled famous artwork from previous eras. American patriots from the "The Spirit of 1776" were recast as "soldiers of the soil" in 1918, bearing hoes instead of muskets, carrying baskets of food instead of tapping drums. They emerge as food-producing patriots protecting American freedom through the act of gardening. Again, through some of the wartime propaganda, Americans—whether native born or immigrants—experienced "memories" of the nation's agrarian roots.

Several different federal agencies and departments promoted youth gardening efforts. The Food Administration promoted the USSGA, emphasizing the value of helping Food Administrator Herbert Hoover by promoting work in school gardens. The NWGC, a private-public partnership between national business and education leaders and the federal government, promoted Liberty and Victory gardens and included youth in its target audience; it also supported the USSGA directly. The USDA also promoted gardening and food conservation programs.

Understanding the Relationship Between History and Memory

At this point, it may be helpful to step back from discussion of propaganda and the tools it employed, and to instead shift focus to view Victory Gardens through the lens of memory. While this book provides a history of Liberty and Victory gardens, history and memory are not the same thing. But how does memory differ from history? Pierre Nora and Marc Roudebush argue that memory and history differ in significant ways. Memory is the animated and living consciousness of a culture; history is a reconstruction or representation of past events.[6] Memory remains in "permanent evolution," and is dialectic in nature. History is a more problematic enterprise. Because it is an "intellectual production," or is by definition a social and cultural phenomenon, it requires analysis and criticism. Alon Confino argues that as a discipline or field of study, "memory has a label more than a content."[7] French sociologist Maurice Halbwachs argues that memory is multiple *and* specific. Because it is so essentially linked to the senses, memory is grounded in "real" things: spaces and landscapes and objects (perhaps not coincidentally, all characteristics of gardens). The multiplicity of memory is reflected in private and collective experiences (again, a characteristic of wartime gardening programs, which represented both personal and public experiences). Because of the multiplicity of experiences, there are many versions provided by the mind's constant reshaping of events.

Memory is more dynamic than history, and this may explain why Victory Garden programs in both world wars remain among the most iconic memories (far larger in memory than in their real presence on the American landscape), and still serve as a cultural touchstone and point of reference for the modern food systems movement. In a cultural sense, memory serves to preserve, to unify, to communicate cultural practices, and to educate. While these are goals shared with the larger historical discipline, memory and history differ in how they are implemented in practice, and ultimately, experienced. While the history of Liberty and Victory Gardens is vital to informing current national policies, it is their memory—and what they represent—that seem to resonate so strongly with Americans today, and which provide the emotional impetus to some engaged in food activism.

Pierre Nora, Marc Roudebush, and Maurice Halbwachs all argue that memory is both cultural experience and practice. Again, while history and memory are inextricably linked, there are distinct differences. History seeks to measure and to quantify. Many of the sources that "quantified" gardening efforts during both world wars are suspect: they reflect, in part, the government's attempts via propaganda to make such efforts seem more successful than they actually were. A primary goal of the historical discipline is to measure rates of change (or continuity) over time. History seeks to identify relationally trends, progressions, and movements. Yet it is important to note that both history and memory are the result of cultural experiences. Lines of inquiry in traditional historical practice reflect in many ways the trends and culture of a larger society.

Both history and memory help us organize information and knowledge in a way that enables us to create "usable narratives to explain the world in which we live."[8] And it is in differentiating and joining the notions of history and memory that we can perhaps best use the power of past gardening efforts to mobilize and organize our contemporary work. By creating from past and present experiences usable narratives, we can inform in ways both practical and spiritual our work in gardens.

David Glassberg argues—and others agree—that the historiography of memory study charts a change not in subject matter, but rather a change in approach.[9] Earlier scholarship focused on a single view of the past (as held by a group or institutions). More contemporary studies primarily focus on identifying and understanding the multiple, faceted nature of memory, and the interrelationships between multiple versions of memory in public settings.[10] This area of study focuses on what anthropologist Robert Redfield calls "the social organization of tradition," a notion that certainly applies to gardening work in home and community settings. The "social organization of tradition" examines how multiple and different versions of the past are expressed thorough institutions and media, and how they compete for influence.[11]

Is memory, then, a heuristic device or a psychosocial construction? Is memory something more organic even, part of our physical-psychological make-up, our genetic material, and the brain's attempt to create a cognitive map for living? We know that memory is linked in intimate ways to our sensory experiences. Gardens are experienced through the senses, and important memories are created by our work in them. Do gardens represent place-based memory, or could they be more accurately termed "lieux de memoire" (sites of memory)?

The consensus among the wide-ranging group of academics engaging in memory study is that memory enables us to create "individual and group identity and moderates behavior while simultaneously defining relationships with the world."[12] Memory, unlike history, (and very much like gardening) is living and active. Pierre Nora argues that memory "is a perpetually actual phenomenon."[13] Memory is also selective (although arguably, history is always selective as well). Memory helps us to organize information and understand the world around us in an organic and personal way that fundamentally differs from the ways in which history helps us understand and categorize past experience.

It is not surprising that foundational pieces of modern memory study were laid during the Progressive Era, a period of great advancement and professionalization in the social sciences, and the period during which the Liberty/Victory Garden model (and in fact, school and community gardening) gained traction. If there is a father of the field of modern memory study, it is French sociologist Maurice Halbwachs, who stated the basic thesis of memory study: that collective memory is a socially constructed notion. Hawlbach's most important work, *La topographie legendaire des evangiles en terresainte: Etude de memoire collective*, was published in 1941.[14]

Another important figure in the field of memory study is Aby Warburg (1866–1929). Warburg, a German art historian, systematically used the concept of social memory in evaluating the transmission of artistic motifs to later societies.[15] His work was greatly influenced by time spent in the United States. His particular interests focused on Native American culture, and the work of anthropologists such as Franz Boas. Warburg enhanced his art history knowledge through study in anthropology and social psychology, a new interdisciplinary form he termed "historical psychology" or "psychology of style." Warburg argued that all human products were simply ancient human memory transmitted through shared symbols. In effect, images become an iconic language of a specific culture. These images have multiple meanings, some of which are deeply embedded. Warburg believed that attempting to understand the collective—or cultural—memory was critical. He differed from art historians who used either aesthetic values or a formalist approach to evaluate art. Instead, Warburg emphasized the importance of social and cultural mediation: art is artifact. Our response is what gives it meaning. Today, the public has an overwhelmingly positive response to the messages and images that inspired citizen gardeners a hundred years ago. (And it should be noted that many of the images produced to promote World War I gardening programs were based on even older images that hearkened to the early years of the nation. In Great Britain, one of the most popular contemporary cultural forms is based on a World War II poster: Keep Calm and Carry On.)

The Importance of Place

Place is inextricably linked with memory, not only in a spatial sense, but culturally. Just as places can build community and reinforce collective memory, so too can the destruction of place destroy communities. This was demonstrated by the 2006 closure of the South Central Farm (also known as the South Central Community Garden) in Los Angeles, a 14-acre community garden. A community of food producers—mostly low-income residents of color—operated an urban garden or farm on city-owned land. The rather informal understandings between the city and the gardeners evolved over time, but the community of producers rooted deeply into the soil and into their collective work. When the city sold the land to a private developer, the community gardeners were evicted amidst protests that gained national attention. The loss of this community-based place for food production became the subject of *The Garden*, a 2008 documentary film that was nominated for an Academy Award. As of spring 2013, the land lies unused and fallow, and the community gardeners have dispersed. The vacant lot cultivation ethos (also called "guerrilla gardening"), which has remained a persistent thread of social gardening practice for more than a century, remains alive and well in Los Angeles, most recently in the work of Ron Finley, a master gardener who has gained attention for his use of public space in gardening. Recently, Finley shared information about his work in a popular TedX talk.

As historian Robert Archibald argues, "civic, neighborhood, and familial life all depend upon shared places that are repositories of common memories and shared experiences."[16] He gives voice to this most eloquently, as he describes the center of a neighborhood shifting away from the locus of a small store to an unanchored consumer (and automobile) society. The small store had not only served as a place to purchase needed goods, but as a gathering spot for a neighborhood, a place where social interactions occurred that defined and strengthened the bonds of community. This certainly describes community gardens. Historian Ray Oldenburg calls these "third places," distinguishing them spatially from the social constructs of home and places of employment. "Third places" provide the social space where the development of community and collective purpose occurs. Archibald argues that these "third" places provide the space that is necessary for the formation of common aspirations and collective memory. I might argue that just as suburbs were a middle landscape linking urban and rural at a pivotal time in our past, gardens can—and often do—serve as important "third places" in communities. As wartime efforts show us, gardens remain powerful in their ability to create common purpose and bridge social, economic, and racial differences.

Places—and perhaps especially gardens—are imbued with specific and unique cultural meaning. David Glassberg argues, "Places are not interchangeable with other places."[17] He describes a process wherein places are made and remade. Building upon a natural landscape makes places; they are then remade culturally, as people attach memories and meanings to them. Glassberg further argues that our sense of place is largely a product of memory. Psychological studies indicate that memory has an enormous influence on how we view our environment; place and personal identity are also strongly linked.[18] The linking of place and personal identity plays out uniquely in America, where much of our national character is defined by our collective history in relation to places, such as "the West." This has been an important theme in American literature (consider the works of Mark Twain, William Faulkner, Louise Erdrich, Wallace Stegner, and Larry McMurtry).

Much of the practice of public historians has focused on the preservation of physical space. Using carefully designed criteria and standards, historians and community members seek out historically "significant" structures and places to preserve or commemorate. Some of these sites are gardens, although ornamental sites are favored over food producing gardens in terms of preservation. These criteria and standards are somewhat clinical. Considered singly, they do not tell us what is "important" about a particular structure or location. Criteria and standards do not assure that what is preserved in a spatial sense reflects what is important to the community in a cultural sense. Hence, the loss of the South Central Community Garden.

In her book *The Power of Place: Urban Landscapes as Public History*, historian Dolores Hayden describes how the languages of those interested in preservation differ and complicate efforts to ensure that public memory is maintained.[19] "Architecture" means the entire built environment to a sociologist; to an architectural critic, it implies structures designed with an "aesthetic intent," a much smaller percentage of the built environment.[20] To the sociologist, the term "neighborhood" implies a web of social networks occurring within a particular spatial network. The architectural critic might use the term only in a spatial sense, defining boundaries and parameters enclosing a certain collection of streets. As we increasingly use technology (and social technologies) to "map" communities, we need to insist that exercise also include mapping a community's food shed, which involves both spatial and social networks. Every community should understand where its food comes from, and also where its food vulnerabilities and opportunities lie.

The social and cultural function of place is critical to understanding memory studies. Collective memories associated with a particular diner where the community gathers may be more significant than the memories associated with a building designed by a famous architect. Again, as those concerned with preservation, our goals must be to consider what memories are important to a community, and what about a place is significant to the community. The lesser spaces, the "third places," may warrant more of our attention and effort. By their nature, gardens are ephemeral, sometimes lasting only a few seasons. But the places that enable a community to produce food must be deemed at least as sacred as the buildings we construct.

Several critical challenges will continue to emerge and need to be addressed by those studying the model of Liberty and Victory Gardens, and especially their re-emergence in our nation's civic life. The contemporary sustainable food systems movement derives much of its strength from sharing stories about the challenges and opportunities inherent in (re)creating community-based food systems. Many of the issues in the movement revolve around the marginalization of certain groups in relationship to the food system; it is not only about food, but also about social justice. In many ways, the food systems movement represents a continuation of the Civil Rights movement, as individuals and communities strive for food access, food sovereignty, and the need to address historical and structural inequities in the food system.

The concept of a meta-narrative (if the meta-narrative ever really existed) has been replaced by multiple versions of the same "history," a history that feels very different depending on your location within the narrative. With a multiplicity of valid stories vying for public space, the challenge for us will be to acknowledge, integrate (when possible) and re-frame larger narratives, while providing opportunities for all stories to be heard. This will be hard work, challenging and often controversial. But as collective memory moves into the realm of public commemoration, the work will become even more critical. It will fall to all of us to identify commonalities and threads of continuity, to weave together the many disparate strands into a recognizable and whole cloth. We must help to preserve, manage and commemorate representative histories within the food system, histories that serve to inform current models and best practices.

There is a great deal of opportunity for all of us to explore the role of gardens in memory and in creating a sense of place. Many Americans seem to feel placeless. We move frequently. Many of our communities are newly created and lack a collective memory or purpose. Many of us are ashamed of the "third places" in our communities: the Home Depots, fast food restaurants, and Starbucks, all characterized by "fast" and conformist architecture. Many communities lack a feeling of spatial or social center, and this is also reflected in social interactions and networks. Perhaps soccer fields and carpools have replaced the corner market as the place where meaningful social interactions and memory are created. In some communities, farmers markets provide this opportunity. "Social life structures territory ... and territory shapes social life."[21] And both social life and territory shape memory.

This represents a wonderful time and opportunity for us to explore how gardens can help reshape social and spatial life in our communities. In fact, it is already occurring.

World War I Posters

The First World War marked the first large scale use of propaganda posters by governments, and all of the governments involved in the conflict produced them. Posters, with easy-to-understand slogans and compelling images, made powerful propaganda tools. The government needed to shape public opinion, recruit soldiers, raise funds and conserve resources, and posters could help do this. In an era before television and widespread radio and movies, posters, newspapers and advertising were mass media.

Modern posters emerged during the 1890s, arising from the La Belle Epoque (1871–1914) and Art Nouveau movements in France.[22] La Belle Epoque—the beautiful era—movement was named in retrospect, after the horrors of World War I. During this period in France (which roughly corresponded with the Gilded Age in the U.S., and overlapped with the Victorian and Edwardian eras in the U.K.), the arts flourished. Two of the most influential individuals on the growth of poster art were Jules Cheret and Eugene

Grasset. Cheret (1836–1932) was a French painter and lithographer whose works reflect the prosperity and optimism of the period. Grasset (1845?-1917) also became a pioneer in the Art Noveau movement. His work was commissioned by a number of American companies, and he created the cover design for the Christmas edition of *Harpers Magazine* in 1892.

Advertising was greatly influenced by the use of color. American advertising pioneer Artemas Ward said of the use of color in advertising that it "creates desire" and was a "priceless ingredient."[23] Skillfully rendered lithographs and advertisements influenced and changed consumer behavior. Advertising cards had been used as early as the 1850s, and catalogs were common. Visual information and advertising thus entered a new era between 1880 and 1915.[24] (Outdoor advertising grew between 1890 and 1915, with increased number of billboards, and the introduction of electric signage.) The emergence of color lithography at the end of the 19th century enabled the cheap, mass reproduction of images. Advertising images improved in catalogs and newspapers, which fed changing consumption patterns in the U.S. The shift of the postal service from a primary purpose of facilitating the spread of information (via letters, newspapers, etc.) to business use was accomplished with parcel post legislation in 1912.[25]

Prior to World War I, posters were used successfully in advertising, and by European governments to support their own efforts during the early years of the war. Although the United States joined the war relatively late, estimates suggest that the United States government printed more than twenty million copies of approximately 2,500 poster designs, far more posters than all of the other nations involved in the conflict printed combined. More than 700 of these poster designs, created by the DPP, were distributed nationally and on a widespread basis. In addition to the nationally distributed posters shown in this book, hundreds of regional and local poster designs were created during the war. The majority of the posters were printed through a process called chromolithography, which produced vibrantly colored and highly moving works that we regard as art forms today. It is important to note that there was tension between those using chromolithography – a chemical process that facilitated the mass production of "art," including advertisements—and those who favored traditional fine art methods. (Off-set printing became the generally accepted mode in the 1930s.) But posters were ubiquitous during the war years. They were challenging and evocative, and seared images into the collective consciousness of Americans of the wartime generation. Posters, along with newspapers and magazines, were the primary forms of mass media during World War I.

In the image *Sow the Seeds of Victory*, rendered by famous artist James Montgomery Flagg and produced by the National War Garden Commission,

Sow the Seeds of Victory! Artist: James Montgomery Flagg (1877–1960). National War Garden Commission, Washington, D.C. (1918). One of the most famous artists of the era, Flagg produced this compelling image of Columbia encouraging Americans to garden (Museum of Ventura County, photographer Aysen Tan).

Follow the Pied Piper. Artist: Maginel Wright Barney (1877–1966). United States School Garden Army (1919). Children carrying agricultural implements follow Uncle Sam as they walk across a landscape shaped like an American flag. Barney, a noted children's illustrator and artist, was also the sister of architect Frank Lloyd Wright (Museum of Ventura County, photographer Aysen Tan).

Americans are asked if they will have a part in America's (assured) victory. Columbia, representing the United States, sows seeds on an empty landscape. The act of sowing seeds is typically female (and reproductive). The furrows on the landscape represent the stripes on a flag, ready to leap to life in Columbia's wake. The poster's tagline, "Every Garden a Munitions Plant," equates gardening and its products to the industrial model that was churning out weapons and other items needed for modern warfare.

In the famous USSGA poster, *Follow the Pied Piper*, created by noted artist Maginel Wright Barney, Uncle Sam, in striped pants, perhaps playing

"Yankee Doodle Dandy" on his fife, leads young children across an American landscape. The boys carry tools, and a young girl, holding a military knapsack with the USSGA logo, sows seeds on newly plowed furrows, echoing a theme of female productive capacity (perhaps the girl is a young Columbia?). The background features a prosperous village or town. The landscape in the background, already under cultivation, appears as an American flag. There is a sense of movement in the poster (an impending storm?), of Uncle Sam taking charge, and the boys looking to him for guidance.

War Gardens Over the Top. Artist: Maginel Wright Barney (1877–1966). National War Garden Commission, Washington, D.C. (1919). A young gardener and his regiment of vegetables go over the top of a trench in an all out effort to encourage gardening. This image in particular evokes the iconic nature of trench warfare during World War I (Library of Congress, photographer Aysen Tan).

The tagline on this vivid poster, "The Seeds of Victory Insure the Fruits of Peace," also created by Maginel Wright Barney, directly ties gardening to world peace and national security. It also delivers the message that peace requires strength. The smaller tagline indicates that this is "A Poster Spreading the Idea of Militant War Gardens," implying that the very land has been mobilized to America's war effort. The poster's headline, *War Gardens over the Top*, addresses the issue of trench warfare, one of the most horrifying and iconic features of World War I. This young boy, holding an American flag, is shown scaling a garden "trench," his weapon a garden hoe. He is "doing his bit" to help the war effort. An army of vegetables, some with mouths opened in a silent scream as they face the horrors of modern warfare, including the possibility of mustard gas, accompanies him.

A companion poster by the same artist was produced later. "War Gardens Victorious" shows the same young boy, perhaps a bit older now, uniformed in a blue shirt and overalls, proudly leading a regiment of smiling vegetables— potatoes, carrots, turnips and pumpkins. A small American flag is tucked into the band on his straw hat, and the vegetable brigade carries a full-sized American flag. They are returning safely from the battlefront to wage a new kind of war that emphasizes the power of gardens in the secured peace.

Join the United States School Garden Army, a poster created by famed artist Edward Penfield, is one of the best known of the World War I posters, and commands a high selling price today. It does not conform to the traditions of many other gardening posters published during World War I, failing to provide a sentimental, almost Victorian depiction of gardening, or a sharply and brightly illustrated work that would appeal to children. Penfield's work, which shows a mannish young woman pushing a wheeled cultivator, challenged gender stereotypes. The young woman is dressed in sturdy and rather unattractive boots and socks. Her hair, which is bobbed, anticipates the "flapper" of the 1920s; she also wears a bifurcated skirt. The poster is not as overtly patriotic as other gardening posters, although the girl's clothing does include red, white, and blue, a military shirt and the USSGA insignia. It also includes the command to "Enlist Now," a strong statement given the recent adoption of the draft. This poster may have appealed to older girls, or served as a bridge to enrollment in the Woman's Land Army Program. The poster also presents a sense of sacrifice: the girl is working by herself, perhaps giving up a fun pursuit to perform her civic duty, meeting the obligation of female citizenship, and what that meant during the wartime years.

Raised 'em myself in my U.S. School Garden, a poster produced for the USSGA by the Food Administration, stressed the grit, individualism and capability of the traditional American boy. A junior entrepreneur, wearing a newsboy's cap and clad in overalls, is illuminated by a bright light (perhaps

Join the United-States School Garden Army. Artist: Edward Penfield (1866–1925). American Lithographic Company (1918). In a different take on youth gardeners, a brooding young woman dressed in a uniform pushes a wheeled cultivator. Her hair and dress foreshadow the ways in which women would use the war to challenge stereotypes (Museum of Ventura County, photographer Aysen Tan).

indicating the boy's energy and unlimited potential). He represents the future of the nation: bright, optimistic, with unlimited possibilities. His rolled-up sleeves demonstrate the "can-do" attitude and self-sufficiency of the American boy, the up and coming "captain of industry." He proudly wears his USSGA insignia, an American flag tie, and a confident and proud grin. This poster would have resonated strongly with American boys.

Raised 'em myself in my U.S. School Garden. A young city boy displays a "can-do" attitude while proudly displaying the fruits of his labor. The sun rises behind him (Museum of Ventura County, photographer Aysen Tan).

"Uncle Sam Says Garden" was a poster that was directed to wider audiences. Produced in 1917, it shows Uncle Sam in the foreground, holding a hoe in one hand, and papers that read "City Gardens" and "Farm Gardens" in the other. These words are clearly meant to synthesize the interests of rural and urban Americans: gardening was a shared activity, a common national goal. A man and woman work in the garden shown, which is in the shape of the American flag. Some of the plants featured in the garden might appear to be stars upon the flag. The woman in the poster wears a long, red skirt and a white shirt; in her arm is something she has harvested from the garden. A subtitle suggests that Americans might wish to garden in order to "cut food costs." Those seeing the poster are urged to write to the USDA for a free bulletin on gardening, suggesting, "It's food for thought." The poster is framed by a brown band, and the bottom right corner features a cluster of richly hued vegetables. Upon careful inspection, the background, featuring trees, actually bears a striking resemblance to leafy green vegetables and also to broccoli stems. The use of Uncle Sam in gardening posters was not as common as Columbia, and in this depiction, he is dressed in clothing covered with stars and stripes, and has

Uncle Sam Says - Garden To Cut Food Costs. **United States Department of Agriculture (1917). As a woman and man garden in the background, Uncle Sam, hoe in hand, offers booklets on gardening for both city and farm gardeners - the federal government offered free brochures on gardening as part of the war effort. It still is food for thought (Library**

a piercing gaze. This poster evokes an earlier era than some of the other wartime posters. For example, the depiction of Uncle Sam is more traditional, and the woman is wearing a long skirt.

Part of the appeal of many of the wartime posters were that they were created by well known artists, who volunteered their time and talents to the war effort. One of the war's most memorable food posters was produced by noted artist John E. Sheridan (1880–1948). Sheridan produced cover art for

Food is Ammunition—Don't waste it. Artist: John E. Sheridan (1880–1948). United States Food Administration (1918?). American cavalry provide the backdrop for this poster, which admonishes the public to conserve food—a primary tactic of the war effort (Museum of Ventura County, photographer Aysen Tan).

the *Saturday Evening Post,* and advertisements for *Collier's Weekly*. His work also appeared in *Ladies Home Journal*. He worked as the art editor for the *Washington Times* and also was on staff at the *San Francisco Chronicle*. His seminal poster, "Food is Ammunition: Don't Waste It," brought home the fact that World War I was both the last old-fashion war and the first modern war simultaneously. In the foreground, a color-saturated basket of vegetables appears. In the background, American cavalry appear on horseback, holding an American flag in front of a white cloud, as an orange sun—or perhaps, the glare of the battlefield—blazes. Faintly shadowed artillery pieces appear upon close inspection. The message—that food was as vital to national security and allied victory as ammunition—was provocative. It is, I believe, a message that might apply to America's current and pressing problem of food waste: our careful stewardship of food is an issue vital to national security.

While many of the USDA and Food Administration appealed to "traditional" American housewives, the USSGA both challenged and reinforced gender stereotypes. While the USSGA challenged stereotypes by encouraging girls to become "producers" and to join its "juvenile food army," it directed some female production to gendered forms, such as food preservation and domestic arts. Some USSGA materials suggest that sewing classes might generate USSGA banners or costumes for USSGA pageants. In addition to posters, lyrics about USSGA service were set to popular wartime tunes; these lyrics occasionally reinforce gender stereotypes. A song written for the USSGA, to the tune of "Over There," indicates that the "lads are hoeing, the lads are hoeing, the girls are sowing ev'rywhere," which seems to reinforce the idea of a typically reproductive role for females and a more active role for males.[26] Yet, the USSGA manuals contain pictures of both boys and girls engaged in gardening work.

Food conservation was a topic of many USDA and Food Administration posters, but posters on this topic were also published by those groups (including the NWGC) that sought to encourage home food production. "Win the Next War Now," produced by artist Leonebel Jacobs, made food conservation patriotic. Those seeking instructions on "home canning and home drying" were instructed to write to the NWGC, directing their inquiry to Charles Lathrop Pack or P.S. Risdale. This poster features a beautifully rendered Columbia, draped in the American flag. In this depiction, Columbia is an ethereal blonde, with a softly rendered Victorian influence. Her expression is proud—perhaps reflecting a duty well met—but she is unsmiling. One hand—its fingers gracefully extended, poignantly gesture to a lush and richly hued display of fresh and canned fruits and vegetables, laid out as upon an altar, reflecting a cornucopia of food abundance. Her other hand is raised above her head, holding a jar of preserves, evoking, perhaps intentionally, the Lady of Liberty, holding up her light.

The focus on youth as a key component of the national wartime gardening programs presaged the notion of "The Child in the Garden is the forerunner of Man in the World"; youth raised up in gardens would become key to the civic life of the nation and the world.

"The Child in the Garden is the forerunner of Man in the World"

The USSGA used a variety of cultural forms to reinforce its message, including posters, its curriculum, songs, and a pageant. One of the most interesting cultural pieces promoting USSGA work was "The Victory of the Gardens: A Pageant in Four Episodes," written for the USSGA by high school teacher Ethel Allen Murphy of Louisville, Kentucky.[27] The pageant was performed by school children, and many of the described visual aspects of the pageant's performance echoed the visual iconography of the USSGA posters. An analysis of this pageant provides additional information about the USSGA and the message it sought to convey to American youth.

Pageants were an important form of cultural life in America at the turn of the century. According to historian David Glassberg, "public historical imagery is an essential element of our culture, contributing to how we define our sense of identity and direction."[28] World War I posters, many of which capitalized on historical themes, clearly sought to define and shape American identity and purpose; according to Glassberg, "pageant writers created the melodramatic equivalent of World War I recruiting posters."[29] World War I mobilization created a variety of new institutions and new ways to use older institutions (including civic organizations). It was a period of uncertainty and change. David Glassberg argues that during a period of transformation, pageants provided a way to "organize the soul of America."[30] (And this notion is also expressed by Wiebe, in his description of a sort of underlying continuity in some streams of American cultural, social, and political life.)

Given the prevalence of pageants, it is natural that this cultural form would be used by the USSGA. Yet, just as wartime transformed so much of American life, wartime also transformed the nature of the American pageant. Simple offerings replaced lavish, professionally produced pageants emphasizing historical themes, with locally produced and easily replicable pageants highlighting allegorical themes.[31] Previously, pageants focused on local histories and themes. With home front mobilization came a need for a common and unified national purpose, and this encouraged the development of themes deemed to be of national importance.[32] Images such as Columbia provided a sort of iconographic shorthand for Americans. The national subsumed the local. Increasingly, pageants also provided places for audience participation, particularly singing, which ostensibly encouraged civic participation, patriotism, and solidarity.[33]

Like others associated with the USSGA, Murphy—the pageant's author—sought to fuse or synthesize rural and urban values. "Something should be said as to the welding of the practical and the imaginative, for both of which a garden holds rare possibilities," she wrote.[34] She saw war gardens as providing a place for "idealism and service," hearkening back to suggestions by Wordsworth and Longfellow of nature as a teacher, and the "wholesome influences" created when man communed with nature.[35] Like others, Murphy saw that gardening could heal the destruction of war. In some British and American military hospitals, gardens were cultivated by healing soldiers, not with the purpose of food production, but because of the therapeutic value of gardening. Even proponents of "militant war gardens" saw gardening as a means to rebuild communities and maintain peace in the post-war era. Just as nature study promised to heal the ills of urban life, gardening might heal the psychic wounds of war. Murphy saw that children might have a foremost place in this healing, writing, "The Child in the Garden is the forerunner of Man in the World."[36] The lessons of the garden, then, might positively influence "the re-shaping" of the post-war world.

The pageant, consisting of four episodes, says fascinating things about America's perception of itself in relation to the rest of the world during World War I. Mother Earth is suffering from the sorrows of war. America must play a vital role in relieving that sorrow. The first episode highlights the seasons, as each attempts to ease Mother Earth's sufferings through dances and play. In the second episode, "The Spirit of Famine," a horrific vision of starving children is shown. These children are weak, "pale, imploring."[37] They are clearly European. Interestingly, the Spirit of Famine represents the only leading male role in the pageant. In this pageant, as in others of the period, the nation state is a strong, young, and female presence.

In the third episode, appropriately entitled "Columbia to the Rescue," America enters the stage. America might have been considered to enter the third act of World War I in terms of military mobilization, and this pageant parallels that idea of America as a latecomer—but savior—to the war effort. Columbia, the youngest of Mother Earth's children, offers her aid. The stage directions describe how Columbia should be costumed:

> She wears a white classic robe girdled in gold. Over her shoulders is draped a beautiful American flag so arranged that the blue-starred part falls over her breast.... On her head is a red liberty cap encircled with a wreath of golden leaves opening in front over a blue band with three stars on it. As she enters, a chorus ... may sing, "Columbia the Gem of the Ocean" ... the Earth Mother blesses her with ... looks of joy.[38]

Columbia is Mother Earth's "youngest and well-beloved child."[39] Unlike the older, and presumably degraded European children of Mother Earth, Columbia is a harbinger of hope. Mother Earth summons all the spirits of nature to assist Columbia in her efforts to feed the world. But it is not enough: Columbia requires the assistance of strong and healthy American children to garden and bring joy and the Spirit of Plenty back to the earth. "Will you help me now to bring joy again to your little sisters and brothers of other countries?" reflects a new understanding of America's increasingly dominant place in the world order.[40] The children agree to assist, and leave the stage, returning shortly in overalls and hats, gardening tools in hand. Nature rejoices. The children chant a song that emphasizes the joy of work.[41]

The pageant culminates in a harvest and a fete to "the Spirit of Plenty," as the children present the "fruits of their labor," and are blessed by Mother Earth, Columbia and the Spirit of Plenty. Representatives from the "Nations" come to pay homage to Mother Earth and Columbia, kneeling and giving "thanks to Columbia." The nations are presumably European and now tributary to Columbia, or the United States. Folk dances and songs from the tributary nations include those from Sweden, Russia, Finland, Hungary and the British Isles.[42] Child dancers, who offer a folk dance representative of each nation, accompany them. The nations take their place alongside, but in a subordinate role to, Columbia. While the American child gardeners remain on the stage—they are Columbia's children, after all—the child dancers representing other nations leave. Columbia is now in the pantheon with Mother Earth and the Spirit of Plenty. Because of her role in providing relief, Columbia is anointed as Mother Earth's favorite child.

This pageant demonstrates the United States' new vision of itself as international savior. In seeking to promote nationalism, the pageant moves beyond traditional American isolationism to incorporate a new vision of internationalism, but on America's terms. The internationalism it presents is shown from the perception of children and through shallow folk representations of other nations. Quaint dances and costumes, the trappings of culture, perhaps, but not a deep understanding of culture in a real sense. Different cultures are quickly shuffled offstage as the predominant American culture of mega-producer and mega-consumer is unveiled, represented by an abundance of agricultural products and strong, healthy, and well-fed children, the products of a successful consumer (and agricultural) society. The vision of internationalism the pageant presents places Columbia in a position around which other nations will orbit. Columbia is not "one of many," but first among nations. Columbia represents America's sense of exceptionalism. That this exceptionalism is demonstrated through the abundance of its land and its ability to produce food is extraordinary. Columbia has taken center stage, and the rest of the world must now wait in the wings.

This form of American exceptionalism shaped the nation's participation in World War II, and also helped to shape international identity post–World War II (in programs such as the Marshall Plan, the Berlin Airlift, and USDA Foreign Agricultural Service work). In the post–World War I world order, America could be counted on to bring food to the world's table.

FIVE

The Pennsylvania School of Horticulture for Women

"The trained hand with the trained mind means mastery and success"—Pennsylvania School of Horticulture for Women fundraising brochure (Ambler Archives, Temple University)

Women were central to the gardening movements that swept across the United States, not only during the World War I campaign, but also in earlier times. Women's work in the domestic sphere and their work in reform efforts provided opportunities for them to shape these programs. But women also used their work in gardening to press for suffrage and fuller participation in the nation's cultural and political life during World War I; the Woman's Land Army of America (WLAA) represented one example of this. To understand what occurred during World War I—and to understand how women strongly influenced the national movement—one must explore earlier efforts, including what might appear to be an obscure horticultural school for women, but which proved to be of national importance in subsequent years.

A full decade before America's entry into World War I, in the winter of 1907, a middle-aged Quaker woman named Jane Bowne Haines completed a thirty-three-page handwritten paper on "Gardening Schools for Women."[1] In it, Haines advocated for an idea that four years later became the Pennsylvania School of Horticulture for Women in Ambler, Pennsylvania (hereinafter "Ambler"). The document Haines wrote was based on her earlier travels in Europe and correspondence she'd engaged in with a number of individuals. A picture of Haines from this period shows a woman with an intelligent, firm and self-assured expression, wearing a lace cravat and a stylish hat adorned with velvet and flowers, secured by a hatpin.[2]

Haines was the daughter of a family that itself seemed to synthesize America's urban and rural interests. The family's wealth was derived from eight generations of farming and allied activities including horticulture, with strong ties to the urban center of Philadelphia. Haines was a descendant of Caspar Wistar, an immigrant from Germany who arrived in the Philadelphia area in 1717. Wistar's home, built in the late seventeenth century in the village of Germantown (now a neighborhood about 8 miles northwest from the center of Philadelphia) was called "Wyck"; it is now a National Historic Landmark.[3] It was the family homestead for generations, remaining under the ownership of the family for 300 years. Wyck was eventually donated by the ninth generation of the family to the Wyck Association, and is now operated as a non-profit organization dedicated to a rich mix of historical preservation; the promotion of healthy, sustainable food systems; and a dedication to what the non-profit terms "innovation, social responsibility, and environmental sustainability." One could easily argue that the life work of Jane Bowne Haines, particularly her work at Ambler, lived out these values.

While Jane herself grew up in Cheltenham, Pennsylvania, where her father owned a fruit and shade tree nursery that Jane and her siblings later inherited and operated, she undoubtedly remained strongly connected to the family's ancestral farm and homestead at Wyck.[4] The Haines were devout Quakers, and were strongly influenced by ideas about educational reform and activism in that area. Jane's later work reflected those sensibilities, as she worked to increase gender equality by providing educational opportunities for women. Jane's work also reflected the central importance of agricultural stewardship (now interpreted as "sustainability") that played out in her family across centuries and generations.[5]

As a child, Haines was a frequent visitor to the family homestead at Wyck, which was a working farm and also contained gardens. (Wyck Historic House, Garden and Farm—an urban farm—is still an important and vital part of its urban neighborhood, providing educational activities focused on food, culture, and history.) Jane is reported to have worked extensively in the rose gardens there, and she became skilled at horticulture. Working alongside her father in the family's nursery business enhanced these skills. After his death, Haines and her siblings ran the business for nearly forty years.[6] The family's work reflected the important role that Philadelphia played in the development of horticulture in America: reportedly among the elder Haines' holdings was one of the original Franklinia trees discovered by noted botanist John Bartram.[7] Also a Quaker, Bartram was a noted botanist, horticulturist, and explorer. His garden is considered by many to be the nation's first significant botanical collection and garden. He was one of the founders of the American Philosophical Society. Like Wyck, Bartram's Garden, remains a thriving enterprise, hosting visitors at its site in Philadelphia, proving that agriculture can endure and thrive in urban settings.

The Haines family believed in education for women. Jane enrolled at Bryn Mawr College, where she graduated with a degree in history and economics in 1891. She continued her graduate education there, receiving a Master of Arts.[8] Later, Haines enrolled in a library sciences program, earning a certificate from the Library School in Albany, New York, in 1899. She worked in the Library of Congress for a short time between 1900 and 1903. Haines was unusual for her time, not only in terms of her educational attainment, but also in terms of her professional work.

Emma and Jane's Travels: Southern California and "Atlantic Crossings"[9]

Haines wasn't the first or only woman interested in creating a horticultural school for women. Between 1884 and 1886, Cleveland resident Emma Adams traveled to Southern California, penning a series of letters that provided a glimpse into the status of women, agriculture, and community development.[10] In her letters, Adams strongly connected career and educational opportunities in agriculture with the possibility of improving the status of women. An avid horticulturalist, Adams desired to create a horticulture college for women.[11] Other women saw a need as well. In 1901 Judith Eleanor Low opened Lowthorpe School, a horticultural school for women, in Groton, Massachusetts.[12] (Lowthorpe School is an excellent reference point for Ambler. In 1917, the school fielded a baseball team called the "Farmerettes.") Haines was aware of the activities and organization of the school at Lowthorpe; she refers to it in "Gardening Schools for Women."[13]

Unlike Adams, Haines looked abroad for inspiration, traveling to Europe in 1906. She did not engage in a grand tour.[14] Instead, Haines' agenda led her to visit a number of female-oriented horticultural schools and demonstration farms. As was the case in the school garden movement, Europe had a much longer tradition than America of educational and associational work for women interested in gardening and horticulture. As early as 1797, Finland formed an Agricultural Women's Organization. In 1899, the Women's Agricultural and Horticultural International Union of England was founded at a gathering of the International Council of Women (ICW).[15] What Haines saw in Europe—and her own experience of working on her family's farm and alongside her father in their family nursery—led her to believe that there could be for women the "opening of a new field of labor" that would enable them "at once to profit by a new employment."[16]

During the period of Haines' trip, the British Women's Agricultural and Horticultural International Union of England (which provided the model for the American Woman's National Farm and Garden Association, WNFGA) held its first annual show. It is possible that Haines attended this exhibition, although the evidence is not conclusive. Around this time, Haines collaborated and corresponded with a key figure in the American gardening community, Louisa Yeoman King. King was one of the founders of the Garden Club of America in 1913. She served as the first president of the WNFGA (from 1914 to 1921). She was a prolific gardening writer and among the most well-known woman gardeners in the U.S. during the interwar years.[17] King also had traveled in Europe, had met and corresponded with those involved in women's horticultural efforts in Europe, and was a driving force behind women's garden club activities both in Michigan and nationally. She also was a highly respected gardening writer. King's work in women's civic organizations provides one example of the active engagement of club women in reform activities utilizing community and school garden programs. It makes sense that the Progressive thrust of many of these women's organizations influenced women's interest in educational opportunities in the field of horticulture.[18] The Progressive Era was a period of education, reform, and associational growth, with national networks and affiliations gaining traction, and sharing knowledge with one another.

"The beginning was inauspicious"[19]

The next few years led Haines to the realization of her dream through the creation of a school of horticulture for women. She shared that vision: "Our dream was of a place where earnest minded women could live and dream, where they should not be expected to do household work, but should give their whole time to learning under competent teachers to become competent workers, bearing out the maxim: the trained hand with the trained mind means mastery and success."[20]

The founding of the Pennsylvania School of Horticulture for Women at Ambler was a seed that gave life to other female enterprises of national importance. The work at Ambler bears similarities to a genealogical project, for it proved to be the nexus of numerous and tangled relationships among individuals and associations. Ambler linked seemingly disparate impulses, including urban-rural relations, professional specialization, scientific agriculture, woman's rights, reform efforts, labor, and higher education for women. Progressive touches were evident in Ambler's organization and implementation; the Ambler experience was both "prophetic and particular."[21]

Ideas about creating a horticultural school for women—and what the program of study might be– were gathered by Haines in "Gardening Schools for Women."²² This document, a manifesto of sorts, provides a comprehensive survey of women's horticultural education shortly after the turn of the twentieth century and foreshadows the creation of her horticulture school, Ambler. Haines conducted painstaking research; her survey discusses horticulture education activity for women in England, Scotland, Belgium, Italy, Germany, Russia, Austria-Hungary, Spain and the United States. Her study provides detailed descriptions of educational models, sites, acreage, operations, crops, curriculum, admission policies, educational philosophy, faculty, employment opportunities, living arrangements, and even some student demographics (class, age, rural or urban, etc.).

The curriculum of the school she founded was influenced by what Haines learned through her travels and correspondence. Most surprising was that the curriculum was not strictly—or even largely—influenced by the rural experience of farming.²³ (And this notion would hold true of World War I programs such as the USSGA.) This makes sense for many reasons, including Haines' personal experience in horticulture. In this respect, the school she imagined was similar to the nature-study movement, Country Life Movement, and wartime gardening programs: it derived from largely urban understandings of what was rural. It sought to carve out a new landscape of economic and employment opportunities for women, a sort of middle ground or landscape that synthesized urban and rural ideals, philosophies, and practices. In her survey of women's horticultural schools, Haines referred to this as "a new field of labor," but it was much more than that.²⁴ As expressed in "Gardening Schools for Women," Haines was concerned about the widely held notion that women could not be successful at hard physical labor.²⁵ She disagreed. Haines herself had worked in the out-of-doors, and knew otherwise. She was deeply worried about the negative effects that office and factory work had on women. Hers was a reformer's interest.

In 1910, just a few years after her trip to Europe and the completion of her paper, Haines shared her vision with colleagues from Bryn Mawr. Together they raised funds to purchase the 71-acre McAlnon family farm, with the express purpose of creating a woman's horticulture school. In 1911, the Pennsylvania School of Horticulture for Women at Ambler opened. (There is some confusion over the date of Ambler's founding. While the school was chartered by the Commonwealth of Pennsylvania in 1910, it did not open its doors to students until February of 1911. Reports on the number of students who entered Ambler for the first term vary depending upon the source.) It was located less than twenty miles from Philadelphia, accessible from the city by railway, which was by design: Haines clearly intended to open up "country pursuits" to urban, well educated women like herself. In 1910, Haines said:

> Believing thoroughly in the principle of horticultural training for women, and that the time for founding such an institution is now come, a number of people have associated themselves together with the purpose of opening, in the near future, a school for the practical training of women in gardening and kindred subjects. The purpose of the school is to offer educated and earnest minded women who have a love for the country life and an aptitude for country pursuits, practical training in horticulture.... The first students in the school will have much of the fun, for to them will be given an insight into the foundation of things; the laying out and planting of the gardens and grounds, and the creating of custom and precedent so dear to all schools and colleges.[26]

Her attendance at Bryn Mawr having impressed upon Haines the value of customs and traditions to creating continuity across the life of institutions, she sought to articulate a greater purpose for the institution that she and her colleagues were designing. One custom that Ambler created was to reconnect women to the land. This provided one precedent for the work of the WLAA during World War I.

Building a Cold Frame

The "place to live and dream" Haines intended can be seen as a cold frame for women's aspirations to move from the domestic to the professional sphere. A cold frame is a simple gardening structure that protects small plants and seedlings, enabling them to thrive in adverse conditions. In many ways, the Pennsylvania School of Horticulture for Women at Ambler provided a cold frame for the movement of women into horticulture and the realm of food production Haines saw as distinctly fit for women. It also provided a sheltered space for the WLAA to form only a handful of years later, as wartime mobilization advanced the agenda of woman's rights. What might appear to us to be a place where elite women could learn about gardening was actually envisioned by its female creators as a place where women might create new kinds of employment opportunities for themselves, new kinds of places for professional work, and a new kind of middle ground where women could claim a leadership role that encompassed and honored their work in both the domestic and public spheres.

The history of gardening is better understood when it is considered within the framework of domestic and public spheres, and also when it is considered in relationship to the history of agriculture. While histories of gardens and gardening are seldom included in agricultural literature, again, the etymology of the words indicates we ought to consider them together. An understanding of where gardening traditionally fit into the discipline of agriculture is vital to understanding both the Ambler experience and woman's wartime gardening work. Understanding the etymology of the terms "agriculture" and "horticulture" reveals something about the domestic location of gardening, and helps us to locate within a larger context the program at Ambler and what was in part generated by seeds sown there—the WLAA.

The word "agriculture" is derived from the Latin "ager" (field) and "cultura" (cultivation). "Horticulture" is derived from the Latin word "hortus" (garden). These origins convey the differences in scale, spatial and cultural understandings between agriculture and horticulture that have persisted through the years. Agriculture is the larger discipline and includes many things, including producing crops and raising livestock. Horticulture is a field within that discipline, and includes "growing fruits, vegetables, flowers, or ornamental plants."[27] The physical measurement associated with agriculture is "acre," implying the cultivation of many plants. In the Progressive Era, the increasing focus on scientific agriculture assumed the use of certain technologies to farm larger acreage, technologies that typically fell under male dominion (including tractors, which were increasingly coming into use).[28] Horticulture's role in the lives of people, communities, and societies is poorly understood, as is its relationship to agriculture. P.D. Relf defines horticulture in a comprehensive way, including as the art and science of plants resulting in the development of minds and emotions of individuals (a Progressive era take), the enrichment and health of communities (a goal of the modern Good Food movement), and the placement of the notion of "garden" across civilization. Liberty Hyde Bailey is considered to be the "Father" of the modern horticultural and Extension movements, authoring more than 65 books on various topics relating to agriculture and education. Bailey, an agrarian, was actively involved in the Country Life Movement, and suffused Jeffersonian ideals of the importance of agriculture, higher education, and the notion of civic engagement linking all.[29] Again, the relationship between horticulture and agriculture is unclear to many, but I would consider all gardeners to be horticulturists, but not all horticulturists to be gardeners.

Gardens strongly link with the domestic sphere, but women work—and have worked—in all scales of growing enterprises. American women have always labored on farms and participated in agricultural endeavors. However, through much of our nation's history their contributions have been largely overlooked, their efforts unseen, their voices unheard, their work classified as part of their domestic responsibilities, ignored because of their gender and/or race.[30] Agriculture was considered by many to be primarily male work. There was significant resistance to women's entry into the field in a formal, articulated way outside understandings of the domestic sphere, or outside of the vital (yet marginalized) agricultural work performed by women of all colors in all regions of the country, including the South.

The physical referent of horticulture, a subfield of agriculture, is a "yard," a unit of measure easily contained within the span of a woman's arms. Hortus, the garden, provides a sense of agriculture on a domestic—and hence, female—scale. "Science and art" are an integral part of both definitions. Perhaps it was the nature (initially, artistic), the location (gardening was located within the domestic sphere) and the scale of horticulture that provided an entry point for urban women into the field. In a spatial sense, gardens often have been understood as a middle landscape between conceptions of rural or wilderness and urban experience, akin to parks. Culturally, "hortus" has generally fallen within the female, or domestic sphere in American experience, although at various times the field of horticulture has been contested terrain.

Landscape architecture is a related but different field of agricultural study and practice (and some would argue that in a contemporary understanding, it is not closely aligned with agriculture at all), incorporating aspects of horticulture and several other disciplines, including art.[31] Landscape architecture also provided a way for women to gain access to new kinds of employment opportunities and was inextricably linked with the Ambler experience.[32]

Haines' school intended to train women in horticulture and landscape, building on past work to extend women's work in the area of practice. The experience of Ambler's early years is the perfect place to pause and look both forward and backward, for Ambler's founding represented both a continuation of earlier trends in American women's experiences with horticulture, and a jumping-off point for a future increasingly marked by the woman's rights movement and women's professional entry into a field that itself was growing more structured, disciplinary, and scientific. Thus, larger social themes and impulses became intertwined in the practice of horticulture.

The Program

In her essay describing gardening schools for women, Haines began by defining terms. In 1907, school gardening and nature education were important topics among a certain group of Progressives, including educators, some government officials, and social reformers of all kinds.[33] School gardening and nature education were thought to ameliorate the ills of urban life. These reformers also viewed nature study and school gardening as providing a way to "Americanize" immigrant students. It was the golden age of school gardening and Haines was determined to differentiate "garden schools" (higher education for women) from "school gardens" (for children), describing them as being in "no way connected."[34] In this, of course, she was wrong. The two movements were from the same rootstock: Progressive reform agendas.

Like the founders of the WLAA (some of whom were associated with Ambler), Ambler's founders hoped to provide an education that would lead to employment opportunities beyond nursing, teaching and stenography, occupations that were viewed by some as "devitalizing." Haines herself termed the lives of stenographers and clerks as "hard and unhealthy." The kind of work that Haines envisioned for women held rewards; one of the school directors that Haines visited in England remarked on careers in horticulture: "if ... she is patient and hard-working, she will find it not only remunerative, but intensely interesting. It will give her more freedom and independence of thought and action than the profession of hospital nurse or private secretary."[35]

Haines was influenced by the work she saw at the Horticultural College in Kent. She also used ideas gained from the Lady Warwick College in Warwickshire, England. Haines corresponded with its warden, Edith Bradley, as early as 1905, and visited the school while traveling in England during 1906.[36] From its prospectus, one gets a sense that in some ways, Lady Warwick College was a finishing school. Class mattered: the addition of a tennis court was much anticipated.[37] Later, Ambler would struggle to maintain a balance between being a serious enterprise and catering to the elite.

Haines defined a horticultural school as "an industrial school for the teaching of the art of horticultural and some allied subjects which can usually be profitably undertaken along with horticulture."[38] While Ambler offered short courses, the diploma was awarded only for the completion of a two-year course of study (forty weeks per year and a total of forty-two semester units). Admission requirements were rigorous, and included the completion of a high school degree or passing an examination that, in addition to English and mathematics, might include French, German, Latin, physics, physiology and/or history.[39]

In the European model, many horticultural schools for women were intended to provide professional post-secondary education. While they were hands-on and practical in focus, most were not strictly vocational schools. Some catered to middle- and upper-class women. Again, class differences informed the European experience. One of Haines' European correspondents wrote about the ability of women horticulturalists to "be brought in contact with cultured people" through their work.[40] Class divisions had always existed in women's gardening work—both in Europe and the United States—and as mentioned previously, class played a role at Ambler, as well. (Class considerations also arose during the Woman's Land Army experience in World War I, both in the United Kingdom and the United States.)

At its inception, Ambler's core curriculum focused strongly on horticulture. The overlap between horticultural and landscape art (later to become "landscape architecture") is significant, and, as time progressed, Ambler's curriculum expanded to include more elements of landscape architecture. This was probably due to the influence of Elizabeth Leighton Lee, who served as the school's director from 1915 to 1924. Lee was a noted landscape architect and consultant to the Garden Club of America.

The curriculum reflected the urban influence of Ambler's leaders; courses that were more rural in focus (such as "rural economy" and "care of animals") were less central to the overall curriculum, and were generally elective. Prospectus and curricular descriptions from the period 1919–1930 reflect fewer instructional hours devoted to purely "rural" topics and indicate the elective nature of these courses. The curriculum also was influenced by the professional experiences of its female leaders. Ambler offered a two-year degree program as well as "short courses" of a term's length (or less). The Spring Short Course of 1913 offerings included plant life, soils and fertilizers, garden planning, floriculture, woody ornamentals, vegetable growing, forcing, fruit growing, insects, and fungi and marketing.[41] Some topics that might be considered more "traditional" farming instruction (i.e., poultry, dairying, larger-scale field work) were not included in this particular short course.

In this newly created middle ground, small-scale and specialized agricultural enterprises were encouraged that could presumably enable women to be self-employed or employed in a key role as a specialist in smaller commercial operations. The resulting landscape, again, was neither wholly urban nor rural, but a synthesis of the two. The work at Ambler, while it synthesized Progressive and urban themes of modernity, science and efficiency, hewed to a pro–Agrarian strain of thought, emphasizing love of the outdoors and embracing a controversial view that hard work and physical activity would strengthen the bodies and moral fiber of young women. Ambler students were required to pass a health examination as part of the admission process. Reports from the early days indicate that a local doctor surveyed the health of the students on a regular basis. In later years, it was reported that some Philadelphia doctors recommended enrollment at Ambler to improve the health of their patients; regular review of participants' health was also a feature of life in the WLAA, which is discussed in Chapter 6.

The efforts of Ambler, then, reflected a larger national effort to synthesize the (presumably) best attributes of urban and rural life.[42] Ambler represented a sort of "rural urbanity" in a period of urban ascendancy.[43] Haines wished to "aid ... in broadening woman's sphere in horticultural work," and to instill "leadership and responsibility."[44] These were adopted as goals of the WLAA when war came, although they were secondary to the message of wartime mobilization.

Specialization in Agriculture

Ambler's curriculum followed a larger trend of specialization within the discipline of agriculture that resulted in new, distinct programs and areas of practice in forestry, landscape architecture, and horticulture. Colleges created programs in these areas at a rapid pace, as the profession became more "scientific" and rationalized.

Bernhard Fernow, who served as chief of the Forestry Division of the USDA, founded a forestry school at New York's land grant agricultural college, Cornell, in 1898.[45] Yale founded its forestry school in 1900; Gifford Pinchot, who succeeded Fernow as chief of forestry, and who later became a strong supporter of Ambler, funded it.[46] (Pinchot was also active in the Country Life movement.) Harvard developed two specialized agricultural programs in short order: landscape architecture (1900–01, founded by Frederick Law Olmsted, Jr.) and forestry (1902–03, developed by Nathaniel Shaler and Gifford Pinchot). Ambler's development of a specialized curriculum for women can be understood as part of the larger movement and trend towards specialization.

The rapidly growing wealth of scientific knowledge and the trend of professionalization led to increased specialization in many professions. Specialization locked women out of some fields, but provided opportunities in others, including landscape architecture and horticulture. It can be argued that Ambler strove to define horticulture as an area of professional practice that could be claimed by women, a sort of female dominion in agriculture, similar to that described by Robyn Muncy in relation to social reform.[47] Margaret Rossiter describes a similar process in relation to the development of the home economics field.[48] The field of dominion was small and very specifically defined, but because of the nature of agriculture, women found ways to extend their work in the profession. While she doesn't use this term, Rossiter argues for something that could be defined as a female dominion of sorts in her discussion of a kind of "women's work" that enabled the development of a scientific field around home economics that made significant gains in the period between 1910 and 1920.

There was overlap with home economics in Ambler's curriculum, which provided some courses in this field. Rossiter argues that by 1910, a "new rigidity set in," there were fewer opportunities for women in emerging fields. Women were limited to previously defined areas of practice and study. Because by its very nature, horticulture—which combined art and science—straddled amateur and professional spheres outside of the academy, and women found a place of entry. Mariana Griswold Van Rensselaer was one such woman. The author of the best-selling *Art Out-of-Doors: Hints on Good Taste in Gardening*, she bridged with her work the "informed, but initially not a scholarly or professional, interest in fine buildings and landscapes."⁴⁹ America's entry into World War I provided additional opportunities for women to enter new professional fields.

While some rural women attended Ambler, the majority of its students came from urban and suburban settings. This infusion of urban and suburban women into horticulture and agriculture continued through World War I, when the WLAA placed more than 20,000 largely urban and suburban, college-educated women as laborers in the nation's agricultural sector.⁵⁰ (The trend also continued into the interwar years: noted California architect Myron Hunt commented upon the number of women working as landscape architects in his introduction to Winifred Starr Dobyns's 1931 book, *California Gardens*. Some of those were graduates of the Lowthorpe School.⁵¹) A number of the WLAA's founders and leaders were Ambler students or graduates. Prominent among them was Mary "Edith" Diehl, who was also active in the WLAA. During World War I, more than two hundred new students per year entered Ambler's gates, many of them enrolling in short courses to prepare for wartime service on the home front.

Understandings of class played a role in the Ambler experience. Ambler's students were described as "educated women who have a love for country life and an aptitude for country pursuits."⁵² In fact, many of Ambler's students, especially those who enrolled in the short courses that were offered there, represented the Philadelphia elite.⁵³ While an early fundraising campaign for Ambler included a Cornell Reading-Courses booklet entitled "The Young Woman on the Farm" as a gift to prospective donors, it is important to understand that Ambler's primary audience was not rural women. When it raised funds, Ambler targeted Progressive-leaning individuals who were "lovers of Horticulture and ... believers in the education of women."⁵⁴ Special luncheons were held at the Ritz-Carlton in Philadelphia, not down on the farm.⁵⁵

Progressive Influences

The Progressive Era saw great interest in horticulture, both in Europe and in the United States, which was reflected in exhibitions, conferences, gardening literature, and the formation of civic organizations supporting gardening and horticultural pursuits.⁵⁶ This coincided with aspects of the Country Life Movement, which was emphasizing Extension education. Urban women increasingly stretched the understanding of the domestic sphere construct in relation to agriculture through business ventures in horticulture. In the late nineteenth century a number of women became particularly active—and successful—in seed catalog ventures and trials, among them C.H. Lippincott,

Jessie R. Prior, Emma V. White and Theodosia Burr Shepherd.[57] Others enjoyed notable success in landscape architecture (originally called landscape art), including Kate Sessions, an "amateur" who created the landscape at San Diego's Balboa Park, and Ellen Shipman, who was named the "Dean of Women Landscape Architects" by *House and Garden* magazine in 1933.[58] Much more of women's para-professional work in horticulture took place within the context of reform movements, such as garden-based education for city children, tenement and vacant lot gardening efforts, and city beautification.[59] Lacking ready access to professional agricultural training (again, some colleges limited their enrollment to men), women either found male mentors, or cobbled together their own education.[60]

During this period, there arose professional associations and civic organizations that contributed to an ethos of professionalization and formalization of training and standards in the field. Federal legislation provided support for scientific agriculture, and the body of knowledge surrounding agricultural science grew exponentially, supporting the trend to professional specialization.

An historical analysis of the work at Ambler helps us understand the issues of early twentieth century progressivism; the tensions and ascendance of consumer-based culture and urban life; the trend toward specialization in science that created more discrete and distinct fields of professional practice; and as a subtext, a concern with the advancement of woman's rights. On some level, the work at Ambler explores how women pushed the domestic location of gardening into a more visible location, where they could practice as professionals and do work that many considered the domain of men.

Gardening as Part of the Domestic Sphere

Gardening and some aspects of ornamental horticulture historically have fallen within the domestic sphere in America. Colonial kitchen gardens were tended by women, and in addition to providing for a family's needs, sometimes provided a point of entry into the market economy for women, who might sell excess product for profit. Throughout the nineteenth century, the "cult of domesticity" was promoted to middle-class women; within that construct, gardening values were relegated to the domestic sphere. In her seminal book, *The Bonds of Womanhood: "Woman's Sphere" in New England, 1780–1835*, historian Nancy Cott explores the notion of "separate spheres" and "The Cult of True Womanhood" through her analysis of 18th and 19th century New England women. Cott argues that "separate spheres" combined with the dynamic of the "bonds of womanhood" to provide opportunities for women to bond together, even as they were kept apart from men. Cott's work also explores how the work of women in the area of social reform enabled them to develop new opportunities for leadership.[61] (And this was certainly true of the WLAA.) Gardening for household consumption might be considered "industrious housekeeping."[62]

To women of means, gardening was sometimes depicted as a leisure activity, with a focus on ornamental horticulture and home beautification. Some of the early literature about gardening was written by wealthy and prominent women, and purchased by middle-class urban women. The publication of *An American Woman's Home* in 1869, written by Catharine E. Beecher and her more famous sister, Harriet Beecher Stowe, met with immediate success, even in a market saturated with books about domestic life (which included gardening).[63] The Beecher sisters sought to "professionalize" or elevate work on the domestic sphere, and to remind women of its great moral value, its ability to reform. (And these kinds of values carried through to the work of the WLAA in World War I.) The Beecher sisters contended, "If the parents and children were united in the daily labors of the house, garden, and fruit culture, such thrift, health, and happiness would be secured as is but rarely found among the rich."[64]

Advancing Women

The work at Ambler was important in advancing the cause of women: the campus is identified in a National Park Service survey as a site of significance to the woman's rights movement.[65] Is it a coincidence that Martha Van Rensselaer, the first female professor at Cornell University, and a dominant force behind the development of the home economics field, was involved with Ambler?[66] Or that Mira Lloyd Dock, a renowned female scientist and the first woman to sit on a state forestry commission, was also a strong supporter of Ambler?[67] Certainly not. While Ambler's faculty included some men, women—including its own graduates—taught many of its courses. Until 1953, a woman consistently held the position of school director. In 1919, Ambler's board of directors consisted of twenty-five prominent citizens: all were women.[68] Fifteen of them were unmarried. This was a woman's school, and women claimed leadership roles.

Ambler was a generative place, not only in the sense of propagating plant material, but also in fostering relationships and the kind of Progressive networks and associations that had far-reaching effects; this influenced wartime programs such as the WLAA, the USSGA and the Liberty/Victory garden efforts of the NWGC. Three organizations of vital importance to women in horticulture—and the advancement of women in general—claimed roots at

Ambler: the Garden Club of America (1913); the Woman's Farm and Garden Association (1914); and the Woman's Land Army of America (1917).[69] Ambler was seemingly where all roads met, at least for Progressive women interested in agriculture and horticulture.

Federal Legislation, Scientific Agriculture and Professionalization

There were other influences on school gardens, city gardens, garden cities and woman's horticultural schools. The Morrill Land Grant College Act of 1862 (which donated federal lands to each state to create colleges of agriculture and mechanic arts, serving as the origin of America's public higher education system and today's land-grant university institutions) provided educational opportunities for men and women, although women did not at first enroll in great numbers. Legislation such as the Hatch Act of 1887, which created the federal system of state-run agricultural research stations, provided support for scientific agriculture, and the body of knowledge surrounding agricultural science grew exponentially. The Second Morrill Act (1890) also endowed the land-grant university system by creating colleges for African Americans in the former Confederate states, further democratizing higher education and contributing to the wealth of scientific knowledge.

Congress' passage of the Adams Act in 1906 doubled funding to agricultural research stations, while requiring a new funding commitment from state sources. The infusion of federal and state capital facilitated an ever-growing trend of agricultural research, education, and innovation, and generated increasing interest in American agriculture. Enormous amounts of literature regarding agriculture (including horticulture and gardening) in the form of bulletins, journal articles, and information booklets became readily and widely available to many Americans, including women and educators working with children. These funds also fueled the interest in the nature-study movement; its primary advocate was Liberty Hyde Bailey from Cornell.

The Smith-Lever Act of 1914 provided for the creation of the United States Cooperative Extension Service (CES), which sought to increase the efficiency of production agriculture and at the same time, impart urban values relating to the domestic sphere into rural homes. The passage of Smith-Lever in 1914 was certainly facilitated by the findings of the Country Life Commission. Smith-Lever sought to improve, reform and change rural life. Smith-Lever also sought to create a single extension service from the two systems of agricultural extension and education that had developed and were operating simultaneously in the U.S. One strand of extension work had focused on short-courses and farmers institutes run by the land grant universities. A second strand of extension work had been developed by the USDA, and focused in the South on field demonstrations that controlled pests (such as the boll weevil) and in the North on farm management. As part of the Smith Lever Act of 1914, the two systems of extension were combined together into Cooperative Extension, which created a federal, state and county funding formula for Cooperative Extension, which persists to this day.[70] The CES was a direct result of efforts of Country Life advocates; the model has been enduringly successful because of its focus on building the economic strength of farmers through scientific methods promoting industrial agriculture.[71]

Among its corps of county agents was a new generation of college-educated female home economists who worked in rural settings, increasing the contact and interchange between urban and rural, especially on social and domestic issues. Although the language of Smith-Lever suggested the desirability of placing female agents in counties, placement of women Extension agents lagged behind the placement of men, due to the emerging nature of the field, and lack of resources and the relative lower priority placed on the rural home as opposed to production agriculture. World War I gave a boost to the numbers of female extension agents, who made important contributions in teaching food preservation (among other things) to rural women and girls, sometimes working simultaneously on behalf of the Food Administration.[72] An urban construct seeking to alter rural life, CES also intersected with movements such as those represented by Ambler and the WLAA by providing technical training in agriculture for women. Some Ambler graduates went on to work as Extension educators.

Even prior to the passage of the Smith-Lever Act in 1914, Cornell and other land grant institutions developed strong extension programs that targeted women through demonstration work, short courses, and "reading and correspondence courses"; some of these correspondence courses were developed by Martha Van Rensselaer. There were numerous publications available about school and home gardening. There were also women's gardening clubs and associations, which grew in number during the Gilded Age and Progressive Era. Popular magazines included gardening information. Widely available commercial seed catalogs provided another source of information. Enrollment in public agricultural colleges, at least in the United States, was generally open to women, although certain obstacles often made female study impractical. With these options, why did Haines and others feel that new (female) institutions were needed?

There were several reasons. Haines was strongly influenced by her experience at Bryn Mawr, and sought to replicate the model of the independent women's college. Haines believed that women did not enroll in public agricultural colleges because of the distance from their homes, and also because of the lack of course and degree specialization. Ambler provided a specialized course of study that might appeal to women seeking professional training. In her survey, Haines repeatedly writes, "the [agriculture] field is very broad, however, and there is room for many more schools ... the demand for them will continue and will ensure their establishment." Because of her close personal and professional relationships with women practicing in specialized fields of agriculture, including landscape architecture and forestry, Haines was aware that there was room for women in specialized fields, and she sought to carve a niche for women in that location. (Mira Lloyd Dock, Elizabeth Leighton Lee and Gifford Pinchot, all of whom were involved in the growing specialization and professionalization of fields such as forestry and landscape architecture, were affiliated with Ambler.)

The professionalization of science in America and the increased number of opportunities in higher education strongly influenced women's experience in horticulture. Women played an important role in bringing about the professionalization of horticulture and landscape architecture. But progress towards professionalization was not a straight march forward. Gardening and landscape was first embraced by many Americans as a leisurely (albeit well-informed) pursuit, and not as an area of professional specialty. Ultimately, this created tension between generalists and their increasingly specialized successors as an area of "professional" practice emerged. It also created tension between well-informed amateurs and the emerging "experts."

Even today, the lines of personal expertise and professional practice blur in landscape architecture and horticulture in an uneasy way. Professional designations matter little; actual skill matters more. "Amateurs" from the Rose Society may know more about the cultivation and care of roses than a scientist from a land grant university. Cultivating landscape is both "science and art." The blurring of personal expertise and professional practice provided an opening for women seeking professional recognition, and they took it.

Propagation: Woman's Rights, the WNFGA and the Woman's Land Army

Ambler was a generative place, peopled by dynamic women, and several organizations (and even a movement) arose from the connections made there. In 1913, a conference on "Agriculture as a Means of Livelihood for Women" was held at the campus.[73] Approximately two hundred women and men from New England and the mid–Atlantic states attended the conference. Others came from as far away as Indiana and Michigan; some reportedly walked the eighteen miles from Philadelphia to attend. Most of the speakers were women, who tackled a variety of topics, including agricultural training and employment opportunities for women, the similar work in Great Britain that might provide a model for American efforts, forestry, and the uses of horticulture in reform work.

That afternoon, a national association, the Women's National Farm and Garden Association (WNFGA) was formed. Based on a successful British organization, the WNFGA undertook an advocacy role for Ambler, and proved vital to encouraging urban women to enter the field of agriculture by providing scholarships and continuing educational opportunities. The WNFGA was a hybrid civic and professional organization, with a membership that was involved in many aspects of social reform, including the suffrage movement. Some of the WNFGA's members were familiar with the woman's land army movement in Britain, and they began to converse as early as 1915. It was significant that women were linking the advancement of woman's rights and work on the land. Many of the conversations about land army work prior to and during World War I were gathered, conceptualized, and implemented at WNFGA conferences in 1917 and 1918, breathing life into the WLAA, which trained and placed more than 20,000 women as agricultural laborers during World War I.

While the WNFGA provided vital support and start-up funds for WLAA units during World War I, it was Ambler that provided some of the valuable training and resources needed by the WLAA's leadership. One of Ambler's first graduates, Mary Edith Diehl, became an important part of the WLAA's national organization, serving as head of one its largest camps. The WFNGA and Ambler proved to be the "glue" for the national land army movement by using their vast and impressive network of personal and professional alliances to spread the land army gospel.

Outcomes

Despite its "inauspicious beginning," Ambler grew and prospered for many years. After it opened, a number of capital projects were quickly undertaken, some built partially with student labor.[74] The addition of Elizabeth Leighton Lee, who held the position of director from 1915 to 1924, added to the school's prestige. Lee was one of the first women in the United States to practice landscape architecture. While some claim that Lee was the first practicing female landscape architect in the nation, this is hard to document, because many practiced without professional certification. Lee was, however, a highly regarded landscape architect in the Philadelphia area. World War I provided a boost in Ambler's enrollment. Excitement and a sense of purpose surrounded the school. Women flocked to the campus to prepare for home front service.

In part as a result of Ambler's work and the WLAA, women's post-war interest in horticulture did not decline. In the ensuing decade, a number of conferences on women and agriculture were held. Jane Haines and Elizabeth Leighton Lee attended one such conference, "Women in Agriculture and Country Life," held at Amherst in October of 1920.[75] In a letter thanking Amherst's president Kenyon Butterfield (he had previously served on the Country Life Commission) for his invitation to attend, Haines wrote, "We feel that we received much of value as well as of pleasure from our attendance. These we hope can be transmitted into something profitable for our own modest School of Horticulture."[76]

The institution's progress may be gauged through a series of school booklets and prospectuses published through the years. In 1929, a new dormitory was built to accommodate fifty students.[77] Grainy black and white photos show students engaged in apple harvesting. The text of the prospectus describes a variety of gardens, including colonial, formal (developed in 1925), native plant, and experimental. Ambler acquired fifty acres of farmland to use for the cultivation of general crops and pastureland, but farm subjects continued to be "elective."[78] The 1929–30 prospectus included a large list of alumnae and students; they hailed from Pennsylvania, Maryland, Washington, D.C., New York, New Jersey, Connecticut, Massachusetts, Michigan, Virginia, Tennessee, Nebraska, Indiana, Illinois, Colorado, Oregon, and even New Zealand and England.

Probably no person other than Jane Haines had a greater impact on Ambler than Louise Bush-Brown, who served as Ambler's director from 1924 to 1952. A graduate of Ambler, she also held a teaching degree from Horace Mann Teaching College, and had completed coursework in the School of Horticulture at George Peabody College.[79] Bush-Brown's husband, an early graduate of Harvard's landscape architecture program, also served on Ambler's faculty.

Bush-Brown encouraged international enrollment; Ambler's student body eventually included women from Japan, China, West Germany and Australia. She also established partnerships with other educational institutions, including Smith College, to increase the degree-earning capacity of Ambler's students. Bush-Brown was instrumental in adding the "Farmer's Journal" to Ambler's offering; this magazine was published during the 1930s and helped to fund the school's operations. Ambler was a place central to women and horticulture; an anonymous history of the school refers to Ambler's "Camelot" atmosphere.[80]

Ambler's curriculum expanded, and reflected further specialization within the field and refinement within topics. For example, by 1929, two courses totaling 240 hours of coursework ("trees and shrubs" and "woody ornamentals") replaced the single 120-hour "woody ornamentals" course offered in 1919. Course descriptions grew increasingly precise and technical in nature, reflecting the increasing specialization of the profession. The school retained its applied research focus, utilizing a combination of "classroom lectures supplemented by practice and project work."

Despite its many successes, however, the institution was crippled by its inability to offer professional and advanced degrees. Ambler offered a superb training program, but in a world where degrees and professional certification were growing increasingly important, the school became less relevant, its students less able to compete. After the retirement of Bush-Brown in 1952, obstacles to the school's continued success mounted, including meeting state accreditation standards, plummeting enrollment and financial difficulties. The school's first male director, Jonathan French, replaced Bush-Brown in 1953. In 1958, Temple University acquired the school, dedicating it as the Temple University Ambler campus. Today, Ambler, as it is still called, boasts one of the most respected landscape architecture programs in the nation.

Endings

Like the school garden, city garden and garden city movements, Ambler was a product of its historical environment. It was strongly influenced by a number of impulses, including varying reform agendas, European models, woman's rights, and avid interest in educational opportunities for women and trends of professionalization and agricultural specialization. Federal legislation also influenced the development of Ambler, as did Progressive Era philosophies. The various gardening movements feeding into national gardening programs during World War I were shaped by these impulses, and in turn, added something to each of them.

The imprint of the Progressive Era is easily seen in Ambler, with its emphasis on scientific management, technical training, and highly ordered existence. For example, Ambler's literature is replete with schedules, and highly specific detail about coursework, the arrangement of living quarters, conduct, etc. While Ambler represented a typical prescriptive Progressive Era program in many ways, it was a bit different. Unlike the other movements of school gardens and community gardens found more than a century ago, which have persisted and are even experiencing a major resurgence today, the experiment of woman's horticultural schools such as Ambler has not survived. But by its very existence, Ambler provided a new and different meaning for woman's work in agriculture and horticulture.

As the WLAA did during World War I, Ambler strongly challenged stereotypes about the proper role of women in the labor force and their role in the agricultural sector in particular. The success of the Ambler "farmerettes" (as the WLAA participants came to be called in World War I) defied deeply held beliefs about the potential of middle and upper-class urban women to be successful at hard physical labor and the appropriateness of a certain class of urban females working outside of the domestic sphere. A further challenge was the residential nature of Ambler's degree program; women lived and worked with other women, freed from the authority of men.

All of these elements were replicated in the WLAA program during World War I; in fact, the WLAA was born of Ambler, a school that took for its formative mission "agriculture as a means of livelihood for women." The theme of woman's rights is threaded through the Ambler experience. It is not the primary theme perhaps, but it resonates and echoes in many ways. As women sought increased political, educational, social, and economic opportunities, schools such as Ambler provided places of accommodation and advancement. Ambler enabled women to live together in community, and to direct their own affairs. It provided opportunities for women to study science and for other women to serve as faculty and in leadership roles. It enabled women to challenge widely held stereotypes about their physical limitations and to work with their hands. It prepared several generations of women for new occupations, for self-employment, and for more lucrative work.

By nearly every measure, Ambler was an extraordinary success. But as women gained greater equality and more opportunities, they simply outgrew the need for such institutions. The presence of these institutions at a critical time in American history, however, helped set the stage for one of the most controversial—yet successful—home front mobilization efforts in World War I: the Woman's Land Army of America.

Wyck, the historic homestead of Jane Bowne Haines' family, remains an important part of Philadelphia's current food and agriculture scene. It is now an historic house, garden and farm, and a National Historic Landmark. As the city has grown around it, what was formerly rural property is now a vital part of Philadelphia's urban environment, educating a new generation about the opportunities inherent in growing food in urban spaces. With the creation of the "Home Farm" in 2007, the formerly rural aspects of Wyck have ceded to a "newer" American impulse: urban agriculture. Wyck grows food and hosts a weekly onsite farmer's week from June through November. It provides an outdoor interactive classroom and green space to educate children and adults about all aspects of the food system. It provides a "safe place" for young neighborhood residents to experience nature in a sometimes-troubled urban environment. A family archive and historical collection is located in the historic buildings; it includes thousands of family documents and material objects, including documents written in Jane Bowne Haines' own hand. Wyck is one of those rare historical sites that actively fosters relevance by linking history with current practices, in this case, using its historic farm to promote a topic of great interest to contemporary audiences: urban agriculture. Through the trajectory of this single farm and family, one can see the evolution of the American food system, the links between reform and gardening, and also the ways in which women took advantage of opportunities to expand their work into new areas of professional practice when America entered World War I.

SIX

"Sisters of the Soil": The Woman's Land Army of America

"Over there, over there,
Send the word, send the word, over there
That the girls are farming, the girls are farming
The weeds are falling everywhere.
Get a rake, get a hoe, get a pitch fork, get a shovel, get a hoe,
We'll be planting, we're going to be planting
And we won't stop planting till there's taters over there!"

"Planting crops to win the war.
Kaiser Bill's Afraid, Hindenburgh is dismayed,
Watch that Yankee maid learn a trade, use a spade.
Soon a farmer she will be
Planting crops for liberty."

"America, we are the girls for you,
America, you'll find us staunch and true,
With a hoe upon our shoulder,
And a pitch-fork in our hand.
America, we'll do our bit for you,
No matter what the cost,
For if we're sent to Red Bank,
Or out to San Francisco,
America, you're our boss"
—Farmerette song, to the tune of "Over There"
(Emma L. George Papers, Library of Congress)

On February 24, 1918, the *New York Times* published an article written by a young woman named Helen Kennedy Stevens.[1] Stevens, a college graduate, was not a professional journalist. Rather, she had been earning her wartime living as an agricultural laborer in an organization called the Woman's Land Army of America (WLAA). Two photographs of Stevens appeared in the article, side by side. In one, the carefully coiffed Stevens wore the elegant attire of a young socialite.[2] In the other photo she wore overalls and carried a hoe over her shoulders. Her article was obviously written to provide a human face for the "farmerettes" who were challenging stereotypes of "appropriate" work for women. In it, Stevens described her life as a land worker in great detail, and with great humor: turnips "ruined" her disposition, she reported.[3] (The play between socialite and farmerette appeared in other places. An article reporting the debut of Grace Vanderbilt, daughter of General and Mrs. Cornelius Vanderbilt in Newport Rhode Island in July 1918, included as a sub-heading "Farmerettes Sell Fruits." In addition to reporting details of the dinner and dance at Beaulieu, the article reported that fruits, vegetables and flowers had been sold in a public square by "farmerettes," heading by the Misses Ethel and Violet King, Helen Cameron and Ruth Thomas.[4])

But from her words, it was clear that Stevens loved being a "farmerette" and found much meaning in the work. "Every morning, when you started off, it was with a feeling of adventure—no telling what might happen before you got home," she said, although the "home" she described was an agricultural labor camp, far from the domestic life to which young women of her status were typically accustomed.[5] "No one minded taking chance," Stevens reported.[6] And indeed, thousands of young women like Stevens took an enormous chance by stepping out of their traditional roles to join a home front mobilization effort that challenged many Americans' understandings of the proper role of women, and which argued against deeply held beliefs about the kind of work that women were capable of. Women like Stevens leveraged Progressive impulses and the exigencies of wartime to bring about changes that enabled women to gain greater access to technical education and specialized training. Brought together within the crucible of World War I, these impulses gathered form and resulted in the WLLA, a little-known, yet highly significant chapter in the history of the Progressive Era.

Mobilizing a Woman's Land Army

Like the national draft that called millions of American men into military service during World War I, the WLAA officially organized in 1917. The "Army" in the title clearly marked the collective nature of the work and indicated the nation's wartime footing. But the term "Army" also reflected the importance of the work to the nation's security. Unlike the draft, however, and unlike other national wartime gardening efforts, such as the USSGA, the WLAA was purely a non-governmental organization, although it interacted with various government entities and institutions.

As noted by historian Christopher Capozzola, the relationship between "state and civil society was particularly blurry" during World War I.[7] In the absence of a large federal government with many functions, voluntarism flourished, creating public-private partnerships to aid the mobilization effort.[8] Women's organizations played an enormous role in America's successful home front mobilization during World War I. Women's membership in clubs with local, state, and national affiliations aided their entry into wartime work and brought them into partnership with the government.[9] The WLAA provides only one example of this phenomenon, but it is an important one. The WLAA had some relationship with the government and its mobilization efforts, but there was also some distance between the two.

Many historians have discussed in their work the non-statist aspect of many World War I home front mobilization efforts, i.e., the quasi public-private partnerships that these efforts represented. Other historians have discussed the voluntary nature of such work. Christopher Capozzola introduces a third element to this discussion: the reminder that even voluntary work was labor, albeit unpaid.[10] The WLAA offered challenges to existing societal structures not only because of the nature of the work and its location outside the traditional domestic sphere, but because its members were "paid" labor.

The idea of women in land service was based on the female land armies already in existence in the United Kingdom and Canada (at war since 1914). Earlier conversations about the need and desirability for female agricultural labor in the United States had occurred among various women's groups and civic organizations, and woman's agricultural training and labor was a subject of continual investigation and prospecting at places such as the Pennsylvania School of Horticulture for Women at Ambler (Ambler).

Women's civic organizations in general had anticipated the eventual need for mobilization on the American home front prior to the United States entry in the war, some through participation in European relief efforts.[11] The need for a national woman's land army in the United States had been articulated among many groups, including the leadership of a fairly new organization, the Women's National Farm and Garden Association (WNFGA), which was formed as a result of a meeting held at Ambler.[12] These conversations anticipated that America would be entering the war, and that women might have an important role to play on the home front, through gardening and food production and conservation, among other things.

There was a disconnection between perception and practice in America vis-à-vis women and gardening. Gardening was an activity pursued by women of all classes, some out of interest, and many out of necessity. It was an activity tended to by women in both rural and urban settings. Class divisions arose around the kinds of gardening work considered appropriate for women. Programs such as the WLAA helped to bridge class divisions, as well as divisions that existed between urban and rural experience.

It is important to understand that certain kinds of gardening and horticultural activities were depicted as "appropriate" activities for women, falling clearly within the domestic sphere. Here was the point of entry and challenge for women to contest the boundaries of separate spheres; it also provides part of the rationale for the WLAA, whose work generally was not part of the domestic sphere. Lines between personal expertise and professional practice had been blurring as women moved into fields such as landscape art (later to become landscape architecture).[13] The work of the WLAA sought to remove the boundaries altogether.

In Service to the Nation and the Land

In February, 1917, a representative of the National League for Women's Service Agriculture Committee asked the secretary of the WNFGA, Hilda Loines, if that organization might be willing to help organize a woman's land corps based on the British and Canadian models, a program to be called a "Land Service League."[14] One of the primary goals of such a League would be to "foster mutual understanding between city and country women," and to discourage rural depopulation by keeping rural populations on the land, "happily occupied."[15] Thus, wartime gardening and agricultural mobilization efforts also sought to allay concerns about the relationship between urban and rural in American life and to soothe the tensions that existed between these two spheres, as well as to address concerns about the perceived loss of a traditional producer ethic in an increasingly urbanized and consumer-oriented society.

In March 1917, Loines brought that request to the WFNGA's board. They approved, and agreed to provide a nominal amount of funding to develop a training "school" in New York City.[16] With a declaration of war on Germany imminent, there was a sense of urgency in the request and in the work. In the weeks following the declaration of war on Germany by the United States, Loines, on behalf of the leadership of the WNFGA, wrote to President Wilson and Agriculture Secretary David Houston, providing a "plan for universal service" of the home front population not mobilized for military duty.[17] This plan included a number of domestic efforts, including gardening and food preservation. The plan also demonstrated the interconnectedness of Progressive leaders by endorsing the USSGA proposal being floated by P.P. Claxton from the Bureau of Education.[18] Thus, Woodrow Wilson and his staff would have had an opportunity to see a range of potential home front responses that involved gardening, food and agriculture.

Again, the plan the WNFGA shared contained items relating to agricultural education for children and suggested food preservation and conservation measures that could be implemented to help the nation accomplish wartime goals. The WNFGA letters also suggested that as wartime "necessity," grain be diverted from distilleries to human consumption.[19] Clearly, old reformers die hard. But in addition to conserving food, the WNFGA proposed something more novel: the idea of recruiting women to produce food within a larger, more industrialized context. The idea of a woman's land army movement was a centerpiece of that production plan.

The concept of a woman's land army in America, which had surfaced as early as 1915 (during a period of labor shortages in agriculture) received a boost early in 1917, when famed British propagandist and woman's rights advocate Helen Fraser came to deliver a series of nine lectures about woman's war work in Great Britain at Vassar College. These lectures electrified American coeds in the closely affiliated women's colleges of the Northeast; standing-room only crowds of young women packed lecture halls and spilled out to adjoining areas to hear Fraser speak. The Vassar College newspaper reported, "Miss Fraser, here's to you! We don't need to say that we liked Miss Fraser and everything she had to tell us. The way we followed her around, and packed every room in which she spoke."[20] Shortly after her appearance at Vassar, Fraser's lectures were published in a book entitled *Women and War Work*, which was widely distributed.

At the next national conference of WNFGA, its fourth, held in Chicago in October 1917, reports of woman's land army service in England and Canada were provided and a WNFGA Land Service Committee was formed. As a result, the WNFGA's general secretary, Hilda Loines, resigned her position to help drive the organization of the Land Army effort. Loines' work was critical to the WLAA's formation. As WFNGA secretary, she had corresponded with a similar British woman's organization (the Woman's Farm and Garden Union, founded 1899), and was aware of what was occurring overseas. Like Ambler's founder, Jane Haines, Loines was a graduate of Bryn Mawr. She had also attended a horticultural school. Loines was the daughter of a well-known suffrage leader in New York.[21]

Loines helped organize a meeting of the WNFGA Land Service Committee in December 1917. The committee met at the New York YMCA that cold December, to further develop the agricultural workforce proposal.[22] The successes of the woman's land army work that had occurred during the previous summer (1917) through a trial camp at Bedford, New York—and the creation of twelve smaller camps—was shared at the meeting. A number of organizations were represented, including the New York State Council of Defense, the Garden Club of America, the WNFGA, the YMCA and the Woman's Suffrage

Party of New York.²³ Although the aims of each organization differed, all saw the value in placing women in agricultural work.

The Nature and Location of Woman's Work

The creation of the WLAA in World War I ultimately recruited nearly 20,000 largely middle-class urban and suburban women to enter America's agricultural sector to work as wage laborers between 1917 and 1919.²⁴ Efforts similar to the WLAA, and that would ultimately tie into WLAA work, actually began as early as 1915, when regional agricultural labor shortages occurred. Women had always worked the land, of course. However, the active recruitment of urban women into a (largely) female-managed workforce to labor in tasks such as sowing and harvesting, was a new and—to some—a disconcerting idea. That these women were also young, many college-educated and living in community with other like-minded women outside the authority of men, challenged contemporary stereotypes relating to women's role and work all the more.²⁵

And the concept of "work" was vital to some organizers of the WLAA, who hoped that the standardized labor practices and uniform wages provided in other sectors of employment (including manufacturing industries), could be successful in agriculture. WLAA workers would be paid for their labor; in this they differed from many of the other wartime mobilization efforts organized by and utilizing women. The WLAA sought identification with government (at all levels), as a contributor to the nation's labor needs during wartime.

A memorandum found in the Cora Call Whitley papers at the Iowa Women's Archives details "Relations of the Woman's Land Army with Federal and State Departments."²⁶ This vital document lists the "assurances" of cooperation and collaboration that the WLAA had received from federal and state departments, assurances that might ease resistance to the organization's work. The first item listed? A discussion of the relationship between the WLAA and the Federal Department of Labor.²⁷ The relationship with this agency is described as being one of "cordial cooperation." John Densmore, a Federal Department of Labor employee who was in charge of "the problem" of farm labor, had agreed to coordinate WLAA work with his department. From the USDA, the WLAA had "the assurance of advice and information from.... Farm Help Specialists."²⁸ However, in exchange for cooperation from the USDA and a "cordial reception," the WLAA pledged to "ask, in every case, the advice of the County Farm Bureau Agent before placing units."²⁹ This was telling, for at that time, County Farm Bureau Agents were government employees representing the newly developed United States Cooperative Extension Service.

The Cooperative Extension Service was legislated, but had itself begun as a quasi public-private relationship between land grant institutions, counties, the federal government and the privately organized Farm Bureau. Another telling thing: County Farm Agents were exclusively male.

The WLAA also sought to organize in each state by working through mobilization work managed by women, primarily the Woman's Committee of the Council of National Defense.[30] President Woodrow Wilson formed the Woman's Committee of the Council of National Defense in April 1917, shortly after the declaration of war on Germany. The purpose of the Woman's Committee was to coordinate women's *voluntary* work for the wartime effort on a national basis. In typical Progressive fashion, the Committee tapped into existing networks of professional associations and affiliations locally, at the state level, nationally and into the large national club movement exemplified by organizations such as the General Federal of Women's Clubs.[31] They also sought—and apparently received—"assurances of cooperation" from individual state chairs of national defense and food production and home economics.[32] A period document provides a snapshot of the organization's status, describing six classes of readiness.

Class 1, described as "states which are organized or organizing," included California (with two efforts, northern and southern); Connecticut; Colorado; District of Columbia; Illinois; Kansas; Maryland; Massachusetts; Michigan; Minnesota; Missouri; New Jersey; New York; Oklahoma; Pennsylvania; Rhode Island; Tennessee; Vermont; and Virginia. "Class 2" was defined as those states which were considering organizing. "Class 3" consisted of states where Woman's Land Army organization had been deferred; "Class 4" included those states in which the work was occurring, but independently of the Woman's Land Army. "Class 5" states were defined as those where decided interest "has been awakened." Finally, "Class 6" represented those states to which letters were sent but to which there have been no replies. (Of the twelve states listed as Class 6, six were Southern, a region where the WLAA had less success.) For each state, a "chairman" (really, a chairwoman, as all contacts were female) and contact information was provided. The organizational affiliation of the state chairmen—when provided—demonstrates the breadth of interest in the WLAA. The state chairmen represented a chamber of commerce in Los Angeles; Woman's Committee, State (and National) Defense Councils (the majority of chairmen indicated this affiliation); the WNFGA; a board of education; and groups already under the WLAA umbrella.

There is evidence that the WLAA offered not just wartime mobilization, but also the prospect of a more long-term response to labor needs, at least in some states, such as California. The University of California played a crucial role in anticipating wartime agricultural labor shortages and at least peripherally, in helping the WLAA gain traction, just as that institution proved instrumental to foundational work informing the USSGA.

In most historical documents from this time, reference to the University of California indicates the flagship campus at Berkeley. Berkeley was—and is—the state's agricultural college, although the University of California campuses at Davis and Riverside are now also considered "agricultural" campuses. But that lay far in the future, as in 1906, the University of California opened a university farm in Davisville, on the site of the present UC Davis campus, with the intention of providing a practical, hands-on experience on a working farm for the agricultural students at the Berkeley campus. The University Farm served for several decades as a northern division of UC Berkeley. Short courses were offered for both men and women as early as 1908, and in 1909, the first students from Berkeley arrived. The first regularly enrolled female students arrived from UC Berkeley in 1914. During World War I, the College of Agriculture established and conducted short courses for women (four weeks duration). At the request of the WLAA, the College of Agriculture conducted a special class for women machine milkers at the University Farm. The University of California's 224-page annual report from July 1, 1918, to July 15, 1919, provides an extensive listing of wartime efforts and classes relating to agriculture conducted by the University of California.

Agricultural labor was an ongoing concern in California, which featured—and still does in many areas—crop patterns that require intensive labor. In 1918, the University of California's Agricultural Experiment Station at Berkeley issued "A Study of Farm Labor in California," also known as "Circular 193."[33] The storied Agricultural Experiment Station at the University of California Berkeley was also the publisher of the earlier Circular 46 on school gardens, which helped that movement gain national traction. The Agricultural Experiment Station was also where Babcock and Stebbins, whose work was instrumental to the formation of the USSGA, had engaged in research and Extension work. It was a nationally known and respected unit, and the work that came out of it received great attention.

The 1918 study—Circular 193—described the labor shortage of 1917, the difficulties presented by the drawdown of the "best class of farm labor" due to the military draft and mobilization and "suggests the urgency of immediate steps to improve existing conditions."[34] The study also indicated that plans were being made to "mobilize women for such work as they can do."[35]

Another University of California labor study was conducted during this period. In the summer of 1917, a group of women students from the University's Department of Economics assisted in surveying firms to assess needs for female labor in different economic sectors, including agriculture, and to solicit ideas on how women (presumably women's organizations) could facilitate recruitment should a labor shortage occur.[36] The project's mentor was Mrs. Sydney Joseph; she later became chair of the Northern California Division of the WLAA. Joseph was not a neophyte; according to a letter to the editor of the *Republic* magazine that appears in the Emma L. George archives, she had received "university training in economics."

Another woman key in facilitating this project, Katherine Phillips Edson, was also instrumental in the WLAA's activity in California, and had ties to the University of California.[37] Edson had contact with Dr. Hunt, who served as dean of the College of Agriculture at the University of California (again, at the flagship campus at Berkeley). As such, Dr. Hunt managed all the Farm Advisors (the Cooperative Extension staff, also sometimes referred to as Farm Bureau Agents), located in many California counties. In this role, Hunt would have been well informed on the status of agricultural labor needs in each county. Edson also consulted with one of the University of California professors, Dr. Adams, who co-authored "A Study of Farm Labor in California" (Circular No. 193). Adams also served as the USDA's "Federal Farm Agent" for California. In February, 1918, Hunt and Adams "decided it be might be necessary to use women as agricultural workers during the 1918 season." It is important to note that Edson was also a significant player in a variety of social justice and reform movements in California, had connections at the highest levels of governmental and non-governmental institutions, and proved instrumental to the WLAA operation in that state. Edson was also a board member of the California Federation of Women's Clubs from 1910 to 1916. She also was appointed as a special agent to the California Bureau of Labor Statistics. She was an appointee on the California Industrial Welfare Commission, a position that enabled her to encourage changes in labor practices.

The California survey indicated that there might be an agricultural labor shortage in 1918 if production rates were normal.[38] The California study was part of a national undertaking conducted by the National League for Women's Service; Edson was also the California State Chairman for this organization.[39]

The Organization of Work

The organization of the WLAA's work reflected Progressive impulses of efficiency, management, and organization. The WLAA sought to allay concerns about women working as agricultural laborers by developing a highly structured program. As its associative nature, the college affiliation and connections to state and national surveys suggest, the WLAA represented a Progressive form of labor mobilization.[40] In this, the WLAA was strongly influenced by the principles of scientific management and efficiency, which characterized one stream of labor organization during the Progressive Era. President Theodore Roosevelt had stated in 1909 that one of the "three great requirements of national life" was to be "efficient," and theories of managing production with the goal of increasing national efficiency abounded.[41] Frederick Winslow Taylor published his famous work, *The Principles of Scientific Management*, in 1911.[42] The idea of efficiency became "entwined into the culture of nation."[43] This culture of scientific management and efficiency was seen in the organization of the WLAA program and other wartime mobilization efforts. However, because of their grassroots nature, other wartime gardening efforts (such as the Liberty/Victory Garden program), were much like overflowing gardens, more organic in nature, and less easily contained within the more orderly processes emerging in the developing wartime bureaucracy.[44] The WLAA, with a focus on providing paid wage laborers in production agricultural settings—and not as volunteers—was more readily organized. Like soldiers, WLAA members would enlist and volunteer for service (which male soldiers did, at least prior to the draft), but also like soldiers, their work would not be purely voluntary: they would receive wages.

A prospectus published by the national WLAA office in March 1918 expressed the era's attention to scientific management and efficiency. It detailed not only the mission of the organization, but also how it ought to be structured and implemented at the national, state, county and local (unit) level.[45] Nothing was left to chance. In the paragraph describing the Unit System, which is what WLAA working groups or camps were called, a multitude of items are described: the form of supervision; the need for cooperative housekeeping; where women should live; who should employ them; etc. Paragraphs describing county committees, the nature of work, types of women employed, payment methods, period of employment, and financing were clear and explicit. The camp reports produced by the WLAA are equally detailed. The WLAA was a model organization, in many ways, or at least an organization that sought to enable its ideals and practices to be easily replicated.

The notion of female labor brought with it issues that challenged many Americans. The thought of middle class daughters physically laboring in agriculture was contrary to both modern and Victorian expectations of domesticity and feminine ideals, and ran counter to aspirational values of a growing middle class. While middle class women had worked in challenging circumstances in settlement houses and in other venues, and while a certain "shop girl" culture existed that incorporated single working women into the workforce, WLAA participants were not generally immigrant factory workers or working class women; they were women of a certain means embracing hard, physical labor in the male-dominated sphere of agriculture.[46] The leaders of the WLAA movement knew they were bucking a strong public perception that women were incapable of hard physical labor, and notions that such activity would damage their health. To counter these claims, the vast number of reports the WLAA produced—both official, and the unofficial recounting of the work that appeared in the media—constantly referred to the health of WLAA participants.

A single 1918 report produced by the WLAA provides an exhaustive list of references to the health of female participants:

- in many cases, women of delicate health who have taken up work on the land have been thereby restored to health;
- the greater number found the work a source of health and pleasure;
- the girls said they never had a healthier, happier summer;
- the college girls proved especially well able to stand the physical strain of hard labor;
- every member ... left the farm in the best of health with increased weight; and
- they were a healthy, happy community.[47]

Pictures showing the WLAA members at the Wellesley Camp being led in marching drills by a Marine cadet and doing push ups were taken and circulated, to demonstrate that the women ("farmerettes") were being properly prepared for the hard physical labor that lay ahead.[48] It is one of the few instances where a man is shown leading the female farmers.

Was the physical aspect of the WLAA a modern impulse, or something contrary to that? Was it a reaction to—or a repudiation of—a quickly modernizing society that was becoming more consumer-oriented and more removed from its producer roots and values? In some ways, this physical reconnection to the land, this vigorous life and physical engagement, challenged modernity, but in a Progressive way that appeared to create something new by evoking the old: America's connection to the land and its perceived origin as a nation of farmers. Former president Theodore Roosevelt, a leading American figure who played an important role in advocating woman's agricultural work during World War I, was a staunch supporter of American vigor, believing that "a race must be strong and vigorous."[49] But in attempting to demonstrate this American virtue, by tackling work that required great physical vigor, WLAA participants were challenging strongly held beliefs about woman's roles and capabilities. Unlike other kinds of home front mobilization efforts that brought Americans back to the land, such as the Liberty/Victory Garden and USSGA programs (which also had stated goals of Americanizing the immigrant), there was a real and palpable tension surrounding the work of the WLAA. Was it because of the gendered aspect? Or because the effort was not entirely voluntary, but rather, involved women entering the workforce as paid labor in a non-traditional work sector? How the WLAA organized and structured its work and operations not only reflected Progressive impulses, it was also clearly intended to allay concerns and challenges to the organization.

Roosevelt was a supporter of woman's rights, and he did support the work of the WLAA. "Much can be done by law towards putting women on a footing of complete and entire equal rights with man—including the right to vote, the right to hold and use property, and the right to enter any profession she desires on the same terms as the man.... Women should have free access to every field of labor which they care to enter, and when their work is as valuable as that of a man it should be paid as highly."[50] Roosevelt had different attitudes toward American women who were seeking full citizenship than he had for "others," i.e., immigrants. In his work, historian Matthew Frye Jacobson explores modern nationalism by examining a host of issues, including economics, labor and immigration. While seemingly far removed from the WLAA, Jacobson's exploration of American concern with certain populations and their "fitness for self-government" can perhaps be extrapolated and applied to American women who were struggling to gain full citizenship during this period. Major national players, such as Theodore Roosevelt, helped shape this national conversation. During World War I, when there was a labor shortage—and some tensions with foreign agricultural laborers—WLAA participants (an "other" of sorts), stepped in, in some cases, to replace immigrants (a different kind of "other").[51]

For middle class families who might also be struggling with issues relating to class divisions, the WLAA's 1918 "Women on the Land" report shared that in England, even "titled women work in the dairy farms and in the stables."[52] (This was also an observation made by Jane Haines in her paper on "Gardening Schools for Women," penned in 1907.) Issues relating to the ability (and desirability) of middle class women working in agriculture, as well as class issues, were challenges to the WLAA. The WLAA's director of recruiting, Ida Ogilvie, said that the WLAA provided "one of the most interesting of experiments in Democracy. To break through class barriers has hitherto been easy for men; the Land Army camp shows to women the unreality of such distinctions ... and illustrates these principles through the unhampered use of muscle and brain. The Spirit of the Land Army is the true substance of the democratic idea."[53] Just as the leaders of the NWGC envisioned Victory Gardens as strengthening democracy, the founders of the WLAA saw their organization as making a substantial contribution to civic life.

Female Citizenship During Wartime

Women in America did not have the vote in federal elections at the outset of World War I. A number of states granted voting rights to women prior to the passage of the 20th amendment. In general, Western states were more progressive in granting female suffrage.

Society and WLAA advocates responded to objections facing the WLAA's premise and work by constructing temporary frameworks of identity and purpose that enabled the acceptance of women into the kinds of war work—in this case, providing physical labor in a field dominated by men— which challenged the notion of separate spheres.[54] Like the "female dominion" of maternal and children's welfare work described by historian Robyn Muncy, the WLAA operated without the day-to-day involvement of men. But, unlike the women who provided leadership for settlement houses, whose work could be understood within a framework of reform, and thus be considered acceptable and within the domestic sphere, the work of the WLAA was somewhat different. Authority for agricultural labor, including its organization and management, was beyond the domestic sphere, universally regarded as a rough-and-tumble domain of men.[55]

The exigencies of wartime and other historical American social constructs made non-traditional work permissible. In her work, historian Laurel Thatcher Ulrich describes "Deputy Husbandry," which argues for a certain degree and kind of fluidity in gender roles during times of emergency and hardship. In this construct, communities would permit women to step out of traditional roles to support and further their husbands. In his work, John Mack Faragher describes the suspension of traditional, gendered roles and the creation of temporary equity to help families successfully navigate difficulties as they made their way West. Both of these constructs provide an increased understanding of female citizenship on the World War I home front.[56] Under this construct, the desire of an urban, college-educated woman to engage in common agricultural labor could be attributed to patriotism and altruism, an eagerness to serve, and personal sacrifice, simply a natural part of the huge wave of voluntarism that swept the nation and was assiduously promoted by the Committee for Public Information during World War I.[57] The motive of patriotism thus served as a lubricant for urban women seeking work in agriculture through the WLAA. Society's understanding was that wartime needs permitted women to adopt new identities and work in non-traditional roles in the public sphere temporarily, "until the boys come back," as one WLAA recruitment poster stated.

Some female wartime workers, who refused to accept the temporary role assigned to them, contested the provisional nature of this "social contract."

While wartime allegedly granted temporary citizenship to women in certain roles—women were struggling to gain the vote during this period, and couldn't truly be considered to enjoy the benefits of full citizenship—there was resistance to programs such as the WLAA, which sought to place female workers in areas traditionally claimed by men. While the federal government needed agricultural laborers, it only hesitantly accepted, but did not fully embrace, the WLAA.

Resistance to the WLAA was overcome in many cases because the WLAA delivered what it promised: a reliable, inexpensive, and motivated labor force. The media was charmed with "the farmerettes." Reports published in newspapers, journals and magazines were nearly unanimous in their approval. More importantly to the success of the program, farmers raved about their female workers.

Women's motives for WLAA participation drew more deeply from purposes other than the public portrayal of patriotism and self-sacrifice, although the notion of the obligation of citizenship and service was a driving force for many women. As many historians have argued, American citizenship in earlier times was perceived not just as consisting of a set of rights, but also of explicit obligations.[58] For white, native men, those obligations might consist of paying taxes and voting. Less explicit obligations of citizenship might be understood as the responsibility to educate one's children, and for women of a certain economic means, to participate in civic life through participation in voluntary organizations. Clearly, wartime needs and the "obligations" of mobilization provided an opportunity for women to attempt to expand the limited notion of female citizenship in America into a real and full citizenship in the public sphere. It might be argued that America's entry into the war, combined with the social and political circumstances of the American home front, created a new obligation to actively express patriotism through participation in voluntary mobilization efforts. Active expressions of patriotism became a social norm; to act otherwise was to be suspect; there was a strongly coercive feel to many of the home front mobilization efforts.

While patriotism was clearly a factor in WLAA participation, economic opportunity (especially for those WLAA members who were seasonal trade workers), the chance to receive specialized training and a desire for adventure provided additional—and in some cases stronger—motives to patriotism. According to a brochure published by the Woman's Land Army of America in 1918, 11 percent of WLAA members were classified as trade workers. There is also strong evidence that certain WLAA units organized as a further expression of the woman's rights movement, as young women sought to prove that they could perform the same work as men, and deserved to be paid the same wages. Individuals, and in certain cases, specific WLAA units, used the "cover" provided by wartime to advance an agenda of economic advancement, new employment and educational opportunities, and expanded rights for women. The historical record strongly indicates that some women balked at the notion of temporary and provisional rights and economic independence; they continued to work in agriculture after the Armistice was signed.

Whatever their motive for participation, or whether their entry into the field of agriculture was temporary or permanent, for many women, participation in the WLAA proved to be an experience that they valued. While individuals in the federal government were initially mixed in their receptiveness toward these woman agricultural laborers, farmers and program proponents valued the contributions of the WLAA.

Progressive Impulses

As was the case with the other wartime programs, a number of Progressive reform agendas found their way into the WLAA's work, including woman's suffrage and civic beautification through gardening, which were linked through the organization's challenge to the place of gardening in the domestic sphere. Like the Ambler experience, the WLAA pushed the understanding of women, gardening and the location of that within the domestic sphere, enlarging that understanding to include paid wartime work that challenged traditional female roles. The organization built upon the avid interest in America and Europe vis-à-vis horticulture and gardening in general (this was the era of expositions, many of which featured horticultural exhibits). For example, the Panama-California Exposition in 1915–1916 was held in San Diego, California. It featured a variety of horticultural and botanical wonders, including a Botanical Building.[59] There was also an interest in education for women in the field of horticulture specifically.

Like the work at Ambler, the WLAA also reflected and amplified the trend towards professionalization and specialization, including in the field of agriculture. Its work was also influenced by federal legislation that shaped scientific agriculture and agricultural education through land grant institutions and government-funded research stations. This legislation was facilitating the movement of increasingly technical information in a variety of fields, including horticulture, food preservation and home economics from land grant institutions to general audiences. In some ways, this information flow democratized the fields of agriculture and horticulture and made them more accessible to women. The information flow also made possible efforts such as the WLAA.

Progressive Era philosophies, particularly those emphasizing institutional forms and the nature of the rural-urban interface, including civic organizations, and the impulses expressed in the Country Life Movement also influenced the WLAA. Civic and reform movements, including the woman's rights movement, as well as the British wartime experience, also greatly informed the WLAA's work. The work of the WLAA emphasized the strong Progressive interest in the relationship between urban and rural spheres; the program itself represents a unique synthesis of urban and rural interests and concerns. Women pursued work in agriculture through the urban-driven constructs of horticulture, professionalism, civic organizations, and woman's rights.

Like other wartime efforts, the WLAA placed public power and purpose in the hands of individuals who were not elected officials, but who were business and professional men—and in the WLAA's case, largely women—drawn from the American upper class and intellectual elite.[60] Many of the individuals who provided leadership for wartime mobilization programs (again, including the WLAA's leadership) were strongly influenced by Progressive thought and shaped by their work in emerging professions, including the social sciences. They eagerly applied their expertise and managerial skills in support of voluntary efforts. World War I provided the perfect "laboratory" in which to play out the experiment of new models of (supposed) public-private cooperation; the WLAA was one such experiment.[61]

Progressive Era influences shaped the philosophy behind the WLAA, not only in terms of formative ideas, but also in modes of delivery and in content; the WLAA more generally bore the imprint of Progressive themes. These efforts sought to educate, to reform, to engage, and to subsume individual concern and promote the greater good by appealing to a sense of patriotism. Content also was based in the language of the emerging social sciences and scientific agriculture. American character was expressed through the best purpose (patriotism) and the best practice (scientifically-based knowledge). The WLAA echoed these themes as well, but also offered a subtler message to those that would hear it: a proposal to advance woman's rights.

Like other wartime programs, the work of the WLAA also emphasized a growing Progressive interest in the relationship between urban and rural spheres. As it became more ascendant, the urban sphere spoke to scientific knowledge, efficiency, and ordered life; the WLAA's para-military unit structure, handbooks, guides and unit reports attest to this influence. The rural sphere was viewed in different ways by urbanites. An anti-agrarian strain viewed rural life as backwards, disordered, and deficient. A pro-agrarian strain, drawn from the very roots of the Jeffersonian Republic, was expressed in some part through the Country Life Movement, and viewed rural life as beneficial, even vital to the survival of the American Republic, and also as an antidote to the ills that plagued modern (read urban) society. While the WLAA blended both pro- and anti-agrarian strains of thinking about rural life and farm work, it favored the pro–Agrarian strain, emphasizing technical training and scientific agriculture and a view (contested by many) that hard work and physical activity would strengthen the bodies and moral fiber of young urban women. While invigorating these women, the efforts of the WLAA also advanced the larger national interest in agricultural production and the uplift of rural lifestyle that played out in both rural and urban settings.[62] Progressive touches were evident in the WLAA's organization and implementation, including the focus on scientific management that characterized the unit structure and camp management.

The WLAA was not a stand-alone effort. Its leadership and larger programmatic purposes overlapped and linked efforts with other wartime work. All of these efforts represented joint partnerships between voluntary civic groups, many of them led by women, and federal, state, and local governmental institutions, although the USSGA effort was more strongly linked with the government. These efforts utilized similar organizational and educational models, and cross-referenced one another. For example, in January 1919, the influential chair of the NWGC, Charles Lathrop Pack, penned an article for *The Farmerette* (the WLAA's newsletter), in which he described the work of the NWGC, and offered greetings and pledges of cooperation to the members of the WLAA.[63] While each of these other efforts was notable for the immediate effects it produced, the barriers it broke down, and the success it enjoyed, the WLAA program offered a much more serious threat to tradition and practice.

The Apple Doesn't Fall Far from the Tree: British Influences

Based on similar programs in the United Kingdom, Canada, and Australia, the WLAA organized women—predominantly young and many college-educated—into a semi-formal, government-sanctioned labor force to respond to severe labor shortages in the agricultural sector. The women's land army movement in America was similar to the British model: it featured a national initiative and a central organizing body. Like the WLAA, the Woman's National Land Service Corps in the United Kingdom corresponded with the United States equivalent of the WNFGA (the British Women's Farm and Garden Union, on which the WNFGA was modeled).[64] By the fall of 1917, these two groups had trained 1,146 "permanent workers."

The goals of the UK woman's land army program differed a bit from the WLAA. The primary goal, of course, was to "ensure the maintenance of the home grown food supply" by recruiting "all classes of women for work on the land." The second goal was "to create a favorable opinion as to the value of women's work in agriculture ... thereby breaking down the prejudices of those ... who are opposed to the employment of women." The third goal was to use land army workers as "organizers of the work of village women," essentially, using them as an example of mobilization, and to provide encouragement for other women to mobilize.

After the first year of operation, it was recommended that the government "itself should initiate a Women's Land Army." With some modifications to the plan, the British government did in fact launch a government-led woman's land army initiative in 1917, although the Land Service Corps continued its own work. By 1918, when British woman rights advocate Helen Fraser—"Our War Loan from England"—delivered nine lectures at Vassar College, the British Land Army of Women claimed 258,300 members, nearly enough to replace the 300,000 male agricultural laborers enlisted in military service during the first eighteen months of the war.[65]

In the United Kingdom, women's work in agriculture was seen as playing into the effort for wider participation of women in British civic life. "The movement has probably caused many people to ask themselves ... whether the experience now being gained by women can be turned to account in furthering the interests of the wage-earning woman," one article reported.[66] The same article discussed concerns about the duration of women's work: "There seems to be no indication at present that the War service of women on the land will increase the number of women labourers when the time comes for a return to normal conditions of labour." (Clearly, the word "normal" is code for a male labor market.)

While sharing a common ancestry born of Anglicized culture and tradition, Progressive voluntarism and feminism, the WLAA program that developed in America differed from the British model in a number of ways. The British message was more inclusive, a general call to assist in the agricultural sector. Several British voluntary associations developed land army programs for women that fell under the general banner of land work, but operated under different names. The British message had to be more inclusive: the labor shortage in Britain was not only much more acute than that in America, but of much longer duration (the United Kingdom had been at war since 1914). The options for foreign agricultural workers on a large-scale that were available to American growers were not available to the British. Overall, the severity of the situation in Britain required stronger measures.

Because it was a general call to service, the British model was much less restrictive in terms of membership, recruiting both rural and urban women and including all female agricultural workers under its banner. Simply by the fact that the British program antedated the American program by several years, it had a larger and broader enrollment. As a result, woman land worker enrollment figures in the United Kingdom were much higher—perhaps ten to fifteen times higher—than in the United States.[67] As in its American counterpart, female health was a primary consideration. "The girls on the land improve in health and increase in weight ... it has improved the physique of our girls—they like it," Fraser wrote.[68] And as in the United States, the public simply liked these women, Fraser reported:

> In the Lord Mayor's Procession in London ... with the men-in-arms of all our great Commonwealth of Nations, with the Tanks and the captured German aeroplanes and guns, the munitions girls and the Land girls marched. No group in all that great array had a warmer welcome from our vast crowds than our sensibly clothed, healthy, happy and supremely useful land girls.[69]

There were differences between the British and American land army experiences, especially in relation to who participated. Who the female participants were is sometimes clear, and sometimes a bit muddier. Unit statistics provide some information. American WLAA participants did include many working class women, among them textile workers, operators and milliners, as well as trade workers with only seasonal employment. The WLAA's newsletter, *The Farmerette*, provided state and unit statistics that might include the number of woman enrolled and their point of origin (i.e., college, trades, etc.); the kinds of agricultural work being done; the failures; physical effects of the work on the women; employers' attitudes toward the women; average wage; training plan; and chief problems. For example, the January 1919 issue provided information about Connecticut, the District of Columbia, and Illinois.[70] Of the 270 workers listed in Connecticut, sixty five percent were classified as college students; seventy percent of the Illinois workers were so classified.

From the enrollment figures of 142 WLAA workers recruited by the Bedford Camp (associated with Barnard College) during 1917, it can be deduced that about sixty-five to seventy percent of the workers had a college affiliation.[71] As the war continued, that composition changed, or is more difficult to deduce. Of 434 workers recruited by the Bedford Camp unit during 1918 (its second year of operation), 139 were classified as college students.[72] An additional 69 were classified as "college graduates." However, other professions requiring some degree of education (including teachers, librarians, dieticians, statisticians, accountants) are identified. Forty-three women identified themselves as being from "trades," but the list also includes other professions that might be considered working class. Because the Bedford unit allowed women to select more than one category of identification (i.e., to double register), true registration numbers are impossible to know, but clearly, the majority of women had some degree of educational attainment. They were also largely single. In the first year, only six members were married, and in the second year, only twenty-two, a stable six percent per annum.[73]

Many American WLAA units developed around private women's colleges, such as Vassar, Brown, Mills (in California), Barnard, Bryn Mawr, Wellesley, Mount Holyoke, Oberlin, etc. Some public institutions, such as the University of California, contributed students to WLAA units. Women's colleges, particularly in the Northeast, were eager to sponsor WLAA units. However, the creation and management of the units by women's colleges and their female deans assured that many WLAA workers were upper-middle and upper class college students, or drawn from college faculty and staff. While class did play a role in the WLAA in America, the influence of class was greater in the United Kingdom's land army; as its first goal, recruitment efforts targeted "all classes" of women, and organizing at colleges and universities was not a primary strategy, as in the United States.[74] The privilege that American WLAA workers enjoyed due to their education and race ensured positive working conditions in states such as California, where agricultural workers had been exploited.

The message of the WLAA in America, whether by design or default, targeted urban women. When rural women are mentioned in WLAA literature, it is usually in reference to a farmer's wife. For example, in a brochure promoting the WLAA to farmers, questions about the impacts of hiring WLAA workers on farmers' wives are included, and assure farmers that the WLAA will bring their own bedclothes, towels and will do their own cooking.[75] In some ways, rural women were an abstraction to the WLAA, and in some ways, the WLAA experience sought to recast what it meant to be a woman working the land. Interestingly, after demobilization, when a new association—the Land Workers of America—replaced the WLAA organization, the invitation to participate became broader. The invisibility of rural women in the WLAA belied the importance of rural women to increased wartime food production, and continued a national practice of rendering rural woman's work in agriculture largely invisible. (The woman's land army work in World War II relied more heavily on the participation of rural women, and the program was much larger.)

The Motivation of Woman's Rights

During her visit to the United States during the early part of 1917, British suffragette Helen Fraser spoke to young American women at college campuses about the World War and its impact on the United Kingdom. She spoke of the many motivations for woman's war work in Britain. Clearly, patriotism was an important motive. But Fraser spoke of other motives relating to the opportunities for higher wages and advancement for women. In one of her lectures, Fraser addressed what the war had "done" for women, focusing particularly on the advancement of the women's rights agenda. She described the growing perception of the value of women's contributions in British society, and the growing recognition of the justness of women's demands for the right to the vote, not as a reward for their wartime contributions, but because they were inherently deserving of full citizenship.[76] Fraser stated unequivocally that women's contributions to Britain's wartime mobilization efforts had facilitated the "conversion" of men (including anti-suffrage politicians)—and the media—to "Women's Suffrage."[77] Fraser was convinced that what had occurred in Britain would occur in the United States. Many of the women who heard her message agreed; it is no coincidence that one of the organizing groups of the WLAA was the Suffrage Party of New York.

In her lectures, Fraser described the political progress of the Women's Suffrage movement in Britain, and "the desire, and the willingness to cooperate" that existed between men and women with respect to securing full rights for women.[78] Fraser attributed this cooperation nearly entirely to the wartime contributions of women. Her descriptions of cooperation between the sexes—and between the classes—presented a new vision of a post-war world that offered greater equality for women. She described the opportunities that war work had provided for women to heal class divisions and to live in community and work with one another. In an America torn by racial, ethnic, class, and gendered strife, this must have been an enormously appealing message.

Fraser articulated the British realization that the gains of women during wartime might not be entirely temporary: British casualties had been appallingly high, and many men would not return from the war. Those who did come home might not return to their former occupations. Women who had experienced freedom, employment, and greater opportunities might not be content to return to their former lives, she anticipated. Fraser saw a vital role for women in the world's post-war reconstruction, not only as a source of moral uplift, but in a tangible way relating to policy and governance. Fraser said, "The war, in fact, has shaken the very foundations of the old Victorian beliefs in the limited sphere of women to atoms."[79]

In *What the War Has Done for Women*, Fraser provides a superb analysis of the advances of women in Great Britain during the war years. She focuses not only on generalities, but also on specifics relating to certain roles, occupations, and trades. For example, Fraser notes the advancement of women to high positions within the British Civil Service, the possible creation of a Ministry of Health at the request of women, and the accumulation of capital by women enabling them to begin their own enterprises.

Fraser's message galvanized American female college administrators and students alike. In addition to appealing to American patriotism and a genuine desire to serve the nation, the British experience demonstrated that wartime mobilization could provide greater opportunities for women. It is probably not a coincidence that one of the first WLAA units was organized by Vassar College, shortly after Fraser's visit. She had issued a call to action, and the women who heard her speak were eager to respond.

Nearly simultaneously, American women received further motivation to organize by noted American and woman's rights advocate Harriet Stanton Blatch, who urged women to organize into a land army to feed the world. The foreword to her book, *Mobilizing Woman Power*, was written by former president Theodore Roosevelt, and described the need for women to assist in the agricultural sector.[80] Blatch wrote glowingly of the success of the 1917 woman's agricultural camps. She also described the frustration of women eager to serve their government, yet failing to receive full acceptance. Blatch wrote of "far-seeing women ... refusing to be in the least crushed by government neglect" and organizing on their own to solve a farm-labor problem.[81] She also noted that one of the groups organizing the WLAA in New York, and ultimately serving on the WLAA's Advisory Council in that state, was the Woman's Suffrage Party. She and others called for the WLAA to be led by women. While patriotism was clearly a motive for WLAA service, evidence such as this proves that the advancement of a woman's rights agenda was also foremost in the minds of at least some of the WLAA's leadership.

The WLAA could free its participants in other ways, its advocates recognized. Ida Ogilvie, a dean at Barnard College in New York City, and the leader of the Bedford Unit (one of the largest and most successful WLAA units), stated that the WLAA had provided an important form of emancipation for women in the physical realm.

> Hitherto the emancipation of women has been mainly in intellectual and political directions. The physical has been absent, except as athletic sport for pleasure. The Land Army movement affords the first opportunity that has ever come to women in large numbers for healthful, useful, physical work in congenial and stimulating surroundings.... The Land Army camp is the first institution founded by and for women, for the work women can do, not modeled on any pre-existing institution for men, nor made by men for what they think women need.[82]

The advancement of woman's rights was not coincidental in the WLAA; it was an important subtext that linked certain parts of the WLAA membership in common cause. Several WLAA leaders, particularly in the Northeast and California, were active in the suffrage movement, in reform efforts and in higher education. For example, Katherine Philips Edson, who led the WLAA's Northern California Unit, was a prominent suffragist and labor rights advocate, focusing on securing a minimum wage, limiting working hours, and improving working conditions for women.[83] Her involvement probably influenced the development of a labor manifesto issued by the Northern California Unit, which reflected quite a different sensibility than units in some other parts of the country. Not only through people, but also through words, the WLAA explicitly linked the interests of woman's rights and the labor movement. Ida Ogilvie wrote, "The Woman Movement and the Labor Movement thus meet in the Land Army Camp."[84] In a world riven by war and labor unrest, these were radical ideas.

Organizational Structure

Again, it should be noted that WLAA participation figures (15,000–20,000) represent only a portion of woman land workers during World War I. In addition to the rural women already working in agriculture for their living—farm operators, wives, migrant laborers, share croppers and others—thousands of other women who worked the land were not included in WLAA rolls. Some thousands also worked the land under the auspices of programs similar to the WLAA. For example, the YMCA sponsored woman land workers. However, the WLAA provided the primary and most-publicized mechanism for women not otherwise associated with farm production to gain entry into commercial agricultural employment during this period.

The WLAA in America developed a national structure, minimally funded and staffed, that made entry into states via the State Councils of Defense, usually through the committee on woman's work. State councils of defense were devised to handle the tasks of home front mobilization that the federal government, alone, could not undertake. Some state councils of defense organized local WLAA units through community-based organizations or institutions, colleges, and/or the YWCA and local civic groups, which worked together to organize, recruit, fund, and manage the work of individual WLAA units.

Women's civic organizations proved vital to funding units, purchasing equipment and covering the start-up costs associated with the venture. Unit capitalization requirements included the purchase of tools and equipment; camp supplies such as cots, bedding, cooking utensils and other household items; transportation costs; training; and a health and/or recreation fund. Often, workers were expected to provide their own uniforms. While unit capitalization was often funded by women's civic organizations, such as the WNFGA, sometimes it was funded through private donations or unsecured loans.

The importance of the WLAA's national structure lay in the personal and professional affiliations and networks of its members, which enabled the organization to get up and running very quickly. The term "unit" not only reflected the nation's wartime footing (by echoing a military term), but also demonstrated that the local work of the WLAA would be organized within a para-military framework and structure. In an interesting parallel to the emerging Cooperative Extension Service (and to the parastate model described by historian Eldon Eisenach), a WLAA unit in America represented a collaboration of national, state and local interests. In the process of formation, no two were exactly alike.[85]

This unit system also corresponded to characteristics of Progressivism that emphasized structure, order, and scientific management. The unit structure provided for systematic training, communal living that assured adequate living arrangements and proper diet, standardized work hours and wages, and organized labor deployment. The unit represented a military-like structure, with a leader transacting all business for the unit (including the negotiation of wages). The costs of room and board (and sometimes health care) were sometimes deducted from wages. Units were managed entirely by women and consisted of as few as four and up to seventy WLAA members.[86] In some ways, units also reflected the demographics of the area where the work was conducted.

For example, a WLAA unit located in an area with a high number of seasonal female laborers might have a higher percentage of non-coeds enrolled, and might operate year-round. A WLAA unit primarily consisting of college students might run a full operation during the summer, but revert to a skeleton crew when school resumed in the fall. There were many variations on the basic model. By the summer of 1918, nearly 1,000 WLAA units were reportedly in operation in at least twenty-one states.[87] According to a synopsis provide by the WLAA's national organization in 1918, the unit size varied tremendously from state to state, and it may be deduced that states used different formulas and methods to calculate what constituted a unit for purposes of reporting.

The WLAA's ability to respond to local needs by moving units around agricultural regions certainly must have contributed to the program's value in the eyes of farmers and growers. Units were collectively managed and deployed into smaller workgroups that traveled to different sites from a "hub" camp to day labor opportunities. Some units, particularly in California and New York, organized smaller satellite camps to reduce travel time to work sites and increase overall efficiency. The kinds of tasks performed by WLAA members varied, but included fruit picking, grading, and packing; hoeing; truck gardening; grain silo work; trucking; thinning, raising, and harvesting vegetables; hay making; general farming; equipment operation; field work; dairying; poultry farming; and livestock management.[88] In California, New Mexico, and New York, much of the WLAA's work focused on fruit production, harvesting, and processing. In Virginia, which sponsored only four WLAA units, young women harvested tobacco in flooded fields, cleared timber, and built a road.

The WLAA's organizational structure called for each unit to provide room and board for WLAA workers within a camp structure. This insistence on providing room and board for its workers broke with the traditional agricultural model, where laborers were fed by (and often lodged with) rural families, creating an enormous amount of additional work during harvest for rural women, onto whom fell the burden of providing food, cleaning, laundry, and even medical services for workers employed on the family farm.[89]

The WLAA intentionally designed its system to limit the impact on rural women (and perhaps also, to maintain more control over the program). Some rural women likely appreciated the female labor force that came with neatly packed lunches in hand. At least one, Mrs. T.D.C. from Cohoes, New York, described her appreciation for the WLAA as "a special help to her sisters living on the farm."[90] This farmer's wife wrote how the WLAA members "were appreciated, being transported ... with lunches in neat paper bags ... never having to come inside the house to cause extra work." The farmer's wife talked about how the help of "the cheerful girls" took the load off rural women for outside work, enabling them to be more productive in their housework and even providing time for some rural sisters to socialize with these new sisters of the soil. The help was described as "spiritual as well as bodily.... They made the day brighter and better for their presence on our Farm."[91]

That the framers of the WLAA desired to supervise the living conditions of its workers was also the organization's attempt to embody Progressive values such as efficiency, organization and scientific management (which played out in nearly every aspect of WLAA life, including diet). Some WLAA units hired college home economics staff to serve as dieticians and cooks. The Bedford Unit, associated with Barnard College, made an art of camp life, publishing precise directions for the placement and construction of tents, a daily schedule, and even a cookbook.

As in the United Kingdom, female-centered management also characterized the American WLAA experience. Like other WLAA units, the Women's Agricultural Camp at Bedford, New York was designed from the outset to be female-centric. Reporting to a local advisory board, the WLAA program was run by Ida Ogilvie, a dean at Barnard, who managed a team consisting of an agricultural professional, a business manager, chauffeur, dieticians and land workers. All were women.

WLAA training was officially grouped into four distinct types. They included hands-on (i.e., "practical instruction") delivered within the unit structure; extended practical courses (usually available at larger WLAA camps, at the "farms" located on some college campuses, or at the WLAA farm in Libertyville, Illinois); Extension and agricultural college courses (termed "scientific training"); and specialized training provided to unit leaders.

Geographic Particulars

The WLAA's early mobilization and the overall success that the program enjoyed in California was probably the result of several factors, including that state's early adoption of female suffrage, concern about a shortage of agricultural labor, and growers' dissatisfaction with foreign-born migrant labor workers. In California, growers were willing to experiment with a new tool that might address the chronic problem of securing labor. Another explanation for the greater militancy of California workers is found in the roster of its state organizing committee, which included social reformer Katherine Phillips Edson and Aurelia Reinhardt, an educator and social activist, who also served as president of Mills College (the first women's college to be founded west of the Rockies). Reinhardt was an early graduate of the University of California and one of the first women graduate students of Yale University.

Employers in California's agricultural sector had experience with workers from different backgrounds, including Mexicans, Filipinos, Native Americans, Japanese, Armenians, and Chinese. The experience had not been trouble-free in the perception of both growers and workers. California growers were clearly interested in a more favorable, and perhaps, native solution. Growers in California were also innovative, willing to try new things. There is strong evidence that some California growers took this female labor source seriously.

Just as the WLAA in California likely benefited from the relatively higher status enjoyed by women in that state, the WLAA in the northeastern United States may have benefited from its participants' high educational attainment and upper middle class orientation. Coeds from elite women's colleges with a tradition of reform and suffrage activity were more amenable to service in the WLAA for a number of reasons, including their economic status. Some educational institutions provided incentives for young women to participate, including specialized training and college credit or approved leave for WLAA enrollment. As regions, the Northeast and the West clearly had less restrictive gender constraints than the South and larger populations of middle class and college educated women.

Recruitment and the Vision of Service

True to the Progressive ethos, the WLAA articulated a desire to educate and inform the public and to share a vision of collective and voluntary service as part of an American creed. This was evident in the recruitment materials. Women were recruited in a variety of ways, although primarily through their affiliation with colleges. Recruitment efforts linked with inspirational speakers were quite effective. Newspaper articles, conferences, and women's civic organizations promoted the program. Nearly every college had a war work committee, and it became a practice at some institutions to extend college credit or offer approved leave for those participating in war work; war work sometimes took precedence over academic work. For example, a University of California annual report for the period July 1, 1918, to July 15, 1919, is remarkable for the focus on war work and the institution's mobilization work, as well as the impacts on the war on the operations of the institution (personnel and students deployed, etc.). The Western College for Women in Oxford, Ohio published a report of its war activities in October 1918. It provides exhaustive detail.

Students attending colleges were easy to mobilize, due to their physical proximity, the nature of these institutions, and in general, the economic and class standing of the students.

Poster art was particularly useful as a recruitment and propaganda tool for nearly all audiences, and the artwork for WLAA efforts is interesting. Posters depict strong women, some wearing military-style garb or overalls, holding hoes. These women portrayed females who were challenging notions of domesticity through their clothing, their work and their living arrangements. At least one poster includes a tagline in much smaller type, "Until the Boys Come Back," directly declaring that the invitation to participate was a limited-time offer.

The WLAA's call for service integrated opportunities to serve the nation, express patriotism, and acquire new skills. One Farmerette song, to the tune of "Over There," said, "Watch that Yankee maid learn a trade." It was a complex message that also considered class and gender. As hoped for, the WLAA was successful at tapping into the concept of "service" that became the focus of emotional and political impulses in America during wartime. The WLAA linked many agendas and impulses: it was educative and vocational in nature; it highlighted and attempted to deal with class and labor issues; it was gendered in a way that challenged traditional notions and understandings of female work during wartime mobilization.

There is more than one reference in WLAA literature that a peripheral purpose, or benefit, of the WLAA was the opportunity to provide a laboratory of sorts in class differences (i.e., working class girls versus coeds), and to prove that class mattered little when the larger goal—presumably duty to country—was shared. Living in community together might provide moral and educational uplift to the working classes and lower barriers to understanding that had long existed between working and elite women. WLAA popular cultural pieces make reference to differences in status. "Nellie was a pedagogue and Sue a social light, but when the Germans sank our boats, They both came out to fight" were words that demonstrated common cause, despite differences in background and education.[92] The WLAA provided entrée for different groups of women to provide service to the nation in the form of agricultural labor.

Wages

The national WLAA organization suggested that wages be negotiated directly with growers by the unit leader (usually an older woman with important academic or social qualifications). Wages were paid to the WLAA unit and then parceled out to WLAA workers, after deductions for room, board and other incidental costs (including unit capitalization). As a national organization the WLAA was conflicted about wages. While the unit formation literature issued by the national organization discussed how wages would be negotiated, and did imply that wages ought to be equal to those received by men working in the same region, it was not pushed equally in each region. In some places, and in some units, wages were clearly not as important as the desire to serve. In other units, particularly in California, wages were central. (In the December 1918 issue of *The Farmerette*, on page 3, one of the "chief problems" listed for both the Northern and Southern California units were listed as "equal pay for equal work" and "fair wages.")

One senses a change in the national WLAA's position on wages during the course of the war, however; by the time of demobilization, the national WLAA organization held clearer, more ambitious goals for labor and wage standards. They set these forth in their national publication, *The Farmerette*.

There were regional variations in wages reflecting local prevailing wage differences. Work that was more physically demanding also warranted higher pay in some instances. WLAA workers in California received higher wages than their peers in the Northeast. In the 1918 annual report provided by the Pennsylvania Land Army, wages for the Chestnut Hill and Huntingdon Valley Units were $15 per month, after board and lodging. These wages represented very modest payment for work. In contrast, in a letter to the editor printed in *Republic*, the Northern California WLAA shared a manifesto describing the "economic standards" that this particular unit had adopted. These standards included a wage scale incorporating equal pay for equal work (based on the existing wages for male workers in the local area); a no competition clause with local labor (including a prohibition on wage undercutting); a maximum workday with standard-scale overtime; weight lifting restrictions; and protection under California's Workman's Compensation Insurance and Safety Act.

These standards reflected the Northern California's group's awareness of themselves not only as individual workers, but also as part of a larger class of agricultural laborers with whom WLAA members felt some solidarity. It may also have reflected that per the December 1918 issue of *The Farmerette*, the composition of the Northern California Division's membership was dominated by workers with supposed economic concerns, and only about 10 percent students.[93] Their demands also reflected a focus on their WLAA work as an important economic activity as opposed to being solely for patriotic service. Writing on behalf of this WLAA unit, Alice Graydon Phillips refers to its membership as "the land workers of Northern California."[94] This is in sharp contrast to the Pennsylvania WLAA's report, which includes at least seven references to WLAA workers as "the girls."

There was tension not only around the issue of wages paid to female agricultural workers, but also with respect to the duration of their stay in the labor market. While some envisioned women as a permanent addition to the agricultural labor force, others were threatened by what women's entry into this area might mean to the male labor force. This was manifested in letters to the editor, and also through the comments of some government officials. The issue of permanence amplified, and for some, further aggravated the issue of wages. In some cases, WLAA workers received lower than the prevailing wage—the *New York Times* referenced "the present unfair wage scale."[95] The wage differential may partly explain farmer's enthusiasm for female workers, and also explains the Northern California Division's insistence on issuing a labor manifesto.

Again, its leaders did not only assert the intentions for the program; its participants' vision also drove the development and outcomes of the WLAA. Unlike other home front mobilization efforts, such as Liberty/Victory gardens and food conservation, the motives of WLAA participants were characterized less completely by voluntarism. In some cases, women simply wanted or needed to earn wages while serving the country. While many college coeds undoubtedly participated for more altruistic reasons, some factory girls and seamstresses (as well as those employed in seasonal work) enrolled in the WLAA for an opportunity for higher wages, regular employment during off times and work that offered greater independence. Some women who favored suffrage chose WLAA work because of the "fresh territory" it enabled them to access and the ability of the nature of the work to challenge traditional stereotypes of woman's role, all while providing a much-needed service to the nation.[96]

Hoeing the Tough Row: Resistance

Some in President Wilson's administration were resistant to the idea of women land workers. The WLAA was held at arm's length by the federal government throughout the war. In 1918, Clarence Ousley, assistant secretary of agriculture for the federal government under David Houston, delivered a speech before the Woman's Committee, Council of National Defense, in Washington. D.C., in which he stated, "It would be extremely unfortunate, I think, if we should get the notion or herald the idea that we have come to such a pass in the United States that we must drive our women to the farms."⁹⁷ The tone of his speech was belittling to women and anti-agrarian in tone. It also failed to acknowledge the vital contributions of rural women in America. Ousley conceded, "There is opportunity from time to time for women to work on the land." He focused on "unmanly" work (i.e., cooks, waiters, clerks, bookkeepers), and suggested that those positions might "well be filled by women," presumably enabling unprepared and untrained urban men the opportunity to serve as agricultural laborers.⁹⁸ Ousley also suggested that the best use for urban and suburban women vis-à-vis rural life was to help in the homes and kitchens of rural farms.

"Is the Woman Needed on the Farm? What the United States Government Has to Say about Farm Work for Women this Summer" appeared in the May 1918 issue of *Ladies Home Journal*.⁹⁹ It described the land army work of 1917 as "some interesting experiments." Both the author and the government appear to be dismissive of land army work; the intent appears to be to influence rural women to do more, to encourage untrained urban women to stay away, and to engage experienced land army women only when all other measures had been exhausted. The article, which ironically used agriculture and horticulture terminology to describe how women were being kept out of work they wished to engage in, continued:

> Woman's eagerness to serve in this war has frequently outrun the Government's ability to place her in the fields of service of her own choosing. Washington has nipped in the bud many a prospective romantic career by its chilling consideration of the facts of a given situation.... And so it is that proposals that the women of America leap overnight almost into the places of the farmers and the "hired men" of America find the Government somewhat cold. Washington sees a great many ways in which women can help in the production of our food, but the suggestion that women from cities seek jobs on our farms is not the first among them. The Government authorities believe that there are many other steps to be taken first before either the interests of farm production of those of the women themselves require the conversion of agriculturally untrained women into tillers of the soil.¹⁰⁰

The author estimated the number of women in American agriculture at 1.8 million who were "engaging in field operations," and claimed that more than one million of those are "negroes, working on Southern cotton plantations." His suggestions for what rural women could do? Create "more and larger vegetable gardens," increase the size of poultry operations, improve the "quality and quantity" of butter production, feed one or two pigs ... all suggestions that put women back squarely in the domestic sphere and increased their already heavy workload. Young farmwomen might help their men folk by driving the horse to town for errands, or riding the hay-rake or cultivator "in an emergency." The article's conclusion: the work of rural women on the farm "creates no social problem." Unsaid? The participation of non-rural women in agricultural work would.

Urban women were largely unaddressed in this piece; they were encouraged to stay away; women "unused to farm ways, unknown to the farm family" are "out of the question."[101] In his favor, the author distinguishes between "untrained" women, and does offer some positive comments about the land army work of the previous summer. "That women can successfully do farm work cannot be disputed…. It was generally agreed that the women workers manifested a better spirit about their work, more zest and enthusiasm, than the casual male farm laborer."

Some of the opposition to the WLAA centered on skepticism of women's suitability for hard physical labor in agriculture and came right from the halls of government. The USDA's Ousley, for example, shared a belief that women were physically unable to be successful in agriculture (except as home economists working in the domestic sphere); he stated, "I will despise American manhood if the great body of our men permit our women to be drafted for these hard tasks of agriculture."[102] Ousley did approve of women engaging in agricultural tasks more closely associated with the domestic sphere, such as dairying and vegetable cultivation.

Some farmers were also—at least initially—skeptical about the strength and ability of non-rural women to contribute in a meaningful way to production agriculture; the WLAA leadership knew this and anticipated hard questions from farmers in their informational brochure.[103] "Are women strong enough to do the heavy work on a farm?" "Are they trained?" "Tell me the different kinds of farm work that women have actually done?"[104] Interestingly, the resistance of farmers was the easiest to overcome; farmers were interested in capable and reliable labor and the WLAA provided it. Again, farmers may have also been persuaded, in some cases, by the lower wages they were able to pay to eager and organized female agricultural laborers.

Farmers offered glowing reports of their experience with the WLAA. "They took great interest in the work, and did the work just as well as the average man, and made good far beyond the most sanguine expectations," one superintendent reported.[105] The WLAA published a brochure that contained farmer testimonials about the value of the WLAA.[106] Farmers from New York, Ohio, Pennsylvania, Vermont, Virginia, California, Connecticut, New Jersey, and New Mexico provided positive comments about the farmerettes. Enoch Miller, a farmer from New Jersey, said that he was able to "plant and cultivate at least one third more" than he would have otherwise. New Mexico farmerettes were credited with saving thousands of dollars of apples. G. Howard Davison, of New York, wrote a lengthy testimonial that provided statistics about the productivity of farmerettes. Most telling was his statement, "I am convinced that I can operate a farm more economically and more efficiently with average men and women than I can with average men alone."[107]

Resistance was sometimes nuanced and complex. Even some individuals who asserted support for the advancement of women were uncomfortable with women working outside of the domestic sphere, or engaging in physical labor. In a letter appearing in the July 15, 1918, issue of the *New York Times*, F. B. Riggs of Lakedale, Connecticut, wrote, "These women cannot stand such work, and if they do not know it now their children will know it later. We do not want to develop a peasant class of women in this country such as is seen with the Poles or Italians ... but we do want more women to engage in agriculture."

While nursing, a celebrated profession for women during World War I, also required great physical strength, it was a more accepted outlet for women wishing to contribute to war work. It allowed women to nurture and heal (and more importantly, to work under the supervision of a male doctor). For many, there was something distasteful about the idea of women engaging in hard physical labor in agriculture and living in all-female communities sans the authority of men.

Some proposals were made to divert WLAA workers to labor in farmhouses, in order to free up rural women to work in the field (this was another suggestion from Assistant Agriculture Secretary Ousley). Based on outdated notions of class, domestic ideology (i.e., separate spheres) and concerns about physical ability, these efforts were firmly resisted by the WLAA, which bridled at the suggestion that rural women were stronger or more capable then urban women. There was also a sense, perhaps, that this was proprietary work as well: woman-directed. WLAA participants sought a certain kind of experience, not only the female-centeredness of the venture, but for many, the opportunity to gain a new and different kind of work experience.

WLAA participants viewed themselves as physically strong. Official reports included resistance to arguments about physical ability by providing measures of weight gain in members as a sign of their continuing health despite the demanding physical labor. In rebuttals to largely male-articulated concerns, WLAA leadership cited the higher mortality rates for rural women as evidence that urban women were stronger than their rural peers. The WLAA also may have resisted the possible diversion of their labor force to domestic use in farm houses based on the specialized training that their members had received, training that had prepared them for other kinds of work, and their desire to gain experience in a new field. There may have been a sense of organizational propriety: the WLAA was a female-centric organization, and may not have wanted to be subordinated to the male-dominated agencies that were managing labor mobilization during wartime.

There was some resistance to the idea of a permanent WLAA presence in labor, sensitivity about the WLAA entering the labor market at the appropriate time and for the appropriate duration. The larger message was clear: women agricultural workers must be a temporary solution. This is in keeping with the understanding of the "temporary" nature of woman's war work. Guidelines from the WLAA's national organization, based in New York, reflected that sensitivity. The following was included in the Northern California Division's statement that "the WLAA of Northern California is designed to supply a need for agricultural labor, not to create a demand for it. Only when a definite labor shortage is demonstrated and reported by the Farm Labor Agent will units be sent into any locality."[108] Since Farm Labor Agents were exclusively male, men could ultimately control the deployment of the WLAA.

Resistance to the WLAA varied by region. Particularly in the South, the land army movement was not able to entirely overcome resistance to the notion of separate spheres, a general distrust of things urban and racialized understandings of who might "appropriately" provide agricultural labor. Mississippi was described as "barren soil" for the WLAA.[109] There were some notable exceptions, however. In August, Georgia, a suffragette and civic leader, Mrs. Clara Mathewson, spearheaded a successful effort to create a white WLAA chapter, although it was not affiliated with a college.[110] To do this, she enlisted the aid of two influential male leaders in the community: the county agricultural agent and a judge; she also secured the support of the local paper.[111] To lend credibility to the effort, and assure that propriety was observed, men younger than draft age (supposedly with guns) would accompany women into the field. The state of Georgia became a "peach."[112] White women of a certain socioeconomic class working in the fields, much less picking cotton, was taboo in the South; the WLAA managed to overcome that notion. However, despite very limited success in the South, WLAA efforts were most prevalent in the Northeast and the West, with strength in some areas of the Midwest. Not surprisingly, WLAA efforts in these regions (particularly New York and California) are among the best documented in the literature surrounding the topic.[113]

Where resistance to the WLAA was overcome it was because the WLAA delivered what it promised: a reliable, inexpensive and motivated labor force. The media was the biggest booster of "the farmerettes" and published reports were almost always approving. For some, "farmerettes" were a pleasant novelty to read about that countered the grim news of life in the trenches and mounting casualties. Some of their stories were also love stories that tugged at the heartstrings: farmerettes laboring over here, in solidarity with sweethearts and husbands serving over there.[114]

Letters to the editor expressing concern about young women harming their chances for childbearing by engaging in hard labor were countered by first-person accounts of the pleasure found in "husky harvesting" and after-work swim parties at the pond, which one WLAA participant termed "the real institution of the camp."[115] WLAA participant and reporter Helen Kennedy Stevens even wrote about the pleasure of "backrubs and massages," a further indication that young women enjoyed the physicality of the WLAA life.[116] Participants wore sunburns and muscle aches proudly, as badges of honor, and made light of physical hardship. Numerous reports speak of WLAA members laboring in heat and other weather conditions that sent male farm workers packing.

First-hand accounts by women mobilized for home front efforts appeared in print media and reinforced the positive nature of women's war work. "We tingled with health and the glow of physical exercise," one participant wrote.[117] In a *New York Times* article appearing in July of 1918, it was reported that physicians were "treating fewer women whose ills are imaginary."[118] War work, including service in the WLAA, was viewed as improving both the health and values of "well-to-do" women. "[Women] are learning the inanities of fashionable fripperies and the real attraction that lies in a healthy body, bright eyes, shining teeth, and an upstanding, graceful carriage that goes with fresh air and exercise and the tonic of work and service."[119] The physical value of the work to women was clear to its proponents. In their view, WLAA work brought roses both to the market and to the cheeks.

Gleanings: Demobilization

Even after the Armistice was signed, women continued to work under the WLAA banner. Their numbers decreased as nearly three million men were demobilized, returned to America, and began to refill the ranks of agricultural labor. Women's motives for participating in the WLAA at this point varied. For some women, continuing the work became a more purely economic issue. In other cases, continued participation might be attributed to a sense of themselves as workers, as well as reflecting an individual's desire to continue working on the land. In an era so sharply defined by worldwide workers movements, some of what occurred during the demobilization of the WLAA and the corresponding organizations in other countries makes a great deal of sense.

For example, when the Woman's Land Army of Great Britain was demobilized in November 1919, losing its governmental help and support, an association of workers called The National Association of Landwomen was formed to take its place; *The Farmerette* reported this approvingly.[120] Its goal was similar to the WNFGA in terms of encouraging women to work in agriculture and horticulture; yet, it also sought to ensure economic advancement for women in the field and to support workers' rights. Many women simply wanted the opportunity to continue employment in their chosen field: agriculture. Organizations such as the United Kingdom's National Association of Landwomen sought to ensure that women would not be forced out of the field, either literally or figuratively.

In ending, as well as in its origins, the WLAA in America was influenced by the British. As they had followed the British lead in founding the WLAA, the American organization followed England's indication to demobilize. The WLAA's leadership dissolved the national organization in January 1920. Saying there was "no longer any demand for the work of the organization," the WLAA's board filed a petition, later approved by the courts, seeking the dissolution of the WLAA corporation that they had formed.

But ... there was a stirring in the sisterhood of the soil, and in May 1920, *The Farmerette* reported an intriguing item of news. The New York Farmerettes, who had provided so much of the initial leadership for the WLAA, had reorganized as the "Land Workers of America," with the dean of Barnard College, Ida Ogilvie, as its honorary president, and *The Farmerette* as its official journal. *The Farmerette* stated:

> The L.W.A. is an organization of WORKERS and has received no outside assistance. Its purpose is to carry on and develop the work and opportunities for women opened up by the Land Army. Membership is open to any woman who has done farm work or who is interested in promoting the employment of women on the land. The organization will be an agency for bringing together employers and workers.[121]

This last issue of *The Farmerette* as the WLAA's official organ provided news of individual farmerettes who were opting to continue their employment in agriculture. Sarah Richardson had gone west to Nebraska to work for the ranch that had employed her as a WLAA worker the previous summer. Linda Schroeder ("Tiny," one of the WLAA's great humorists) was eager to get back to work as a driver. A group of women from the Bedford Unit had worked through the winter, and had been joined by another WLAA member from Illinois. One of them, Mrs. Doble, was working fulltime as an "expert pruner" in orchards. Katherine Sampson had wintered in California and taken a tractor course there, to better prepare her to return to farm work in Nebraska.

Armistice ended the temporary economic citizenship that many American women had enjoyed during wartime. Many women simply withdrew from their work in the public sphere to return to the domestic realm. Ironically, many women were pushed out of the labor force by the same mechanism that had encouraged their entry: a sense of patriotism. According to a Department of Labor report published in 1919, "The withdrawal of women from their work was advocated as a means of providing employment for returning soldiers."[122] It was not patriotic—or ladylike—to deprive a veteran of employment, and this message was transmitted by the government, and through popular culture. The agreement had been "until the boys come home," and indeed, they were coming home. While wartime exigencies had created temporary opportunities for women, post-war "realities" ensured that many of these opportunities disappeared.

The women who participated in the WLAA were transformed by their experience. Many saw themselves as being different physically. "We did not break down or get sick or sun struck.... We went home serene and brown and strong."[123] The WLAA provided a public opportunity for women to test themselves as a group in the physical realm, where they succeeded, dispelling the notion that women were unsuited to hard physical labor. "Perhaps the greatest joy in the work lies in the health and vigor of it," WLAA participant Marguerite Wilkinson wrote in 1918.[124] Others basked in a sense of sisterhood and shared experience with other WLAA members.[125] Like the brotherhood of the battlefield, a sisterhood of the soil developed among the women who served their nation by providing service on the land.

The legacy of the WLAA seems small if measured only by the number of participants, but it is quite important for many reasons. The program proved what its proponents asserted: women were fully capable of organizing themselves and delivering a force of recruits fully up to the demands of agricultural labor. In the process, these women proved capable of managing their own efforts sans the authority of men. They also earned important labor rights, decades before male migrant workers. Through the WLAA, along with many other kinds of wartime work, women had made real claims to full citizenship. The cumulative effect of women's wartime contributions certainly helped to facilitate the passage of the Nineteenth Amendment. The farmerettes also gained acceptance by the government, grudging perhaps, but acceptance, nonetheless: the work of the WLAA was impressive enough that the government reactivated the program as a federal Labor Department effort during World War II. During that time, the program achieved the kind of recognition its leaders had hoped for in World War I: status as an official government program, with estimated enrollments exceeding two million. The WLAA's "girl with the hoe" became in World War I a significant symbol, perhaps not as famous as Rosie the Riveter during World War II, but certainly as meaningful.

WLAA members during World War I also undoubtedly inspired other women into "growing" work, whether to service as home gardeners or to pursue agricultural education and specialized training. In the immediate post-war period, female (and male) agricultural leaders held conferences promoting women's work in agriculture, including an important conference at Amherst.[126] The report from that meeting indicated that an enormous shift in attitudes about the role of women in agriculture had occurred. Educational programs were becoming coeducational experiences as women achieved a greater degree of equality in the field.

The WLAA also increased the status of agricultural labor in some places, at least temporarily. The most important evidence of that came from the Northern California Division, which demanded and received some of the first labor standards in the agricultural sector, including a fixed-length workday, minimum wages and standards of living and working conditions.[127] In its continuing organizational work for the summer of 1920, the national WLAA office spread that development, issuing labor guidelines to those units continuing their work across the country. These guidelines stipulated that growers were responsible for helping workers secure housing, and also delineated work hours, and wage rates, requiring rates to be based on the wages paid to men in the district.[128]

In Vacaville, California, some growers spent several thousand dollars constructing state-of-the-art barracks to house WLAA members. This occurred in California, where agricultural workers were routinely exploited. Growers were willing to accept these standards during wartime, not only because of labor shortages, but probably because these were demands placed by white, middle-class women, backed by a national association with federal, state and university support. Once the war ended, these rights were largely withdrawn, and would not be granted to other laborers (predominantly male and non-white) for many years to come, and then, not without decades of struggle.[129]

Some historians will not entirely agree with this argument. In his 2001 book, *A World of Its Own: Race, Labor, and Citrus in the Making of Greater Los Angeles, 1900–1970*, Matt Garcia argues that the employment of white women and high-school boys (through the Boys Working Reserve) prompted agricultural labor reform, including wage standards and working conditions, as this study concludes. But Garcia also argues that growers regarded the WLAA as a "temporary measure for the war, but not as a permanent solution to the labor shortage problem."[130] That misses the contingency that some saw in the moment that growers in Vacaville levied a self-tax on their fruit products to fund a cooperative investment of $4,500 to build a camp for the WLAA laborers in that community.[131]

There were other clues that more durable change was occurring. It was reported as a news item in *The Farmerette* that a Kansas farmer with three sisters was denied an exemption from the draft, when the judge held forth "that men on farms well provided with feminine workers are not to be exempted on agricultural grounds."[132] Whether this was anecdotal or representative of broader policy decisions, it represented a growing belief that there was an increasingly important—and perhaps permanent—place for women in the agricultural sector, existing outside the roles traditionally delegated to rural women.

In the wake of her experience with the WLAA, Ida Ogilvie, the dean from Barnard College, saw and believed in the promise of future employment in agriculture for women. She saw the possibility of dual paths, with college women perhaps leaving ordinary agricultural labor to women employed in seasonal trade and pursuing what she termed "scientific training and experiment."[133] Ogilvie also felt that the WLAA had proven that the standardized labor practices and uniform wages provided in other sectors of employment (including manufacturing industries), could be successful in agriculture. Ogilvie felt that the land army movement was vital to the United States and would eventually fall under federal control. She was correct on both counts, although her predictions were many years away and would require another national emergency—World War II—to come to fruition.

Ogilvie was proven incorrect in anticipating a need and a place for female labor on a large scale in American agriculture. The advent of technology after World War I reduced labor needs and the working conditions required to secure and maintain white, urban women of a certain social standing as agricultural laborers was not sustainable, as mechanization increased and it became easier (and more profitable) for growers, particularly in the West, to seek other sources of labor.

But, perhaps in part because of the WLAA experience, women moved to claim a place in agriculture, securing greater access to technical education and specialized training. Women became more active in Extension education and carried forward advocacy work with rural men and women to improve production agriculture under the guise of the domestic sphere. Building on the Progressive impulse to synthesize rural-urban America, embodied by organizations such as the WNFGA and the WLAA, women gained ground as professionals, leaders and practitioners beyond the fields they cultivated in the war, in the "middle ground" that their leadership in the WLAA contributed to staking out: the urban-based sphere dominated by horticulture and landscape architecture.

> The pig weed and rag weed have fallen; the potato bug host and cut
> worm army have been completely routed;
> the rank and file
> of strawberries and cherries
> have been safely marshaled to the canneries.
> Victory is assured.[134]

And indeed it was.

SEVEN

Mobilization for Nutritional Defense

Important changes in the food system occurred immediately prior to and after World War I. The Smith-Lever Act in 1914 formalized the Cooperative Extension Service, providing a boost to the effort to make American agriculture more productive. In 1916, a Federal Highway Act provided for cooperation with states in the construction of rural post roads. A Federal Farm Loan Act was also passed that year, as was the U.S. Grain Standards Act. In 1917, the USDA developed official grading standards for potatoes, representing the first standards posed for fruits and vegetable. Scientific advances in agriculture continued at a rapid pace after World War I. Gains produced by mechanization and improvements in agricultural production practices reduced the number of people required to produce the nation's food. During World War I, the Country Life Movement impulse waned, and many lost interest in America's rural life. The 1920 census revealed a new watermark in American cultural, political, and economic life: for the first time in the nation's history, the majority of its citizens lived in cities.[1]

In 1860, near the outset of the American Civil War, farmers made up 58 percent of the U.S. labor force. In 1890, which many historians mark as the beginning of the Progressive Era, 43 percent of "gainfully" employed Americans were engaged in agricultural activity. By 1920, the year that the American Farm Bureau was formed and a national soil classification system developed, only 27 percent of Americans were engaged in agriculture.

After World War I the Bureau of Education discontinued the USSGA program. School gardening continued in fits and starts, but it wasn't a national imperative. The national campaign for Liberty and Victory Gardens was discontinued, but of course, Americans continued to garden, although in smaller numbers. The USDA emerged from World War I with greater reach into the lives of American families. After experiencing a brief downturn in the number of Extension agents (who had been hired under emergency wartime measures), a continuous and growing stream of federal funding and supporting legislation enabled the USDA to continue and expand its efforts on a number of fronts, including Extension work to rural farmers and their families in agriculture, home economics, and 4-H youth development work.

The interwar years and the Great Depression forever changed the face of American agriculture. While most think that the Great Depression began in 1929, in America's rural areas, the economic downturn was felt a full ten years earlier, shortly after the end of World War I. During World War I, American farmers increased production in response to increased demands for food in the global market. The drop in global food demand after the war adversely affected American farmers, plunging America's rural sector into economic distress. During World War I, farmers cultivated existing acreage more intensively, and also brought into production new acreage, assisted by mechanization in the form of tractors and motorized farm vehicles.[2] (Tractors also reduced the number of animals needed to pull plows, thus opening up more acreage for production.[3])

In the near aftermath of the war, other nations resumed agricultural production, international demand declined, American farmers produced a surplus of many agricultural products, and prices plummeted. Individual farmers suffered as the United States entered an agricultural depression (again, a full ten years before the Great Depression—it was as if there were two nations). In addition to having surplus product, many American farmers were saddled with debt from mechanization (in many cases, recommended by the government's agricultural experts).[4]

In 1929, the stock market crashed. But innovations in the food system continued. Hydroponics was invented that year, and the first airplane seeding of rice occurred in California. (California remains one of the nation's leading rice producers, and the industry is still characterized by innovation.) By 1930, when the first Mickey Mouse comic strip ran, Scotch Tape was introduced, and the first frozen Birdseye food products hit the market, only 21 percent of Americans worked in agriculture. That trend accelerated. In the ensuing decade, millions of rural residents were driven off the land by new federal legislation that displaced farmers, a harsh drought, lack of economic opportunities, and the lure of the nation's cities. By 1935, the notions of Jefferson agrarianism seemed outmoded: 2 out of every 5 farmers were tenant farmers.

The federal government tried to help farmers and rural dwellers through a variety of legislative maneuvers and programs. Ambitious programs such as the Tennessee Valley Authority and the Farm Credit Administration were developed. But the farm crisis was complex—and it was not only a farm crisis, but a national crisis as well, because rural and urban are always linked. Surplus product, low prices, diminishing markets, and the Dust Bowl conspired to plunge many rural areas into hard, hard times. Every governmental action that positively benefitted one group adversely affected others. The Agriculture Marketing Act, the Civilian Conservation Corps, the Farm Security Administration, the Soil Conservation Service, the Rural Electrification Administration, and the development of enduring trade agreements are just a few of the things that forever changed the face of American agriculture and reshaped the nation's food system and its psyche.

USDA Secretary Henry A. Wallace (his father, Henry Cantwell Wallace, also served as USDA secretary) became the architect of a new, modern American food system. His work spanned both rural and urban interests. Wallace remains a controversial figure, but the far-reaching implications of his work cannot be underestimated. Under his leadership, the nation reorganized, reordered, and reshaped the relationship between farmers, consumers ... and the state.

There was widespread concern about the nation's nutritional health—especially that of its children; Secretary of Labor Frances Perkins expressed this in 1933. Through reports gathered by employees of the Department of Labor's Children's Bureau, Perkins and other national leaders became aware of the serious and growing issue of childhood malnutrition. Perkins convened a national conference to address this and other issues, and throughout the 1930s, the topic remained at the fore of national policy discussion. A good number of the nation's citizens were hungry and malnourished, despite agricultural surpluses. In his second inaugural address in 1937, Franklin Delano Roosevelt referenced "one-third of the nation" that was "ill nourished," promising bold action to help those affected (and foreshadowing, in some ways, President Lyndon Johnson's war on poverty nearly three decades later).

The nation was very concerned about food and nutrition as war clouds gathered again in Europe. But by 1940, only 18 percent of Americans were involved in agriculture.

Advances and growth in the science of nutrition and dietetics gave traction to the notion of "nutritional defense" as the prospect of a second world war loomed larger and there were clear indicators that the nation's citizens were not as healthy as they should be. Hunger and malnutrition were—and remain—moral issues in a nation of such abundance, but they also represented a challenge to national security and military readiness. (They still do.) Explicit messages linked the health of citizens to the security of the nation. The surgeon general expressed concern about the potential effects of poor nutrition on America's labor capacity.[5] Early Selective Service calls in 1940 resulted in high rejection rates of potential soldiers on medical grounds (many of those rejected had poor teeth, which was considered a sign of poor nutrition). A National Nutrition Conference for Defense was held in May 1941; a new table of Recommended Daily Allowances (RDAs) was made public at that time.[6] This was the first simple daily nutrition guide published by the U.S. government.

America's entry into World War II brought back a version of each of the World War I gardening initiative programs. Within twelve days of the bombing of Pearl Harbor, Secretary of Agriculture Claude Wickard and Paul V. McNutt, administrator of the Federal Security Agency, jointly convened a National Defense Gardening Conference in Washington, D.C.[7] (McNutt was also director of the Office of Defense Health and Welfare Services.) Wickard and McNutt organized a program featuring seventeen speakers. Topics included "Vegetables, Vitality and Victory"; "Developing a National Defense Garden Program"; "The American School System and War Gardens"; "Research in the Nutritional Values of Fruits and Vegetables"; and "Community and Defense Gardens." Recommendations from the participants (working in committees) were gathered into a document—a proceedings of sorts—summarizing the conference.

Former USDA secretary Henry A. Wallace, who was now serving as the vice president of the United States, provided the introduction to the proceedings. Wallace wrote:

> Food is fundamental to the defense of the United States.... On a foundation of good food we can build anything. Without it we can build nothing.... We want to make sure that everyone in the United States has in his diet enough energy, enough bone, blood, and muscle-building food, enough vitamins, to give that feeling of 'health plus'.... We want to make sure that our millions are so fed that their teeth are good, their digestive systems healthy, their resistance to premature old age enhanced through strong bodies and alert minds.[8]

M. L. Wilson, director of Extension for the USDA (he also served as assistant director of Defense Health and Welfare Services), offered opening remarks. He told participants, "What you decide here, and the action resulting from your recommendations ... will play an important part in the national effort to win the second World War."[9] He emphasized the need for Americans "to keep in top-notch condition all the time." Wilson summarized the perception that the nation's circumstances had shifted from food security and supply issues to a battle for American health, saying that "today we recognize that the principal need for gardens is to insure a balanced diet ... essential to have the mass human energy and morale needed to carry on total war." He also noted that the National Defense Gardening Conference was an extension of the national nutrition conference held in May, further linking the nation's nutritional defense to school, home and community gardening programs. Wilson went on to detail the success of the World War I programs and efforts, but acknowledged that there had been "some waste of effort," as gardens may have been attempted in areas where they "could not yield profitably."[10] He promised that advances in scientific knowledge and the experience gained in World War I (and from the British in the previous two years) would inform the development of a more effective program during World War II.

USDA Secretary Claude Wickard noted that Americans "must consider gardening first of all as a part of the food-production program of the Nation ... they can make a vital contribution—if they are well directed."[11] He shared with participants that "more than 6 million farm families of the Nation are now engaged in a Nation-wide program to produce Food for Freedom ... for the first time in the history of American agriculture, we have definite objectives at which we're shooting in the production of all commodities."[12] Wickard urged some caution around the topic of extending garden food production into urban areas, citing concerns about fertilizer and seed supply, and the poor soil quality that might be found in urban areas. However, he also argued for the "tremendous psychological value" of gardening and other activities during wartime. Mixed messages about how Americans—particularly those in urban areas—ought to pursue Victory gardening emerged from this conference.

John W. Studebaker tackled the topic of "The American School System and War Gardens." Like one of the USSGA's strongest advocates in World War I, P.P. Claxton, Studebaker also served as federal commissioner of education. Studebaker began his presentation by sharing personal memories of a garden he tended as a young boy in Iowa. "I learned that gardens, having been planted, must be tended; that the price of production is industry and labor," Studebaker said. He reminisced about the USSGA and other World War I gardening efforts, but made the differences between the World War national gardening programs clear.

> Then the slogan was "food will win the war".... Now the slogan is "food will help win the war and write the peace" ... then the great drive was primarily to increase the production of foodstuffs ... now the gardening phase of the "food for freedom" drive is primarily to improve the quality of home food supplies and ... increase the health and vigor of our people and of our allies. Then the major emphasis was upon thrift and conservation of family resources. Now the major emphasis seems to be on improving family nutrition.... There seems to be no immediate and pressing economic reason for the wholesale encouragement of vegetable gardening by city folk, especially in large cities."[13]

The general objective was "to increase the production and consumption of garden fruits and vegetables for building a stronger and healthier Nation." Studebaker, while minimizing the need for city gardeners, pledged the Bureau of Education's support of national defense gardening goals by promising to contribute the leadership of the Bureau of Education's vocational agriculture and home economics teachers, which numbered nearly 19,000. He felt that the Bureau of Education's "live-at-home" program, offered through its Home Economics and Agricultural Education Services unit, could provide a model by continuing to encourage farm families to produce and conserve what their families would consume. Studebaker felt that war gardens could have a place in rural communities and provide wonderful opportunities for vocational educational students in agriculture and home economics. Studebaker said that the school system's greatest role to the nation's war gardening program was not in contributing to production, but in training school students to be better consumers and improving American dietary standards and habits.

At this conference, a committee on Home, School, and Community Gardens met. Perhaps unknowingly, the very name of this particular committee demonstrated the soundness of the USSGA's policy in World War I, which had been to link school, home, and community gardening efforts. In an interesting parallel to the World War I experience, the chair of this committee was Altee Burpee, the president of Burpee Seed Company, and the cousin of Luther Burbank, who had been such a strong proponent of Liberty and Victory Gardens during the Great War. The secretary of the committee was Mrs. Julius Amberg from the Office of Civilian Defense. This committee affirmed the USSGA model by defining school gardens as a key part of national defense, and located them precisely where the USSGA had: as "those [gardens] worked by children or adults under the supervision of the school. They may be at the home, on school grounds, or on nearby land."[14]

At the outset of World War II, it was estimated that approximately 14.5 million Americans gardened.[15] There is no consensus on the percentage of Americans who engaged in Victory Garden activity during World War II (as in World War I, government efforts to conflate participation figures make it difficult to assess real gardening activity). However, there is a remarkably consistent degree of agreement among historians that World War II saw a significant increase in the consumption of fruits and vegetables on the American home front, in part because vegetables were not among rationed foods. The internment of American citizens of Japanese descent—many of them vegetable farmers—had a real (and certainly) unintended effect on home front vegetable production early in the war.[16] Victory Gardens helped make up some of that production gap. Before the end of 1943, it is estimated that there were as many as twenty million gardens in America, possibly producing 40 percent of the nation's annual consumption of vegetables.[17] This may be the period of highest fruit and vegetable consumption in American history. Like its World War I counterpart, the World War II program served as a point of mobilization for Americans, a point of common purpose that transcended race, class, and geography and proved to be multi-purposed.[18]

The World War II "Food for Freedom" gardening campaign has become a part of our collective history in this nation. It has never been argued, and there is probably no way to quantify it, but it is possible to infer that the phenomenal success of the Victory Garden campaign during World War II was partly due to the fact that many of the adults on the home front had participated in USSGA or Liberty/Victory gardening programs during World War I. These programs would have had a powerful effect on children. They empowered them, they stressed learning by doing and they made them a stakeholder in the war of all wars. Their nation needed their assistance. Their work and their potential was a valued, even necessary part of the formula for victory. Children in World War I, some would have been too old to serve in the armed forces in World War II. So they served the nation as they had been taught in a previous war: they gardened.

The Aftermath: Trajectory

In the aftermath of World War II, it was recognized by the international community that to rebuild nations, agriculture and food would be integral. This echoed the aspirations of those who had worked in the World War I gardening programs, who had expressed the hope that gardens might help rebuild nations and be a tool of peace in the post-war world. Thus, in 1945 the United Nations formed the Food and Agriculture Organization (FAO), which operates under its auspices. The goals of the FAO are simple but simultaneously lofty: to help eliminate hunger, food insecurity and malnutrition; to improve the productivity of agriculture in a way that is sustainable; to ensure inclusivity and diversity in food systems; to reduce rural poverty; and to protect those who are vulnerable from disaster. An important overarching goal of the FAO is to promote global development. The FAO is involved in activities ranging from school feeding programs to direct assistance for farmers. Its work represents a rich mix of Extension education, research, economic development and social justice. It is the sponsor of the World Food Day, which is growing in size and importance each year. It also distributes—internationally—self-irrigating gardening containers that can be set up anywhere, even on inhospitable concrete. As part of its work, it provides instruction on how to conduct effective school garden programs.

In 1946, President Harry Truman signed the National School Lunch Act into law. This created the National School Lunch Program (NSLP). The legislation is named after Richard B. Russell. The NSLP provides free and low-cost meals to American school children. It provided—and still does—a means to prop up food prices by absorbing farm surpluses. Schools receive cash reimbursements and also commodities. The NLSP sought not only to further stabilize the food system, but also to improve childhood nutrition. The legislation was driven in part by concern about the high rejection rate of draft-age men during World War II as a result of poor health. The NLSP was framed "as a measure of national security, to safeguard the health and well-being of the Nation's children and to encourage the domestic consumption of nutritious agricultural commodities" (Section 2 of the Act). The NSLP has come under much criticism for the quality of the food it provides, and it has been amended over the years. Positive changes are being made, but more changes are needed. Some of the policy questions that our nation needs to ask is whether feeding programs belong in the USDA, and also how the current structure favors the distribution of commodities from large producers in the NSLP over locally produced food. Are there other structures that might serve both producer and consumer (read: children's) interests? Childhood hunger and nutrition remained an issue even after the introduction of the NSLP, and the School Breakfast Program was piloted in 1966, and made permanent in 1975.

Each day, then, even as the nation entered a period of unprecedented prosperity in the post–World War II period, millions of American children were fed American agricultural products through the NSLP. The legislation that mandated that grand enterprise was framed in language that linked access to healthy food and good nutrition with national security. Every day, children ate food produced by American farmers. But those eating food and those working the land grew even more disconnected. By 1950, even as the UK was still rationing food as a result of World War II, and as the Cold War loomed larger, only 11 percent of Americans worked in agriculture.

One of the most important pieces of federal legislation—one that has affected the American food system and our daily lives in important ways—was the passage in 1956 of the Federal Aid Highway Act, also known as the National Interstate and Defense Highways Act (Public Law 84–627). It was the largest public works project in American history. It provided a match to states to build highway system, with the federal government providing 90 percent of the funds, and states contributing 10 percent. Eisenhower's decision to sign the legislation into law was based on his own experience as a young army officer in World War I. Eisenhower participated in the U.S. Army's motor convoy across the U.S. The purpose of the convoy was to test road readiness, and the convoy traveled on the historic Lincoln Highway (running from Times Square to San Francisco), which was the first transcontinental road across the nation. Beginning in Washington, D.C., on July 7, 1919, the convoy traveled to Pennsylvania, and then cut across the country to San Francisco, arriving about eight weeks later. On their trip, they encountered roads in disrepair, broken bridges, and poor infrastructure. Eisenhower later wrote a chapter in a book about this experience. His thinking was further influenced by experiences in

Germany during World War II, where that nation's autobahn system demonstrated a model of efficiency and effectiveness that America could not match.

There was widespread support for improved highways. The post-war economic boom in America had led to a rapid increase in car sales, and most Americans were driving on roads built before 1930. With the threats of the Cold War including nuclear bombs, Eisenhower and others were concerned with being able to safely evacuate American cities in the case of war. They also saw the economic opportunities that could arise from an improved highway system.

While the Russians launched Sputnik into space, Americans built roads and highways. This highway system, combined with post–World War II demographic shifts, the GI Bill, the growth of the defense industry, the creation of suburbs, and other cultural and social factors, contributed to the nation's growing prosperity. The growing efficiency of the highway system and cheap fossil fuels also enabled American food products to be shipped longer distances. Convenience foods—many created by wartime necessity—grew in appeal. Because travel was easier, cheaper, and more pleasant, chain motels and fast food restaurants arose along the highways, serving a nation that was becoming more car-oriented.

In 1959, the U.S. created its own version of the FAO: the Food for Peace Program (Public Law 480). Its purpose was to promote the food security of developing countries. This was—and still is—accomplished by the provision of food aid to save lives, to help people recover from crises and to support nutrition and development in impoverished countries. (In some ways, the Food for Peace Program foreshadowed the development of the Peace Corps of 1961.) In a way that was counterintuitive to the Food for Peace Program, agricultural aid and development support was a component of U.S. military involvement in Vietnam. Food, as always, was essential to national security, whether domestically, or with American interests abroad.

When I was twelve years old, I read two books that changed my life. The first was *Bury My Heart at Wounded Knee* by Dee Brown, which highlighted long-standing historical injustices relating to Native Americans. The second was *Silent Spring*, written by Rachel Carson, which had been published ten years previously, in 1962. *Silent Spring* is of course credited with beginning the modern environmental movement, although one can see impulses and aspects of that movement much earlier, in the works of early nature study proponents, such as Liberty Hyde Bailey. *Silent Spring* challenged the use of pesticides, citing damage to the environment. In the same year that *Silent Spring* was published, the USDA's collection of agricultural resources was officially organized into the National Agricultural Library, the food systems equivalent, perhaps, to the Library of Congress.

As in the Progressive Era, a variety of social impulses and movements contributed to the environmental movement, and it is nearly impossible to separate out these impulses, but they affected the food system—and food producers—in significant ways. Food and environment are, of course, inextricably linked. (Today, a popular concept to promote a sustainable food system and a sustainable natural ecosystem is a set of practices called "co-management.") In 1969, as America celebrated Neil Armstrong's walk on the moon, the Environmental Protection Act was passed, and the nation's Food and Nutrition Service (FNS) was established. A wave of legislative activity ensued. In 1970, the Environmental Protection Agency was established. Two years later saw the passage of the Clean Air Act, the Clean Water Act, the Federal Water Pollution Act, the Consumer Product Safety Act ... and the U.S. signed onto the 1952 United Nations International Plant Protection Convention. DDT was banned. The Endangered Species Act was signed in 1975. And by 1975, farmers made up less than 5 percent of the U.S. labor force.

During the social upheavals of the 1960s and 1970s, gardening remained a persistent feature, finding a new location in schools as part of the growing environmental education effort (which, again, echoed the impulses of earlier times). There was a growing interest in organic foods, and many people participated in a movement back to the land, beginning or returning to agricultural enterprises. (This is similar to what we're seeing today.)

With the heightened awareness around food and agriculture, there is no turning back, and the food system will continue to undergo transformation. There are some important questions emerging that are not being addressed, and a national conversation is needed. One emerging issue is the protection of American food production and processing capacity. This is a national security issue. Recently, China has begun the process of acquiring one of the nation's largest meat producers and processors. This should be of concern to all of us, and some in Congress spoke out in protest. But the sale has been allowed to proceed. Recently, the USDA has approved four sites in China that will be allowed to process American chicken. Poultry will be raised in the U.S., sent to China for processing, and then distributed, with some product returning to the U.S. for sale. China's track record on food safety and worker equity issues is poor, and this practice represents risks and an outsourcing model we should not allow. It is troubling.

In 1976, I drove with my father along California Highway 58, towards Bakersfield. It was a hot day, we had the windows down, and my father was observing the speed limit (as always, concerned with safety and fuel efficiency). We rode behind an older Chevrolet pick-up truck that bore a bumper sticker that read: "Agriculture Is America's Oil." Coming off the 1973–74 oil crisis, I found that a particularly resonant way to frame the issue, and I've never forgotten that day, or that moment.

As we move forward into a more transparent era vis-à-vis the food system, there will continue to be many challenges. There are also many opportunities: opportunities to ask better questions, to demand better practices, to correct systematic and systemic wrongs in the food system, and to create a food system that will sustain and enhance human health, while providing for the sustainability of producers, the environment, and providing social equity for all.

Conclusion: Demobilization, the Trajectory of the Programs, and Public Policy Implications for Today

Everyone eats. Everyone is a stakeholder in the food system. In World War I, Americans embraced the idea that they had a personal investment in producing food for the nation by participating in school, home and community garden efforts. "Food will win the war," was the slogan, and in important ways, home front food production made American wartime mobilization efforts successful, and provided models that were adopted later, during World War II. Today America fights other wars on foreign soil, and another generation struggles to reform and transform the American food system, which affects American health and productivity in myriad and important ways, and which is once again recognized as an issue of national security.

The NWGC and the USSGA

Present attempts to reform the food system could have been much less taxing had the wartime gardening programs, and the NWGC in particular, succeeded in the larger mission: creating a lasting sense of urgency and ethos surrounding gardening in America. The Liberty/Victory Garden program built on previous reform movements: nature study, vacant lot cultivation, and gardening efforts that embraced notions of urban reform and city beautification. Wartime gardening had many goals, among them education, improved nutrition and the unification of the American home front. To its proponents, gardening was not only a useful and spiritually uplifting activity that could help the nation win the war; it was also an activity some believed could help keep the peace and feed the world in a post-war era.

Win the Next War Now. Artist: Leonebel Jacobs. National War Garden Commission (1918). Draped in the flag, Columbia raises canned vegetables and offers fresh vegetables and fruits, canned and dried, as a means of winning not only the current war, but future conflicts (Museum of Ventura County, photographer Aysen Tan).

Gardens could make America a better place, helping it to live more fully into the notion of the nation as the "city on the hill," or "the new Jerusalem." The term "City Beautiful," then, might not only refer to the physical improvement of the nation's challenged cities, but could also be understood as beautifying the soul of Americans through a newly understood meaning of the term "service." Within the context of wartime, "making garden cities" embodied notions of reviving America's agrarian ideal, its producer identity, and its civic character. Gardens were also used as a means to synthesize diverse urban and rural experiences. An older social function—gardening—was revived and renewed for new circumstances, through the entirely modern methods of mass media. Gardening folkways were increasingly challenged by knowledge grounded in science, presented by experts. National, state and local networks of individuals, government agencies, and private organizations linked together in new and unique ways to achieve a common set of goals centered around increasing agricultural production through grassroots efforts.

The Liberty/Garden movement during World War I exemplifies Progressive characteristics of reform, organization, and networks of association. Through the lens of voluntary wartime gardening efforts, which represented a private-public partnership, we can see the emergence of the modern state, with its growing reach into the daily lives of American citizens; we can also see how the modern state enabled American citizens to extend their collective reach.

In many ways, the impacts of the NWGC were the most enduring of the wartime gardening programs. By engaging its citizens in the national project of war gardens, the NWGC attempted to recreate the sturdy and thrifty yeoman of America's agrarian roots, transplanting that type and ideal to an urban forum. America's new yeoman was a "city farmer."[1] As Americans face new and increasingly complex challenges with their food system today, the idea of the "city farmer" is gaining new traction under the term "urban agriculture," which is blurring the lines between understandings of gardening and agriculture.[2] A front page article in a Sunday edition of the *Los Angeles Times* in July 2011 indicates that urban "farms"—many the size of large-scale gardens—are taking root in the San Francisco Bay area, facilitated by public policies regarding zoning and food sales. For its 2011 statewide conference, the California chapter of the American Planning

Food ... don't waste it. United States Food Administration (1919). Referred to by some as "Food Commandments," this poster urges Americans to buy locally, a practice that is coming back into vogue today (Museum of Ventura County, photographer Aysen Tan).

Association received three panel proposals discussing gardening and urban agriculture.

In World War I, in addition to framing a new spatial dimension, the type and ideal of the yeoman farmer was reframed: a new prototype, the "soldier of the soil," an activist citizen gardener, emerged. (This is seen today in the impulses of programs such as the Master Gardener Program and Kitchen Gardeners International.) There is a vibrant sense of activism around today's food system projects; citizens are packing city council chambers to talk about backyard chickens and backyard farms. Increasingly, city governments—Oakland, Minneapolis, San Francisco, and others—are responding with local food-friendly policies. Detroit, which provided the prototype for urban relief gardening through its Potato Patches, has emerged again as a leader in developing novel models for urban locales. Richmond and North Richmond, California, the model of home front mobilization in World War II boasts new food production models that are engaging a new generation. (Today, Richmond is home to a National Park Service site honoring Rosie the Riveter, and the World War II Home Front National Park. Like their peers who tend the White House garden, National Park Service staff help cultivate Victory Gardens at the park site, and through community partnerships.) New prototypes for the American farmer are emerging, and they increasingly include urbanites, women, and people of color.

The NWGC and USSGA were decommissioned after the Armistice was signed. Victory editions of the organizations' materials were produced. The organizers of the NWGC and USSGA saw a need for peacetime gardens to help supply food as the world rebuilt. The abrupt shift in gardening rhetoric (from "every garden a munitions plant" to "every garden a peace plant") was apparent. There had been a sense of urgency around wartime gardening; the call to Americans to cultivate peacetime gardens did not prove as persuasive. Gardening continued, but it wasn't a national passion as it was during World War I. The notion of gardening and farming as part of utopian communities did continue to take root in the idea of agricultural colonies that appeared in some places during the post-war period, although they were short-lived. The colonies at Durham and Delhi were an effort to improve rural life in the state of California, which enacted a Land Settlement Act in 1917. Goals of the legislation were multifold and included organizing land settlements and creating model rural communities, using scientific agriculture, and reducing tenant farming. Because it was deemed a success, Progressive reformers turned their eyes to another audience ripe for reform: returning soldiers. A second colony at Delhi was initiated, but never achieved full success.[3] As in the USSGA and WLAA efforts in California, the University of California played a role, with Berkeley professor Elwood Mead (later to be a driving force behind some of the West's largest water projects) providing input based on his experiences abroad. The same idea is finding expression today in communities such as Serenebe, a newly emerging planned community outside of Atlanta, which emphasizes sustainability and features a community organic farm and restaurants that are supplied by that farm. A back-to-land movement swept the nation during the 1960s and early 1970s; a similar movement is occurring again, today.

Americans turned again to gardening in the hard times of the Great Depression. The Depression Era saw the return of all sorts of gardening models located at homes, at schools and throughout communities. They reached the height of popularity early in the Depression years.[4] Gardening during this era was not collected into a national movement with a single programmatic name, like the Liberty/Victory Garden program during World War I, but was a vital activity in many communities.[5] The federal government viewed the activity as significant: it provided some funding for gardening work, and it tracked gardening data through the Federal Emergency Relief Administration. The Extension Service and other organizations provided gardening information to support the nation's citizens.

A national Victory Garden Program returned in 1941; it included school, home, community and workplace gardens. A mere twelve days after the bombing of Pearl Harbor, the USDA and the Federal Security Administration convened the National Defense Gardening Conference in Washington, D.C. That two federal agencies convened this conference, selected the participants, aggregated the recommendations and issued the proceedings, showed clearly how the American state had developed during the interwar years. The Liberty Garden program of World War I, driven by citizens and private organizations with governmental support, was in World War II managed by one of the largest, most powerful and certainly most pervasive agencies in the federal government. The location of the movement had changed; so had the message. The food supply was secure: supplementing agricultural production through home food production was no longer a primary goal. American nutrition was critical, "good food" vital.

Recommendations from the National Defense Gardening Conference were divided into sections that covered farm vegetable gardens; farm fruit gardens; conservation and preservation of fruits and vegetables; home, school and community gardens; conservation of lawns, flowers and shrubs; and educational materials and techniques.[6] There was a strong emphasis in the conference proceedings on human health: on improving it and maintaining it through healthy food habits, including the increased consumption of fruits and vegetables.[7] While there was concern expressed about the anxiety citizens might feel about the possibility of food shortages, "nutritional defense" was a stronger theme. Recommendations called for more gardens ... and "better" gardens.[8]

One of the recommendations that changed history involved the suggestion to change the program's name from the "Defense Garden" to the "Victory Garden Program."[9] The Victory Garden program of World War II proved iconic, and has engaged the imagination of many today, who seek to transform the nation's food system, one garden at a time. Everyone gardened, or knew someone who did.

Where Gardens Lead Us

Gardens lead us places. As a garden-based educator, I have seen people move from gardens into greater engagement with their food system. I jokingly refer to gardening as "the gateway drug to the food system," but there is much truth to this statement. Gardens lead to heightened interest in the food system. In World War I and World War II, there was a call for more gardens. For better gardens. Buried in the quickly organized conference proceedings from World War II were public policy recommendations that would make sense today. They included providing funding and credit to help purchase gardening supplies and equipment, and adopting policies that would provide "adequate productive land for gardens for tenants."[10]

There are modern-day correspondents to the Liberty and Victory Garden programs of World War I and World War II, but sadly, they remain the rarity and not the norm. In February 2009, the USDA launched its People's Garden Initiative, celebrating the biennial of President Abraham Lincoln's birth, and promoting the development of gardens. The flagship People's Garden blooms outside the entrance to the Department of Agriculture's historic Whitten Building. This is sacred space on the National Mall. It is an organic garden. Urban 4-H members, part of a Junior Master Gardener program, volunteer to work in the garden, as children who enlisted in the USSGA program volunteered to work in the nation's gardens nearly one hundred years ago. As part of the People's Garden Initiative, Agriculture Secretary Tom Vilsack has called for all the department's agencies to create gardens and adopt sustainability measures. There have been days when the USDA cafeteria has served local food; it has also incorporated into its menu some of the herbs grown onsite. The USDA is not only talking the talk, but walking the walk with this garden and these efforts: early one morning, as I was headed to the USDA for a meeting, I ran into Bob Snieckus, the National Landscape Architect, putting in a little volunteer time before work.

However, the USDA's People's Garden Initiative has missed an opportunity to provide a grand gesture to the American public. It has been undersold to the public, and for many involved in advocating for gardens, the efforts have fallen woefully short of the emphatic appeal of World War I and World War II programs, the sort of appeal that could move gardening forward again as a national interest, an imperative, even.

There are food gardens cropping up in other public spaces. One month after the People's Garden broke ground on the national mall, First Lady Obama initiated a gardening effort on the South Lawn of the White House. She has used this garden to launch a White House food initiative that is tackling childhood nutrition and obesity. She has shared her family's personal story about food. The food produced in the White House Garden feeds the first family, has been used in official functions and is also shared with Washington, D.C., food banks.

I had the privilege of visiting the White House Garden in September 2009. I stood on the South Lawn with a group of good food friends, eating a sun-warmed Sun Gold tomato, marveling at the fact that this was the first food-producing garden at our nation's first house since the World War II Victory Garden program. The White House Garden is highly visible to the public, and I think its presence at our First House says wonderful things about our nation. I revisited the White House Garden again in October 2012 as part of a tweet-up; the garden has matured and grown more productive in the ensuing years. Its power to inspire awe and patriotism in visitors remains undiminished, and everyone I know who has visited has been profoundly moved by the experience.

Like many in the food systems movement, I credit the existence of this garden not only to the progressive views of the first lady, but also to a quiet gardener from Maine, Roger Doiron. The founder of Kitchen Gardeners International, Doiron was the person who started a social media campaign to encourage the winner of the 2008 presidential election to plant a garden on the South Lawn. Supported in his work by a cohort of the Kellogg Foundation's Food and Society Policy Fellows, and by thousands of other Americans, Doiron successfully got the word out that food gardening was not only an activity suitable for our homes (in particular, at his little white house in Maine), but also an activity we wanted to see at our nation's first house, the somewhat larger White House located at 1600 Pennsylvania Avenue NW in Washington, D.C.

The first lady has also encouraged the opening of a new farmers' market near the White House. She is engaged in the farm-to-school movement. Inspired by the first lady's work, a new campaign to encourage the First Houses in each state—governor's residences—to plant vegetable gardens is underway. In California, First Lady Maria Shriver had such a garden planted at the Governor's mansion in Sacramento.

There are other indications that older, successful models are returning.

The Extension Service, which has been a primary driver of scientific agriculture in the nation, has in some places hired staff to work in positions called "food shed coordinators," a term remarkably similar in name to the World War I food administrators, who helped assess and manage local food needs and supply. The University of California's Agriculture and Natural Resources Division (UC ANR), and home of that state's Cooperative Extension Service, is currently hiring academics to work as food systems advisors and metropolitan agricultural specialists. ANR has also funded through its internal grants program proposals focusing on work in urban agriculture, CSAs, edible landscape, and small farms. In May 2013, UC's flagship agricultural campus, located in Berkeley, launched an inter-disciplinary Food Institute seeking to transform the food system. It is sponsored by four campus departments: The Goldman School of Public Policy, the graduate school of Journalism, the College of Natural Resources, and Berkeley's Boalt Law School. UC Davis—named the "number one agricultural college in the world"—has an Agricultural Sustainability Institute, and recently launched an undergraduate major in that discipline. Students are enrolling in droves, and flocking to work at the student farm located on the campus. An apprentice program at the UC Santa Cruz campus that equips individuals to farm in small-scale, organic operations is turning out a few dozen new farmers each year; it also recently received a major grant from the USDA's Beginning Farmers and Ranchers Program. While most of UC's work remains focused on what some term "industrialized" agriculture, in fact, the institution supports all scales and modes of agricultural production, including school, home and community gardeners. Abraham Lincoln might be very proud of the kinds of work land grant institutions are engaging in more than 150 years after the enactment of the Morrill Land Grant Act.

Traces of the USSGA can be seen in today's robust and ever-growing school garden movement, which is bearing fruit all over the nation. While not mandating the instruction of gardening in its public schools, the State of California passed legislation in the form of Assembly Bill 1535 in 2006, which provided $15 million for school gardening efforts. Oregon passed House Bill (HB) 2800, the Farm to School and School Garden Bill. There are other legislative examples that show the movement has made progress. But across the nation, current public budget difficulties represent a challenge to school garden efforts and their sustainability. In some places, school garden efforts are in retreat, due to increased class size, lack of volunteer and financial resources, and increased demands on teachers to improve student performance on national, standardized tests; it is my deeply held hope that in those places, that trend will reverse.

This is a Sputnik moment for America in terms of science achievement and our future. The future is about feeding eight billion people in 2025, with fewer resources, less political stability, and an unpredictable climate. Gardens can lead us places, and they can lead us, in part, to solutions that will help feed the world.

We should garden in schools more: many studies indicate that school gardens can improve academic achievement in science, among other things. Where space and other factors permit, we should develop school farms. The farm-to-school movement is strong and growing, and where these programs incorporate school gardening efforts and classroom education in gardening and nutrition, they are at their best. One prime example is the Edible Schoolyard, Alice Waters' showcase project in Berkeley, California; there are others, as well, including the farm-to-school program in my community of Ventura, and also in another California community, Davis.

A talented team of Extension educators at Texas A&M University has developed a standards-based gardening curriculum called the 4-H Junior Master Gardener program (JMG) that has been adopted by the National 4-H Council for use nationwide in its youth programs. The program is also taught internationally. 4-H's JMG program teaches across the curriculum, touching on all aspects of science, environment, mathematics, reading, language arts, and nutrition, and also engages youth in community service activities. Youth also need to learn the vital life skill of cooking and preparing food. Individuals such as chef Ann Cooper, the self-styled "renegade lunch lady," work to provide that piece of the puzzle. We have curriculum, engaged communities and a deep need for gardens: what we lack is a mandate by the Department of Education to teach this rich, multi-purposed topic in our nation's public schools.

There is a population of young volunteers eager to support school garden work. The newly initiated AmeriCorps Food Corps program is placing college-aged volunteers in communities to support school garden efforts; the program has just completed its third year of work. The Food Corps program was conceptualized and brought to life by two young activists determined to transform part of the food system: Debra Eschmeyer, a farmer from Ohio and an expert in farm-to-school programs, and filmmaker Curt Ellis ("King Corn"). Like Doiron, the gardener from Maine, both Eschmeyer and Ellis are former Kellogg Foundation Food and Society Policy Fellows. The Food Corps program is already proving to be a successful model, and should be strongly supported and expanded. The school garden battle is one battle Americans can't afford to lose in the larger campaign for a sustainable food system. Healthy citizens are a nation's greatest resource, only one reason that it is imperative that the federal government mandate a spiraled curriculum from K-12 teaching every youth enrolled in America's public schools about the food system and agriculture, healthy living, and environmental sustainability. Every student. Every year. Ideally, every day.

Unlike the NWGC and USSGA, the modern correspondents of Ambler and the WLAA—discussed only briefly in this book—are less clear. But they are present. Across the nation, women are returning to farming, coming back to the land, sometimes after generations away. Many are choosing to specialize in small-scale ventures with community and consumer connections through farmers markets, community supported agriculture and other local food projects. Many women producers are hewing to organics and notions of sustainability. Some of this work appears to draw from the deep civic connections and reform values expressed in earlier gardening movements, such as the Garden City movement. One of these women is my friend Lisa Kivirist, a small-scale organic farmer, innkeeper, and author who lives in Wisconsin with her husband, John Ivanko, and their son, Liam. Kivirist represents an important demographic for the future of American farming: she is a woman, and she is from an urban setting.

Per the most recent United States Census of Agriculture, the number of women farmers has increased nearly 30 percent. More resources are needed to support this movement. The Rural Women's Project (RWP) a venture of the Midwest Organic and Sustainable Education Service (MOSES)—and a project Kivirist works on—advocates for the needs of small-scale female producers. RWP received a 2012 Top Rural Development Initiative Award from Wisconsin Rural Partners on behalf of the program's innovative approaches to women farmer training and outreach.

In Ventura County, where I live, fourth generation farmer Paul DeBusschere and his wife, Julie Morris (an Episcopal priest and self-termed "aspiring farmer"), grow food on the Oxnard Plain, which boasts some of the richest and most productive agricultural land in the world. They secured grant and other funding to create a project called "The Farm," which is linked with the California State University's (CSU) Abundant Table ministry at CSU's Channel Islands campus. DeBusschere and Morris were able to provide housing, health insurance, a small stipend and the gift of farming to young interns. In the first year of the program, all of the interns were female. These young women, predominantly from urban and suburban backgrounds, learned about organic farming, small-scale agricultural operations, how to work at farmer's markets and how to operate a community supported agricultural project. They connected several times weekly with the people for whom they grew food. They kept chickens and lived simply in community together, without men (much like members of the WLAA did, nearly a century ago). None had a degree in "agriculture" from a land grant university. But each of them became, at least for that year, a farmer. They were Cristina Rose Smith, Casey Hopkins, Katerina Friesen, Erynn Smith and Sarah Bagge. They worked with chaplain Sarah Nolan, farmer Paul DeBusschere and his wife, farmer and priest Julie

Morris.[11] Members of the new crop of interns now grow food for Ventura Unified School District's farm-to-school program on land leased from the University of California Hansen Agricultural Center in Santa Paula.

The success of the Abundant Table project has led to other faith-based projects that will have an enormous impact. Bishop Jon Bruno, leader of the Episcopal Diocese of Los Angeles, recently launched an initiative called "Seeds of Hope." The goal is to cultivate wellness in the six counties that the Diocese serves, and to address social justice issues such as hunger, food access, and health disparities. Three million people within the diocesan boundaries are food insecure; the Episcopal Church has great hopes to help meet some of that need through its vision of "farming the diocese" (gardening, urban agriculture, and small-scale farming enterprises). In the next year, the diocese will be conducting a survey of its 139 congregations and dozens of other institutions (including schools, a medical clinic and a children's home) to survey assets that would support this initiative. But work is already being done. An urban orchard has been planted next to a food pantry. A vineyard has been planted at a parish. A parish kitchen is completing certification that will enable it to be used for commercial food production. And young farmers are trained through a church program based in Ventura County.

And these young farmers are needed. Across the nation, farmers are aging, raising the vital question: From where will the next generation of farmers come? Certainly, their ranks will include many women. Again, that is occurring now. The USDA produces an extraordinary amount of data; it conducts a census of national agriculture every five years, twice as frequently as the federal government conducts a census of people. The USDA reported that in 2007 the percentage of American farms with female principal operators nationwide was nearly fourteen percent.[12] In areas of the Northeast and the Southwest, West and Pacific Northwest (and to a lesser extent, areas in the mid–Atlantic), the percentage of women working the land as principal operators is much greater: twenty percent to twenty-five percent, and even higher. While women-only horticultural schools like Ambler will likely never exist again, the role of women in agriculture will continue, and will continue to grow. Internationally, improving the status of women, providing access to education and land and credit, will be vital to assuring the global food supply in the years to come.

In some ways, this book is about memory. The women who worked at Ambler, located in the Philadelphia food shed, are not forgotten. I recently visited Wyck, in the Germantown neighborhood of Philadelphia, where Jane Bowne Haines encouraged other women to claim a place through the act of growing food. The day I visited, a few dozen people had gathered outside to share locally grown food, talk about gardening, past and present, and discuss how history was combining with current practice to create new food sheds. It was about connections and relationships in the food system, learning what from the past could inform the present.

Philadelphia is a city with a long gardening memory and a distinguished botanical history. Historical and contemporary models of gardens of all sizes abound in public, private and shared spaces. The oldest rose garden in the United States (defined as remaining true to its original plan and created in 1824) is located at Wyck, where heritage roses bloom for the thousands of visitors utilizing the site each year. What is probably the oldest botanical garden in the United States, Bartram's Garden, sits serenely on the banks of the Schuylkill River, directly adjacent to a public housing project. It was the home of Quaker John Bartram, citizen farmer, citizen scientist, explorer, who had little formal education but came to be regarded as one of the greatest American botanists.

Early each spring, Philadelphia holds a flower show that serves as a community focal point and draws international attention. In 2005, as part of this important event, Temple University—Ambler developed an exhibit honoring the work of Progressive women in horticulture. Women who peopled the Ambler story, including Jane Haines, Mira Lloyd Dock, Louisa Yeoman King and Elizabeth Leighton Lee were featured. The exhibit was entered in the Flower Show's educational category and featured three living garden vignettes—including a World War I Liberty garden—to signify the individual and collective achievement of these women.

It won the best of show.

Food Access and Security

We are a hungry nation. Among the statistics the USDA collects and analyzes are those numbers that gauge America's hunger and assess food security or insecurity. The numbers are shocking. For many of us working in the realm of food systems, gardens represent a strategy to increase community-based food security and improve human health and nutrition. Access to food is emerging as a basic human right across the globe. This is not only a moral issue, but also an important political consideration; empires rise and fall on food, and food insecurity is a destabilizing force in geopolitical terms.

Former Irish president Mary Robinson is a leading champion of the notion of food as a human right, and is working tirelessly to promote this and the urgent need to address climate change. The United States State Department views hunger and food security as a vital political issue; it sponsors a global initiative in this area, and is also leading a Feed the Future program, which is working with underdeveloped nations to increase food security and

Hunger. Artist: Henry Raleigh (1880–1945). United States Food Administration (1917). The plight of starving Europeans is dramatically depicted in this poster, which pleads with Americans to consume less meat, sugar, and fats so that Allies may receive more aid (Museum of Ventura County, photographer Aysen Tan).

improve human nutrition by helping communities feed themselves. Gardens are a part of this effort.

On a smaller scale, programs such as Cultivate Iowa, an initiative of the Iowa Food Systems Council's Food Access and Health Work Group (FAHWG), strive to promote the benefits of food gardening and produce donations to food pantries and other community organizations. The project's coordinators, Angie Tagtow and Elizabeth Danforth Richey, assessed the perspectives of all those who might be effected by food gardening and produce donations (including potential recipients), to develop a holistic understanding of how individuals, households, organizations, communities and social factors influence gardening in Iowa. Community organizer Jenga Mwendo, founder of the Backyard Gardeners Network, uses gardening and urban agriculture as a tool for increasing food security, community building, neighborhood revitalization and cultural preservation in New Orleans' Ninth Ward. Like Tagtow, Mwendo is also a former Kellogg Fellow.

As hunger remains a persistent issue in the nation, lack of food access is inextricably tied to food quality. Some of the nation's largest corporations have committed millions of dollars to fight hunger. While this is laudable in some ways, activist and community food security expert and former Kellogg Fellow Andy Fisher has a different take on the topic, seeing hunger as a result of public policies such as a stagnant minimum wage, right to work laws, lack of affordable housing, and the effects of globalization. Hunger, Fisher argues, is not a societal problem to be addressed through charity, but rather a reflection of injustice, exploitation, racism and historical and structural inequities. Fisher argues that while we me may be managing hunger (arguably with limited success), we may be moving further away from eliminating it by failing to address its root causes. When Wal-Mart embarks upon a major social media campaign to raise funds for food banks, attention is driven away from Wal-Mart's questionable employment practices, which result in low wages and employees who qualify for programs such as SNAP. Fisher's work is interesting, and holds much promise. Certainly, models such as Cultivate Iowa could help to change this dynamic by creating more resiliency in local communities through the development of gardening efforts that explicitly link with food pantries.

Some have stated that much of the work in the sustainable food systems is reminiscent of the Civil Rights movement. It is, and I would take that one step further: it is a continuation of that impulse.

Ten Recommendations

There are ten things Americans could do immediately that would help transform the food system. Many of these recommendations are based in historical practice. These are teachable moments in our nation's history, but also actionable moments.

1. **Encourage a gardening ethos at all levels, incorporating policy, practice and demonstrating personal value.**
   To paraphrase Gandhi, be the change you want to see in the food system. Buy locally grown, when possible. Know your local farmer ... you'll know a lot more about your food and your community. Eat seasonally

more often. Grow a row for the hungry. Participate in a community gardening activity. Move your backyard garden and make it a front yard garden. Claim an unused space in your community and grow it. Share your gardening skills with youth in your community, at a school or an after-school program, through a church youth group. Volunteer to grow container vegetables at a senior facility. Hearken back to our roots and learn how to preserve what you grow. Think sustainability. Use the World War I and World War II Victory Garden model to enable gardens to move us forward.

While the topic is not covered in enough length in this book, Americans must also focus on food conservation and preservation, and on reducing food waste. The amount of food waste in our nation is staggering; simply reducing that could help address at least part of the nation's hunger issue. World War I and World War II models of food conservation and preservation programs provide a clear roadmap on how to accomplish this task. The Cooperative Extension Service is seeing growing interest in its Master Food Preserver Program, which equips volunteers to train others in communities on food preservation methods, with a strong focus on safety. This kind of expertise and capacity should be developed and available in every American community.

2. **Be radical—and intentional—about land use and zoning policies that support gardening and urban agriculture.**

    Learn more about policies in your community relating to land use, backyard chickens, farm-to-school, etc. Learn more about your local food shed—or begin mapping it using Google maps. Help start—or participate in—a food policy council. (For information on food policy councils, visit the website of the former Community Food Security Coalition at www.foodsecurity.org.) Again, historical models can inform current public policy. We need to create a new understanding of the commons, and the benefits that might accrue to the nation. Look at models such as the Los Angeles Food Policy Council, or food policies developed by cities such as Portland and Minneapolis. Find models that might work in your community, and try to replicate them.

3. **Encourage the development of local, regional, state, and federal policies that support gardening and urban agriculture—and the next generation of farmers.**

    Food is a political issue (in addition to being an economic, social and cultural issue). Vote with your fork. It's a short distance from your plate to your politics. A sustainable food system ought to be part of every political platform, because a sustainable food system is all about children, families, communities, health, food access, economics, green jobs, sustainability and national security. Become a food voter. Insist that every individual running for local, state or national elected office have a food platform. A school board candidate could be asked his or her position on farm-to-school, healthy snacks, and school gardens. A city council candidate could be queried about his or her receptiveness to urban agriculture projects. A state candidate should make known his or her commitment to fully implementing federal programs such as SNAP, and how as a legislator he or she will support sustainable food systems and agriculture at the state level. Candidates for federal office should provide a food platform that clearly explains their position on every aspect of the Farm Bill, and also how they feel about investment in public research and science that support a sustainable food system.

4. **Make nutrition—particularly childhood nutrition—a national priority. Really this time.**

   For decades and decades and decades, American public policy has dealt in fits and starts with the pressing issue of childhood nutrition. While millions of public school students have had access to school lunch through the National School Lunch Act (signed into federal law by President Harry Truman in 1946), and through earlier programs offered by the Works Project Administration, the reality is that much of the food served in our nation's public schools is not of high quality. Other childhood nutrition programs emerged as part of the Great Society domestic program agenda of President Lyndon Johnson; the Childhood Nutrition Act passed in 1966 is the prime example. President Obama signed legislation in 2010 designed to improve the school lunch program and food assistance programs for children and families. These programs have worked, in part, but much, much more is needed. The money provided to local school districts for feeding programs is inadequate. While free and reduced lunch programs assure that the neediest students receive breakfast and lunch (even if the quality is not always the highest), access is not assured during school breaks and over summer in all places. During those periods, students may experience hunger. *A nation that does not address hunger and does not place an emphasis on childhood nutrition risks its national security and its economic future.*

   Mission: Readiness, a non-partisan advocacy organization comprised of former military leaders, has conducted studies that indicate that the number one reason that youth fail in their quest to join the armed forces is because of obesity. This organization views childhood nutrition as an issue paramount to national security. America brought food to the world's table in both World War I and World War II. It's time to bring better food to our own table, to make an investment in agriculture, food system infrastructure and new food system models, models that will more adequately support the health and well being of children, families and communities. Inadequate childhood nutrition can lead to developmental delays. A hungry child has more difficulty learning. This has implications for workforce preparation. Because food access is not only a factor in hunger, but also perversely, a strong factor in childhood obesity, access to not enough food or to poor quality food threatens our health. Think of the economic impacts. Think of the social impacts.

Want to realize a solvent national healthcare system? It is something our nation will never be able to achieve while obesity affects nearly ⅓ of our children. In 2007, it was estimated that the total costs of treating Type II diabetes in the United States was $174 billion (calculate that in today's healthcare dollars). That not only included direct medical treatment, but the costs of disability, work loss, and premature mortality. Childhood nutrition is a moral issue, a social issue, an economic issue and an issue of national security: we must treat it as a national priority. Real national security comes from investing in the health of children, families and communities, and by investing in the production of healthy food.

Americans also need to shift their thinking to an understanding that maintaining a healthy lifestyle is an obligation of citizenship. What I put in my mouth affects you, and our nation. Every food choice matters.

5. Explicitly link school lunch programs with school and community-based gardening efforts and local food projects.

I volunteered in school garden efforts for many years. My single largest frustration was the inability to take what was produced in the garden and serve it in the school cafeteria. While some programs, such as The Edible Schoolyard, have been designed to overcome the barriers—and while farm-to-school efforts may link certain schools and districts with local food projects—there are too many barriers to moving food from the garden into the cafeteria. While food safety is a legitimate concern, common sense policies could—and should—be developed that would make it easier to accomplish this goal.

6. Reconsider certain food acquisition policies for public institutions.

In areas where it is feasible, public institutions should examine whether purchasing locally produced items may be in the best interest of the community, the institution, and the taxpayers. Farm-to-school and farm-to-institution programs at hospitals, prisons and schools can capture dollars for the local economy. They can also provide fresher (and thus more appealing and nutritious) fruits and vegetables to recipients. The Portland public school system currently procures more than 30 percent of the food in its farm-to-school from local sources. That's a significant economic impact for that community.

7. **Begin actively coordinating local food sheds.**

In World War I, Herbert Hoover's Food Administration utilized local food administrators to encourage gardening and food conservation measures at the community level. We ought to do this again today. Every citizen and every local, county, regional and state government ought to have an idea of where the community's food comes from, and should also have a mitigation plan should a natural or man-made disaster occur. We've learned from tragedies such as Hurricane Katrina the dangers of being under-prepared for emergencies. Mapping local food shed—knowing what food is available, where food is grown or might be grown—is vital. With the widespread availability of mobile devices and free social technologies, mapping is becoming easier. Begin with a small Google maps project mapping farmers markets, local farms, and businesses that source locally. Raising awareness about where our food comes from and how it is distributed in our communities may lead to a better understanding of our national food system and food policies, including trade policies. As the world food market grows ever more volatile, access to food supplies will grow even more important. What we don't know can hurt us. Start small, but start somewhere.

8. **Embark upon a fundamental restructuring of agricultural and food policies and the USDA.**

This includes *not* referring to fruits and vegetables as "Specialty Crops." Shouldn't life-giving fruits and vegetables be considered among the most special crops? The policies developed during the New Deal (and before) have not kept pace with new realities and changes in the food system. Current policies privilege certain commodities and certain geographic regions of the United States, and also certain special interests. America's energy policy (or lack of it) plays into this dynamic. We need policies and programs that diversify an aggregated food system, programs that rebuild infrastructure and processing capacity at the local level, programs that draw new, young farmers into agriculture, and policies that work for all scales of agriculture, from a one-acre urban farm to a massive corporate farm.

The question ought to be asked: is there an inherent conflict of interest in federal feeding programs being housed with agricultural programs? We need people to help us find "food truth," to ask challenging questions, and to provoke difficult discussion on complex issues, to help people think beyond their plates.

That's where people such as Melinda Hemmelgarn, a registered dietitian, free-lance writer, award-winning columnist, and radio host come in. Known as "the food sleuth," Hemmelgarn enables alternative and new voices to be heard. Independent scholars such as Raj Patel (he is also a best-selling author and food systems activist) and Ricardo Salvador (Union of Concerned Scientists) play a vital role in helping us critically examine food issues.

9. **Read the Farm Bill and the Child Nutrition Reauthorization Act.**
   The next Farm Bill (actually the Food, Conservation, and Energy Act of 2008) was slated for passage in 2012. It is one of the largest and most-encompassing omnibus bills handled by the United States Congress. The Farm Bill provides the primary agriculture and food policy tools for the United States government. The Farm Bill affects food and nutrition programs, trade policy, environmental efforts, rural development, farm credit, conservation and numerous other aspects of our daily life. It is usually a hotly contested bill, and with the ideological divides present in Congress, Farm Bill discussions seem destined to open up loud—and real—conversations that expose the deep divides in American political and cultural life. These discussions focus more on political ideology (poverty as pathology, cutting the social safety net for poorer Americans, etc.). Elected officials that seek to protect the special interests of the states they represent also dominate the narrative. Lobbyists who seek to further the agendas of the organizations that pay their salaries are equally guilty of failing to see the larger picture. These ideological discussions seldom involve calm and reasoned assessment of the value and impacts of the policies the Farm Bill codifies into law for the entire nation. If politicians won't engage in the critical activity of examining food and agricultural policy, citizens must.

10. **Develop—and mandate—a national curriculum that educates youth about food systems, environment, healthy lifestyle and nutrition.**
    When we fail to educate them about the food system, we leave all children behind. Make food systems education simultaneously a grassroots effort (involving people in communities), a goal of private enterprises (sustainable food systems enhance economic growth), and a series of nationally and locally driven governmental initiatives (public pol-

icy). The need is there. The curriculum is there. Volunteers from the Food Corps and the Master Gardener programs stand ready to assist. What is needed is political will. Any national core curriculum should have at its heart an educational purpose that focuses on the most fundamental of things: food.

I am a Victory Grower. If you are reading this book, it is likely that you are, too. As we imagine where gardens can lead us, as we imagine a sustainable food system that promotes health and equity, I am reminded again of the words Henry Agard Wallace wrote at the outset of World War II, words that exhorted Americans to consider the role they could play in the nation's food system and to engage in the act of growing Victory Gardens for their families, for their communities, for their nation: "On a foundation of good food we can build anything. Without it we can build nothing."

A Final Note

Sometimes, historians experience moments in which abstraction becomes reality, when past fuses with present into something mystical, something greater than the sum of its parts.

It is May 2012. I am part of a group invited to eat dinner at the home of John Ager, uncle by marriage to my friend and colleague Fred Bahnson. Bahnson leads Wake Forest University's new and innovative Food, Faith and Religious Leadership Initiative, which is housed in that college's School of Divinity. Bahnson is a theologian, an author, and an agricultural producer. Bahnson's wife, Elizabeth Bahnson (a well-known and gifted musician), is Mr. Ager's niece.

We have spent the day visiting Anathoth Community Garden (a church-based ministry that Bahnson co-founded in 2005). Anathoth's mission is "cultivating peace by using regenerative agriculture to connect people with their neighbors, the land, and God." A garden seems a most appropriate place to do this kind of work: after all, the Gospel of John tells Christians that Mary Magdalene mistook the risen Jesus for a gardener. *A gardener.* At Anathoth, food for those in need is cultivated, and the notion of first fruits prevails ... the first and best is given to those in need. Not the gleanings: the first and best. This is a theology I can believe in, but to see it in practice is deeply moving.

Later that day, we visit two farms owned by the Ager family. I am humbled by the family's deep commitment to stewardship of the land, and also by the vibrant network of relationships they have built with members of their community. It is an environment filled with respect for the land, respect for the dignity of labor, and with love and passion for the sacred act of growing food, family,

This is what GOD gives us. Artist: A. Hendee. America's great bounty is depicted along with a reminder that by eating less wheat, meat, sugar, and fats, Americans could provide suffering European citizens with more of those staples (Museum of Ventura County, photographer Aysen Tan).

and community. It is an environment that sees what is good and what is possible, and acts upon it. The closeness of this large and extended family is palpable. They value their land, they value their work, and they value one another.

We have been invited to eat a gourmet meal al fresco at John Ager's home, a meal prepared with food produced by several local farms, including two owned by younger family members, farms we visited that day. Mr. Ager lives with his family at Sherrill's Inn, near Asheville, North Carolina. The Inn served as a tavern and stagecoach stop between 1834 and 1909; its initial log structure dates back to 1806. The house is listed on the National Register of Historic

Places. The property came into the Ager family generations ago, and although it is a private residence, the tradition of hospitality continues. We drink beverages standing on the expansive porch, with its view of verdant fields, forests, and the Smoky Mountains. It is stunningly beautiful. I stand quietly at the railing, looking out. I am in awe of the landscape, the hospitality, the sense of timelessness, the experiences of the day.

The house is rich in history; ordinary, modern day items are mixed in with artifacts of great historical significance. Mr. Ager shares family stories and indulges every question the group can offer. He shows us around the house. People wander off. I am drawn deeper into the heart of the home.

In a small back room, one can see portions of the original log cabin; it has been integrated into the larger structure of the home. The room is dimly lit, but it feels alive, and I can imagine the many lives that intersected here. I stand quietly and feel time wash over me: the days, the years, the decades, the more than two centuries of history resident here, the jumble of experiences, the ordinary and sacred things in all our lives. It is a dizzying experience and I take it all in. I spy a small table, with an old photograph album lying upon it. I ask Mr. Ager: "May I look at this?" He is delighted that I am interested, and encourages me to look through its pages. As I turn the aged pages gently, I find two photographs of a World War I Victory Garden, a garden that was grown by ancestors of this family, at this place, as part of the national expression of service to America during a time of national crisis. Faded, but beautifully penned handwriting proclaims: "Our Victory Garden." I am breathless.

Our work in gardens is eternal.

Chapter Notes

Introduction

1. Charles Lathrop Pack, *The War Garden Victorious: Its War Time Need and Its Economic Value in Peace* (Philadelphia: J.B. Lippincott, 1919).
2. Herbert Hoover was appointed by President Woodrow Wilson to lead the newly-formed Food Administration. He organized aspects of the agricultural and food system and encouraged voluntary food conservation and production efforts that targeted nearly every American. See David M. Kennedy, *Over Here: The First World War and American Society* (London: Oxford University Press, 1980) and George H. Nash, *The Life of Herbert Hoover: Master of Emergencies, 1917–1918* (New York: W.W. Norton, 1996). Contemporary accounts of the success of the war garden program (reported by the program's organizers) estimated "conservatively" 5,285,000 war gardens in cultivation. See Charles Lathrop Pack, *The War Garden Victorious: Its War Time Need and Its Economic Value in Peace* (Philadelphia: J.B. Lippincott, 1919), 15. Due to wartime propaganda, it is likely that the statistics provided by Pack and others are somewhat inaccurate. As a result of a number of mobilization efforts, the United States was able to ship 23 million metric tons of food to European allies. See William C. Mullendore, *History of the United States Food Administration, 1917–1919* (Stanford: Stanford University Press, 1941), 41.
3. Amy Bentley, *Eating for Victory: Food Rationing and the Politics of Domesticity* (Urbana: University of Illinois Press, 1998). While Bentley's study focuses on World War II, she provides information about World War I programs. A recent study focusing on Minnesota during World War I is provided by Rae Katherine Eighmey, *Food Will Win the War: Minnesota Crops, Cooks, and Conservation During World War I* (St. Paul: Minnesota Historical Society Press, 2010).
4. John Dewey, "The Social Possibilities of War," 1918. Published under the title "What Are We Fighting For?" *The Independent*, June 22, 1918.
5. Themes of transformation and transition during the Progressive Era that have influenced this work are discussed in the following: David B. Danbom, *The Resisted Revolution: Urban America and the Industrialization of Agriculture, 1900–1930* (Ames: Iowa State University Press, 1979); Eldon Eisenach, *The Lost Promise of Progressivism.* (Lawrence: University Press of Kansas, 1994); Daniel T. Rodgers, "In Search of Progressivism," *Reviews in American History* 10 (1982): 113–32; Robert Wiebe, *The Search for Order 1877–1920* (New York: Hill & Wang, 1967); Robert Wiebe, *Self-Rule: A Cultural History of American Democracy* (Chicago: University of Chicago Press, 1995).
6. Dewey, "The Social Possibilities of War."

Chapter One

1. Alissa Hamilton was a 2008–2009 Food and Society Policy fellow. She is the author of *Squeezed: What You Don't Know About Orange Juice* (New Haven: Yale University Press, 2009).
2. The entire report may be accessed free of charge at the National Gardening Association website, www.garden.org.
3. See Adam Hochschild, *To End All Wars: A Story of Loyalty and Rebellion, 1914–1918* (Boston: Houghton Mifflin Harcourt, 2011); David M. Kennedy, *Over Here: The First World War and American Society* (London: Oxford University Press, 1980); William E. Leuchtenburg, *The Perils*

of Prosperity 1914–1932 (Chicago: University of Chicago Press, 1958); G.J. Meyer, *A World Undone: The Story of the Great War, 1914–1918* (New York: Bantam Dell, 2006).

4. Robert C. Williams, *Fordson, Farmall, and Poppin' Johnny: A History of the Farm Tractor and Its Impact on America* (Urbana: University of Illinois Press, 1987).

5. Meyer, *A World Undone*.

6. John M. Barry, *The Great Influenza: The Epic Story of the Deadliest Plague in History* (New York: Viking, 2004).

7. See Meyer, *A World Undone*; Tammy Proctor, *Civilians in a World at War, 1914–1918* (New York: New York University Press, 2010), 59, 71; Matthew Stibbe, ed., *Captivity, Forced Labor and Forced Migration in Europe During the First World War* (London: Routledge, 2009), 49–81. The use of civilian and prisoner of war labor was widespread during World War I; among the nations engaged in this practice were Russia, Austria-Hungary, and Great Britain.

8. Meyer, *A World Undone*.

9. Steve Lopez, "In the weeds of bureaucratic insanity there sprouts a small reprieve," *Los Angeles Times*, August 20, 2011.

10. Alisha Coleman-Jensen, Mark Nord, Margaret Andrews, and Steven Carlson, *Statistical Supplement to Household Food Security in the United States in 2010*, AP-057, U.S. Dept. of Agriculture, Economic Research Service, September 2011.

11. Life Sciences Research Office, S.A. Andersen, ed., "Core Indicators of Nutritional State for Difficult to Sample Populations," *The Journal of Nutrition* 120 (1990):1557S-1600S.

12. Coleman-Jensen, Nord, Andrews, and Carlson, *Statistical Supplement to Household Food Security*, Table S-17, 31.

13. Rich Pirog and Andrew Benjamin, *Checking the Food Odometer: Comparing Food Miles for Local Versus Conventional Produce Sales to Iowa Institutions*, Leopold Institute for Sustainable Agriculture, Iowa State University, July 2003.

14. Lincoln's Milwaukee Speech, An Address by Abraham Lincoln Before the Wisconsin State Agricultural Society in Milwaukee, Wisconsin, September 30, 1859, http://www.nal.usda.gov/lincolns-milwaukee-speech (accessed 06/12/2013).

15. http://www.sarep.ucdavis.edu/ (accessed 06/12/2013).

16. http://www.wkkf.org/what-we-support/healthy-kids/food-and-community.aspx#2 (accessed 06/12/2013).

17. http://www.agcensus.usda.gov/Publications/2007/Online_Highlights/Fact_Sheets/Demographics/farmer_age.pdf (accessed 06/12/2013).

Chapter Two

1. Louse B. Wilder, "A Call to the Hoe," *Good Housekeeping*, April 1918, 47.

2. Ibid. Emphasis in original.

3. Charles Lathrop Pack, "Making a Nation of Garden Cities," *Garden Magazine*, May 1918.

4. Laura Lawson, *City Bountiful: A Century of Community Gardening in America* (Berkeley: University of California Press, 2005), 118; Charles Lathrop Pack, *The War Garden Victorious* (Philadelphia: J. B. Lippincott, 1919), 46–52.

5. This is referred to in numerous government and media publications. See P. S. Risdale, "The Garden and the Government," *The Touchstone*, March 1918, 537.

6. Wilder, "A Call to the Hoe," 47.

7. Alfred C. Lane and O. S. Morgan, "Gardening on Sunday: Two Letters," *The Outlook*, May 23, 1917, 158.

8. Christopher Capozzola, *Uncle Sam Wants You: World War I and the Making of the Modern American Citizen* (Oxford University Press, 2008). See also Christopher Capozzola: "Uncle Sam Wants You: Political Obligations in World War I America," (Ph.D. dissertation, Columbia University, 2002) and P. S. Risdale, "The Garden and the Government."

9. A Victory Garden Program also operated during World War II (1941–1945). The effort was convened by the United States Department of Agriculture.

10. See Pack, *The War Garden Victorious*, 15.

11. David B. Danbom, The Resisted Revolution: Urban America and the Industrialization of Agriculture, 1900–1930 (Ames: Iowa State University Press, 1979): 25.

12. Pack, "Making a Nation of Garden Cities," 183–186.

13. Pack, *The War Garden Victorious*, 15.

14. Danbom, *The Resisted Revolution*, 99–101. David M. Kennedy, *Over Here: The First World War and American Society* (London: Oxford University Press, 1980).

15. Danbom, *The Resisted Revolution*, 99.

16. Ibid., 74.

17. Ibid., 36–37.

18. See Frederick Jackson Turner, *The Frontier in American History* (1920). These ideas are also based on essays and papers produced by Turner as early as the 1890s. Turner delivered a seminal speech on this topic at the World Columbian Exposition in Chicago in 1893.

19. Danbom, *The Resisted Revolution*, 20, 46, 120.

20. William Frieburger, "War Prosperity and Hunger: The New York Food Riots of 1917,"

Labor History 25, no. 2 (1984): 217–239. See also Lawson, *City Bountiful*, 24–26.

21. Robert Wiebe, *The Search for Order 1877–1920* (New York: Hill and Wang, 1967).

22. Ida Clyde Clark with P. P. Claxton, *The Little Democracy: A Text-Book on Community Organization* (New York: D. Appleton, 1918), xiii. Ida Clyde Clark also wrote *American Women and the World War*. P. P. Claxton was the federal commissioner for the Bureau of Education, and was involved with the work of the USSGA and the NWGC.

23. Ibid.

24. See Richard Abbott, "The Agricultural Press Views the Yeoman: 1819–1859," *Agricultural History* 42 (1968): 35–48; Clifford Anderson, "The Metamorphosis of American Agrarian Idealism in the 1920s and 1930s," *Agricultural History* 35 (October 1961): 182–188; W. Burlie Brown, "The Cincinnatus Image in Presidential Politics," *Agricultural History* 31 (1957): 23–29; P. Gerster and N. Cords, "The Northern Origins of Southern Mythology," *The Journal of Southern History* 43 (November 1977): 567–582; William Grampp, "A Re-Examination of Jeffersonian Economics," *Southern Economic Journal* 12 (1946): 263–282; Alfred Griswold, *Farming and Democracy* (New York: Harcourt, Brace and Company, 1948); William Hesseltine, "Four American Traditions," *Journal of Southern History* 27 (1961): 3–32; Richard Hofstadter, "The Myth of the Happy Yeoman," *American Heritage* 7 (1956): 43–53.

25. David Potter, *People of Plenty: Economic Abundance and the American Character* (Chicago: University of Chicago Press, 1954).

26. Thomas Joseph Bassett, "Vacant Lot Cultivation: Community Gardening in America, 1893–1978" (Ph.D. dissertation, University of California, Davis, 1979): 13–14.

27. Potter, *People of Plenty*. Potter makes a strong argument that the fertility of American soil shaped American character.

28. Bassett, "Vacant Lot Cultivation," 9–12. Lawson, *City Bountiful*, 23–26.

29. Ibid. Lawson, *City Bountiful*, 25. See also Melvin G. Holli, *Reform in Detroit: Hazen S. Pingree and Urban Politics* (New York: Oxford University Press, 1969).

30. Holli, *Reform in Detroit*, 70–72. See Lawson, *City Bountiful*, 23–24, 28. A table provided by Lawson lists thirty-one American cities in eighteen states (and the District of Columbia) that had vacant lot cultivation associations between 1894 and 1927.

31. Bassett, "Vacant Lot Cultivation," 9–12; Holli, *Reform in Detroit*, 70–72; Lawson, *City Bountiful*, 25.

32. Holli, Reform in Detroit, 72.

33. New York Association for Improving the Condition of the Poor (AICP), "Cultivation of Vacant Lots by the Unemployed," *AICP Notes* I, no. I (1898): 27–28. Also cited in Lawson, *City Bountiful*, 27. See also H. Patricia Hynes, *A Patch of Eden: America's Inner City Gardens* (White River Junction, VT: Chelsea Green, 1996), x.

34. Bassett, "Vacant Lot Cultivation," 43; Lawson, *City Bountiful*, 93–97; James L. Machor, *Pastoral Cities: Urban Ideals and the Symbolic Landscape of America* (Madison: University of Wisconsin Press, 1987), 47–49.

35. Machor, *Pastoral Cities*, 47–49.

36. Pack, "Making a Nation of Garden Cities."

37. Bassett, "Vacant Lot Cultivation," 44.

38. Ibid., 48; Lawson, *City Bountiful*, 93.

39. Witold Rybczynski, *A Clearing in the Distance: Frederick Law Olmsted and America in the 19th Century* (New York: Simon & Schuster, 1999); Machor, *Pastoral Cities*, 168.

40. Machor, *Pastoral Cities*; Rybczynski, *A Clearing in the Distance*.

41. Alexandra Eyle, *Charles Lathrop Pack: Timberman, Forest Conservationist, and Pioneer in Forest Education* (Syracuse: State University of New York, 1992), 142. See also Pack, *The War Garden Victorious*, 1.

42. Eyle, *Charles Lathrop Pack*, 133–139.

43. Ibid.; Pack, *The War Garden Victorious*, 10.

44. There is no consensus on this idea. See William J. Novak, "The Myth of the 'Weak' American State," *American Historical Review* 113, no. 3 (2008): 752–771; Brian Balogh, *A Government Out of Sight: The Mystery of National Authority in Nineteenth Century America* (Cambridge: Cambridge University Press, 2009).

45. Eyle, *Charles Lathrop Pack*, 177.

46. Pack, *The War Garden Victorious*, 8.

47. John R. McMahon, "The War Garden Campaign of 1917," *The Country Gentleman* 82, no. 45 (1917): 1722.

48. Ibid.

49. The National War Garden Commission, "War Gardening and Home Storage of Vegetables" (Washington, DC: National War Garden Commission, 1919).

50. Eyle refers to Pack as a "timber tycoon"; among his contemporaries was Fred Weyerhauser. See Eyle, *Charles Lathrop Pack*, 84. While Pack came from a wealthy family, he was successful in his own right.

51. Eyle, *Charles Lathrop Pack*, xv. Eyle cites *St. Mary Academy 1898–1973* (Lakewood, NJ: St. Mary's Academy). Eyle notes that Pack's wealth was "on a par with John D. Rockefeller and Jay Gould."

52. Char Miller, review of *Charles Lathrop Pack: Timberman, Forest Conservationist, and Pioneer in Forest Education* by Alexandra Eyle, *Journal of American History* (June 1995): 294.
53. Eyle, *Charles Lathrop Pack*, 84–86.
54. See Conference of Governors Proceedings (Washington, DC: Government Printing Office, 1909).
55. Pack, *The War Garden Victorious*, 8–9.
56. Ibid., 1.
57. Ibid., 9.
58. See Jane Smith, *The Garden of Invention: Luther Burbank and the Business of Breeding Plants* (New York: Penguin, 2009).
59. Pack, *The War Garden Victorious*, 26–27.
60. Vrooman served as assistant secretary of agriculture during the war era. David E. Hamilton, "Building the Associative State: The Department of Agriculture and American State Building," *Agricultural History* 64, no. 2 (1990): 207–218.
61. Frances Duncan, "The Easy Wartime Garden," *The Ladies' Home Journal* 35 (March 1918): 36.
62. Pack, *The War Garden Victorious*, 102; Lawson, *City Bountiful*, 188. Victory Gardening also occurred during World War II on the Common.
63. Lawson, *City Bountiful*, 117. See City of San Francisco, "All Out Food Production: Victory Gardens 2008+," http://www.sfvictorygardens.org/ (accessed 06/14/2013).
64. Pack, *The War Garden Victorious*, 102. The Boy Scouts of America also details its role in this gardening place during World War I. Boys Scouts of America, "United States Boy Scouts: World War I Activities (1917–1919)," http://histclo.com/Youth/youth/org/sco/country/us/chron/1910/bsa-ww1.htm (accessed 06/14/2013).
65. See *The Touchstone* (August 1914): 399.
66. Pack, "Making a Nation of Garden Cities," 186.
67. Judah L. Magnes Museum, Western Jewish History Center, Lubin, David (1849–1919), papers 1875–1982, Box 5, Folder V, Q.
68. Bassett, "Vacant Lot Cultivation," 6; Lawson, *City Bountiful*, 24–26.
69. Pack, *The War Garden Victorious*, 96.
70. Ibid., 10.
71. "Crop Prolific on Small Lot: Jack's Wonderful Beanstalk Has Little, if Anything, on Harriet's," *The Los Angeles Times*, September 2, 1917: I11. Young Harriet Johns harvested 1,769 beans from four seeds.
72. Pack, *The War Garden Victorious*, 53–67.
73. Pack, "Making a Nation of Garden Cities," 184.
74. Ibid., 185.
75. Pack, *The War Garden Victorious*, 53–55.
76. Bentley, *Eating for Victory*, 122–124.
77. Lawson, *City Bountiful*, 68.
78. Ibid., 135.
79. J. H. Francis, "The United States School Garden Army," in *Advanced Sheets from the Biennial Survey of Education in the United States, 1916–1918*, Bulletin No. 26 (Washington D.C.: Department of the Interior, Bureau of Education, 1919).
80. Pack, "Making a Nation of Garden Cities," 183.
81. Rae Katherine Eighmey, *Food Will Win the War: Minnesota Crops, Cooks, and Conservation During World War I* (St. Paul: Minnesota Historical Society, 2010), xi.
82. K.D. Hall, J. Guo, M. Dore, and C. C. Chow, "The Progressive Increase of Food Waste in America and Its End Impact," *PLOS ONE* 4, no. 11 (2009): e7940. Doi: 10.1371/journal.pone.0007940.
83. Harvey Levenstein, *Revolution at the Table: The Transformation of the American Diet* (Berkeley: University of California Press, 2003); Author unknown, memo, April 1919, Bureau of Human Nutrition Records, RG 176, Subject Correspondence of the Chief of the Bureau (Alfred True), 1917–30, Box 595, pg. 141.
84. Levenstein, 8.
85. Ibid., 137.
86. Ibid., 137–138.
87. Eighmey, *Food Will Win the War*, 29.
88. Pack, *The War Garden Victorious*, 12.
89. Ibid., Frontispiece.
90. This was produced by the National War Garden Commission and featured an upright shovel. See Pack, *The War Garden Victorious*, 35.
91. David Kennedy's classic book, *Over Here: The First World War and American Society* (New York: Oxford University Press, 1980).
92. Ibid.
93. National Archives and Records Administration, "Herbert Hoover Presidential Library and Museum," Biographical Sketch of Lou Henry Hoover, http://www.ecommcode.com/hoover/hooveronline/LHH_WEBSITE/WebPages/Service%20to%20Women%201917-1928/1918-14.htm.
94. Warren McArthur, "Hoe! Hoe for Uncle Sam," *Illustrated World* (1918): 369–370.
95. Mrs. Arthur Chester, "Women's Work in the War: Given Before the Garden Club of Greenwich, Conn.," *The Touchstone* 1 (1917): 298–300; "Expert Advice on Garden-Making," *The Touchstone* 1, no. 3 (1917): 317.
96. Frances Duncan, "The Easy Wartime Garden," *The Ladies' Home Journal* 35 (March 1918): 36; Dudley Harmon, "The Second Year War Gar-

den," *The Ladies' Home Journal* 35 (February 1918): 46; Dudley Harmon, "Planning the Individual Garden," *The Ladies' Home Journal* 35 (February 1918): 46.

97. "War Garden Campaign in New England Towns, *New York Times*, February 16, 1919, 51.

98. Ibid. See Grace Tabor, *The Suburban Garden* (New York: Outing, 1913).

99. See Kathryn Kidder, "Thrift in Little Gardens: Number Four," *The Touchstone* 1, no. 4 (1917): 388–391; Cabot Ward, "Giving the People What They Want: Number Four in the Series: Help Your Country with a Food Garden," *The Touchstone* 1, no. 4 (1917): 399–407.

100. Pack, *The War Garden Victorious*, 10.

101. Ibid. See pages 38, 46, 48, 50, 54, 86, 94, 126.

102. Ibid., 90. See Pack, "Making a Nation of Garden Cities," 185.

103. For an excellent description of the Council of National Defense, please refer to William J. Breen, *Uncle Sam at Home: Civilian Mobilization, Wartime Federalism, and the Council of National Defense 1917–1919* (Westport, CT: Greenwood Press, 1984).

104. Ida Clyde Clarke, *American Women and the World War* (New York: D. Appleton, 1918). Also cited in Lawson, *City Bountiful*, 122.

105. Martha A. Nolan, *A Chronicle: The History of Woman's National Farm and Garden Association* (Fremont, OH: Lesher, 1986).

106. Amy Bentley, *Eating for Victory: Food Rationing and the Politics of Domesticity* (Urbana: University of Illinois Press, 1998).

107. Ibid., 2. See also Drew Gilpin Faust, *Mothers of Invention: Women of the Slaveholding South in the American Civil War* (Chapel Hill: University of North Carolina Press, 1996).

108. Bentley, *Eating for Victory*, 115.

109. See United States Department of Agriculture, National Defense Gardening Conference, December 1941.

110. Danbom, *The Resisted Revolution*.

111. Pack, *The War Garden Victorious*, 97.

Chapter Three

1. "The World's News in Today's Times Covering the Globe," *The Los Angeles Times*, July 7, 1917, p. 11.

2. *The Los Angeles Times*, various. See also National Environmental Satellite Data, and Information Service, a historical records website, published by the U.S. Department of Commerce, National Climatic Data Center, http://www.ncdc.noaa.gov/oa/ncdc.html (accessed 2/21/2010).

3. "Crop Prolific on Small Lot: Jack's Wonderful Beanstalk Has Little, if Anything, on Harriet's," *The Los Angeles Times*, September 2, 1917, p. III.

4. "Fourteen Thousand Children Working War Gardens Here," *The Los Angeles Times*, March 24, 1918, p. III.

5. Ernest B. Babcock, *Suggestions for Garden Work in California Schools*, Circular No. 46 (Berkeley: University of California Press, 1909), 11. The positive impacts described by Ms. Rogers are substantiated by current research in garden-based education. See also J. Alexander, M. North and D. Hendren, "Master Gardener Classroom Garden Project: An Evaluation of the Benefits to Children," *Children's Environments* 12, no. 2 (1995): 256–263; D.E. Bunn, "Group Cohesiveness is Enhanced as Children Engage in Plant Stimulated Discovery Activities," *Journal of Therapeutic Horticulture* 1 (1986): 37–43; and T.M. Waliczek et al., "The effect of school gardens on children's interpersonal relationships and attitudes toward school," *HortTechnology* 11, no. 3 (2001): 466–468.

6. Babcock, Suggestions for Garden Work in California Schools.

7. Ibid.

8. Ibid., 5. Emphasis in original.

9. For more information, see G. Leydard Stebbins, *Ernest Brown Babcock: A Bibliographic Memoir* (Washington, DC: National Academy of the Sciences, 1958). Available online at books.nap.edu/html/biomems/ebabcock.pdf. The bibliography of Babcock's relevant work includes Ernest Babcock and L. H. Miller, *Outline of Course in Nature-Study* (Los Angeles: Los Angeles Normal School, 1906), 1–16; Ernest Babcock, *Information for Students Concerning the College of Agriculture of the University of California*, Circular No. 52 (Berkeley: University of California Agricultural Research and Experiment Station, 1906), 1–18; Ernest Babcock, *Suggestions for Garden Work in California Schools*, Circular No. 46 (Berkeley: University of California Agricultural Research and Experiment Station, 1909), 1–48; Ernest Babcock, "Agriculture in Secondary Schools," *The Nature Study Review* 5, no. 8 (1910); Ernest Babcock, "Co-operation between the Schools and the College of Agriculture," *University of California Chronicle*, 13 no. 3 (1910): 1–10; Ernest Babcock, "Agriculture in California Schools," *Sierra Education News*, 6 no. 1 (1910); Ernest Babcock and Cyril A. Stebbins, *Elementary School Agriculture* (New York: Macmillan, 1911).

10. John Amos Comenius advocated for school gardens in the seventeenth century. See C.M. Weed and P. Emerson, *School Garden Book* (New York: Charles Scribner's Sons, 1909); M.R.

Sealy, "A garden for children at Family Road Care Center," unpublished master's thesis, Louisiana State University and Agricultural Mechanical College, 2001; Aarti Subramaniam, "Garden-Based Learning in Basic Education: An Historical Review," *University of California 4-H Center for Youth Development Monograph Series*, Summer 2002; Alfred Charles True, *A History of Agricultural Education in the United States 1785–1925* (Washington, DC: United States Government Printing Office, 1929), 3–4.

11. Subramaniam, "Garden-Based Learning in Basic Education: An Historical Review." Jean-Jacques Rosseau (1712–1778) stressed the importance of incorporating nature as an essential component of education. See also Daniel Desmond, James Grieshop and Aarti Subramaniam, "Revisiting Garden-Based Learning in Basic Education," published by the United Nations Food and Agriculture Organization and the International Institute for Educational Planning, 2004, 25–36; True, *A History of Agricultural Education in the United States 1785–1925*, 2–3.

12. Subramaniam, "Garden-Based Learning in Basic Education: An Historical Review," 2–3; and Desmond, Grieshiop, and Subramaniam, "Revisting Garden-Based Learning," 25–27.

13. Maria Montessori, *The Absorbent Mind* (New York: Dell, 1912). Translated from the Italian by Claude A. Claremont.

14. Babcock, *Suggestions for Garden Work in California Schools*.

15. Subramaniam, "Garden-Based Learning in Basic Education: An Historical Review," 2–3; Desmond, Grieshiop and Subramaniam, "Revisting Garden-Based Learning," 25–27; Laura Lawson, *City Bountiful: A Century of Community Gardening in America* (Berkeley: University of California Press, 2005), 53.

16. Desmond, Grieshiop and Subramaniam, "Revisting Garden-Based Learning," 25–27; Lawson, *City Bountiful*, 60–61. Lawson argues that the Putnam School effort served as a "catalyst" for a national school garden movement.

17. For more information about The Food Project, visit http://thefoodproject.org (accessed 6/16/2013).

18. Lawson, *City Bountiful*, 62–65; Greene, Among School Gardens, 28.

19. Lawson, *City Bountiful*, 52; Greene, *Among School Gardens*, 3.

20. Lawson, *City Bountiful*, 52.

21. Greene, *Among School Gardens*, 3.

22. See Lawson, *City Bountiful*, 52. Lawson cites an original report prepared by James Ralph Jewell, *Agricultural Education Including Nature Study and School Gardens*, Bulletin 2 (Washington, DC: Department of the Interior, Bureau of Education, 1907), 30. Jewell's report is also cited in Babcock, *Suggestions for Garden Work in California Schools*.

23. Louise Klein Miller, *Children's Gardens for School and Home, a Manual of Cooperative Learning* (New York: D. Appleton, 1904).

24. Ibid., vii.

25. Jacob Riis, "What Ails Our Boys," *The Craftsman*, October 1911, 8.

26. Greene, *Among School Gardens*.

27. Ibid., 7. Charles Lathrop Pack described them as links in a chain of democracy. See Pack, *The War Garden Victorious*.

28. Ibid., 4.

29. Ibid., Introduction.

30. Ibid., 4.

31. Ibid. The school farm was the centerpiece of the site when it opened in 1902; it closed in 1932.

32. For an excellent discussion of the history of Extension and rural resistance to its methods, see David Danbom, *The Resisted Revolution: Urban America and the Industrialization of Agriculture, 1900–1930* (Ames: Iowa State University Press, 1979). As an interesting postscript to this footnote, historian Alfred Charles True argues that the precedent of using public land to support public education began as early as 1787. See True, *A History of Agricultural Education*, 20–22.

33. Ernest B. Babcock and Cyril A. Stebbins, *Elementary School Agriculture: A Teacher's Manual to Accompany Hilgard and Osterhout's "Agriculture for Schools of the Pacific Slope"* (New York: Macmillan, 1911).

34. Cyril A. Stebbins, *The Principles of Agriculture Through the School and the Home Garden* (New York: Macmillan, 1913).

35. Liberty Hyde Bailey, *The Nature Study Idea*, 3d ed. (New York: Macmillan, 1909); Liberty Hyde Bailey, *The Training of Farmers* (New York: The Century Company, 1909).

36. Babcock, *Suggestion for School Gardens in California*; Jewell, *Agricultural Education Including Nature Study and School Gardens*.

37. Liberty Hyde Bailey, *The State and The Farmer* (New York: Macmillan, 1908).

38. Liberty Hyde Bailey, *The Country-Life Movement in the United States* (New York: Macmillan, 1911); Theodore Roosevelt, "Rural Life," *The Outlook* 95 (1910): 919–22; Horace Plunkett, "Conservation and Rural Life: An Irish View of Two Roosevelt Policies," *The Outlook* (1910): 260–64.

39. Danbom, *The Resisted Revolution*.

40. Jewell, *Agricultural Education Including Nature Study and School Gardens*.

41. Historian O. L. Davis reports that during World War I the Bureau of Education and the United States Department of Agriculture were engaged in an "inter-agency territorial squabble" over whose territory school gardening programs were, and that an agreement was not reached until two days after the Armistice was signed. O.L. Davis, "School Gardens and National Purpose During World War I," *The Journal of the Midwest History of Education Society* 22 (1995): 115–126.

42. Lawson, *City Bountiful*, 64.

43. Philander P. Claxton, United States Bureau of Education Commissioner, School Garden Association of America Annual Report (New York: School Garden Association of America, 1916), 2.

44. Lawson, *City Bountiful*, 65; O.L. Davis, "School Gardens and National Purpose During World War I," 10; "School and Home Gardening," *School Life* 1 (1918): 4; *Report of the Commissioner of Education for the Year Ended June 30, 1918* (Washington, DC: Government Printing Office, 1918), 128–132.

45. Michigan State University Libraries, *School Gardening in the Early 1900s*, http://libguides.lib.msu.edu/content.php?pid=46894&sid=446374 (accessed 06/14/2013).

46. Lawson, *City Bountiful*, 65; O.L. Davis, "School Gardens and National Purpose During World War I," 117.

47. Lawson, *City Bountiful*, 65–66; C.D. Jarvis, *Gardening in Elementary City Schools*, Bulletin 40 (Washington, DC: Department of the Interior, Bureau of Education, 1916).

48. Lawson, *City Bountiful*, 66.

49. For information about childhood and education during this period, see Patricia Albjerg Graham, *Community and Class in American Education, 1865–1918* (New York: John Wiley and Sons, 1974); Joseph E. Illick, *American Childhoods* (Philadelphia: University of Pennsylvania Press, 2002); Lisa Jacobson, *Raising Consumers: Children and the American Mass Market in the Early Twentieth Century* (New York: Columbia University Press, 2004); Herbert M. Kliebard, *The Struggle for the American Curriculum, 1893–1958* (Boston: Routledge and Kegan Paul, 1986); David I. Macleod, *Building Character in the American Boy: The Boy Scouts, YMCA, and Their Forerunners, 1870–1920* (Madison: University of Wisconsin Press, 1983); Viviana A. Zelizer, *Pricing the Priceless Child: The Changing Social Value of Children* (New York: Basic Books, 1985).

50. Scott J. Peters, "'Every Farmer Should be Awakened': Liberty Hyde Bailey's Vision of Agricultural Extension Work," *Agricultural History* 80 (2006): 190–219; Andrew Rieser, *The Chautauqua Moment: Protestants, Progressives, and the Culture of Modern Liberalism* (New York: Columbia University Press, 2003).

51. Ethel Gowans, *Home Gardening for City Children of the Fifth, Sixth, and Seventh Grades*, United States School Garden Army (Washington, DC: Government Printing Office, Department of the Interior, Bureau of Education, 1919).

52. C.A. Stebbins, *A Manual of School-Supervised Gardening for the Western States*, United States School Garden Army (Washington, DC: Department of the Interior, Bureau of Education, 1920), 49.

53. See William J. Breen, *Uncle Sam at Home: Civilian Mobilization, Wartime Federalism, and the Council of National Defense, 1917–1919* (Westport, CT: Greenwood Press, 1984); William J. Breen, "Mobilization and Cooperation Federalism: The Connecticut State Council of Defense, 1917–1919," *Historian* 42, no. 1 (1979): 58–84; William J. Breen, "The Mobilization of Skilled Labor in World War I: 'Voluntarism,' the U.S. Public Service Reserve, and the Department of Labor, 1917–1918," *Labor History* 32, no. 2 (1991): 253–272; Christopher Joseph Capozzola, "Uncle Sam Wants You: Political Obligations in World War I America," Ph.D. dissertation, Columbia University, 2002, 150; Robert D. Cuff, "Herbert Hoover, The Ideology of Voluntarism and War Organization during the Great War," *Journal of American History* 64, no. 2 (September 1977): 358–372.

54. Lawson, *City Bountiful*, 65–66; O.L. Davis, "School Gardens and National Purpose During World War I," 117.

55. Charles Lathrop Pack, *The War Garden Victorious: Its Wartime Need and Its Economic Value in Peace* (Philadelphia: J. B. Lippincott, 1919), 9. See Chapter Two.

56. Davis, "School Gardens and National Purpose During World War I."

57. Gowans, *Home Gardening for City Children*, 33.

58. Davis, "School Gardens and National Purpose During World War I," 118–119.

59. Gowans, *Home Gardening for City Children*, 9, 13, 17.

60. Stebbins, *United States School Garden Army: A Manual of School-Supervised Gardening for the Western States*, 40. This tag line also appears in numerous other USSGA publications.

61. Davis, "School Gardens and National Purpose During World War I," 117–118; "The United States School Garden Army," *School Life* 1 (1918): 2; Lawson, *City Bountiful*, 127.

62. See Sarah T. Barrows, "Teaching English to Immigrants: Some Suggestions on Methods

and Materials" (Columbus: Ohio Branch, Council of National Defense, ca. 1918).

63. Babcock and Stebbins, *Elementary School Agriculture*, p. xx. Emphasis in original.

64. Ibid., viii.

65. Lawson, *City Bountiful*, 70.

66. Nature-Study Review, 1912, cited in Lawson, *City Bountiful*, 72.

67. Babcock and Stebbins, *Elementary School Agriculture*.

68. Ibid., viii.

69. Ibid., ix.

70. J. H. Francis, "The United States School Garden Army," in *Advanced Sheets from the Biennial Survey of Education in the United States, 1916–1918*, Bulletin No. 26 (Washington D.C.: Department of the Interior, Bureau of Education, 1919).

71. Report of the Commissioner of Education (Washington, DC: United States Department of the Interior, Bureau of Education, 1918): 183–186.

72. Ibid.

73. See "Ann Street School Doing Its Bit," *Ventura Star*, September 21, 1917, 1; "Crop Prolific on Small Lot: Jack's Wonderful Beanstalk Has Little, if Anything, on Harriet's," *The Los Angeles Times*, September 2, 1917, II1; Staff, "Win the War, Mass Nation's Forces To Grow More Food, School Children are to Play a Huge Part in the Campaign for Greater Production," *The Los Angeles Times*, May 31, 1918, II11; Staff, "Work for Local Woman to Organize School Children in Western Cities," *The Los Angeles Times*, September 19, 1918, II6; Staff, "War Gardens Town's Hobby, Armies of School Children Plant for Prizes," *The Los Angeles Times*, April 29, 1917, II6.

74. Charles W. Eliot, letters to P. P. Claxton, April 18 and April 27, 1918, Historical File, 18701950, Office of the Commissioner of Education, Department of the Interior, U.S. National Archives.

75. *Report of the Commissioner of Education* (Washington, DC: United States Department of the Interior, Bureau of Education, 1918), 183–186.

76. Ibid.

77. "Living Civics," *The New York Times*, 10 August, 1920, p. 11.

78. Francis, *Bulletin 26*.

79. Ibid., 6.

80. Department of the Interior, Bureau of Education, *The Fall Manual of the United States School Garden Army* (Washington: Government Printing Office, 1918), 5.

81. Francis, *Bulletin 26*, 1.

82. Davis, "School Gardens and National Purpose During World War I," 120.

83. Cyril A. Stebbins, *School-Supervised Gardening for the Western States*, Department of the Interior, Bureau of Education, United States School Garden Army (Washington: Government Printing Office, 1918), 38–39.

84. Robert H. Wiebe, *The Search for Order, 1877–1920* (New York: HarperCollins, 1967), 287.

85. Ibid.

86. Ibid., 287–293.

87. Ibid., vii.

88. Stebbins, *School-Supervised Gardening for the Western States*, 39–40.

89. Ibid.

90. Ibid.

91. Ibid., 40.

92. Department of the Interior, Bureau of Education, *United States School Garden Army Fall Manual*, 24.

93. Ibid.

94. Ibid.

95. All USSGA manuals use the term "garden educators" in addition to "teachers."

96. Francis, Bulletin No. 26.

97. Ibid.

98. Francis, *Bulletin No. 26*; Davis, "School Gardens and National Purpose During World War I."

99. John W. Studebaker, "The American School System and War Gardens," United States Department of Agriculture, National Defense Gardening Conference Proceedings, December 1941.

100. Francis, Bulletin No. 26.

101. Cyril A. Stebbins, *School-Supervised Gardening for the Western States*, Department of the Interior, Bureau of Education, United States School Garden Army (Washington: Government Printing Office, 1918), 40.

102. Gowans, *The United States School Garden Army's Home Gardening for City Children of the Fifth, Sixth, and Seventh Grades* provides an excellent example of this. In her acknowledgements section, Gowans thanks various educators, Extension staff and industry representatives for their assistance in preparing the courses.

103. The USSGA funded field organizers in a regionally organized system to further its goals.

104. In a reflection of changing times, the Future Homemakers of America changed its name to Family, Career and Community Leaders of America in 1999.

Chapter Four

1. Report of the Commissioner of Education, 183–186.

2. Shawn Aubitz and Gail F. Stern, "Ethnic Images in World War I Posters," *Journal of American Culture* 9, no. 4 (1986): 83.

3. See George Creel, *How We Advertised America* (New York: Harper & Brothers, 1920), 4–5.

4. Gary A. Borkan, *World War 1 Posters* (Atglen, PA: Schiffer, 2002), 5.

5. Cyril A. Stebbins, *School-Supervised Gardening for the Western States*, Department of the Interior, Bureau of Education, United States School Garden Army (Washington: Government Printing Office, 1918), 27.

6. Pierre Nora and Marc Roudebush, "Between Memory and History: Les Lieux de Memoire," *Representations: Special Issue: Memory and Counter Memory* (Spring 1989), 7.

7. Alon Confino, "Collective Memory and Cultural History: Problems of Method," *The American Historical Review* 102, no. 5 (1997): 1388.

8. Robert Archibald, *A Place to Remember: Using History to Build Community* (Walnut Creek, CA: Altamira Press, 1999), 24.

9. David Glassberg, *Sense of History: The Place of the Past in American Life* (Boston: University of Massachusetts Press, 2001), 8.

10. Ibid.

11. Ibid., 9.

12. Archibald, *A Place to Remember*, 29.

13. Nora and Roudebush, "Between Memory and History," 8.

14. Maurice Hawlbachs, La Topographie Legendaire des Evangiles en Terresainte: Etude de Memoire Collective (Paris: University of Paris Press, 1941).

15. Confino,"Collective Memory and Cultural History: Problems of Method," 1390.

16. Archibald, *A Place to Remember*, 17.

17. Glassberg, *Sense of History*, 123.

18. Ibid.

19. Dolores Hayden, *The Power of Place: Urban Landscapes and Public History* (Cambridge: MIT Press, 1995).

20. Ibid., 4.

21. Hayden, *The Power of Place*, 23. Quote attributed to Michael Dear and Jennifer Wolch.

22. Borkan, World War I Posters, 2002.

23. Willam Leach, *Land of Desire: Merchants, Power, and the Rise of a New American Culture*. (New York: Vintage, 1994), 45.

24. Ibid. 50.

25. Ibid. 184.

26. A number of historians assess the impact of war on gender roles, including Cynthia Beeman, Stephanie Carpenter, Lynn Dumeril, Marilyn Holt, Katherine Jellison, Joan Jensen, Penny Martelet, and Margo McBane. There is little in literature, however, pertaining to how wartime programs targeting school-aged girls may have challenged traditional stereotypes.

27. Ethel Ann Murphy, *The Victory of the Gardens: A Pageant in Four Episodes, for the United States School Garden Army* (Washington, DC: Government Printing Office, 1918).

28. David Glassberg, *American Historical Pageantry: The Uses of Tradition in the Early Twentieth Century* (Chapel Hill: University of North Carolina Press, 1990), 1.

29. Ibid., 216.

30. Ibid.

31. Ibid., 213.

32. Ibid., 218.

33. Ibid., 220. *The Victory of the Gardens* also provided opportunities for the audience to sing.

34. Murphy, *The Victory of the Gardens*, 4.

35. Ibid., 3.

36. Ibid.

37. Ibid., 7.

38. Ibid., 15–16.

39. Ibid., 16.

40. Ibid., 18.

41. Ibid., 19.

42. Ibid., 8, 19, 21, 22.

Chapter Five

1. Jane Bowne Haines, "Gardening Schools for Women," February 1907. Personal document. From the Wyck Papers, collection of The Wyck Association, held by the American Philosophical Society, Philadelphia, Series 11, Box 296A, Folder 137.

2. Martha A. Nolan, *A Chronicle: History of WNF&GA* (Fremont, Oh: Lesher, 1985).

3. See Valencia Libby, "Jane Haines' Vision: The Pennsylvania School of Horticulture for Women," *New England Garden History Society Journal* 10 (2002): 44–52.

4. Libby, "Jane Haines' Vision," 45.

5. Libby, "Jane Haines' Vision"; Nicole Juday, personal interview with the author, January 24, 2010; "The Trained Hand with the Trained Mind," docent notes from Wyck Gardens tour, author and date unknown, from Wyck ephemera files, provided by Nicole Juday.

6. Libby, "Jane Haines' Vision"; Nicole Juday, personal interview with author, January 24, 2010; "The Trained Hand with the Trained Mind," docent notes from Wyck Gardens tour, author and date unknown, from Wyck ephemera files, provided by Nicole Juday.

7. Docent notes from Wyck Gardens tour, author and date unknown, from Wyck ephemera files, provided by Nicole Juday. John Bartram, an American Quaker, was a noted botanist, horticulturist and explorer. Bartram's Garden, still in existence and hosting visitors in Philadelphia, is considered the first American botanical collection. Bartram was one of the founders of the American Philosophical Society.

8. Libby, "Jane Haines' Vision"; Nicole Juday, personal interview with author, January 24, 2010; "The Trained Hand with the Trained Mind," docent notes from Wyck Gardens tour, author and date unknown, from Wyck ephemera files, provided by Nicole Juday.

9. Daniel T. Rodgers, *Atlantic Crossings: Social Politics in a Progressive Age* (Cambridge: Harvard University Press, 1998). Rodgers argues for European influences on many aspects of American social, cultural and political life during the Progressive Era.

10. Emma H. Adams, *To and fro in Southern California* (Cincinnati: W.M.B.C. Press, 1887). Digitized version found in the Library of Congress, http://memory.loc.gov/cgi-bin/query/h?ammem/calbkbib:@field(NUMBER+@od1(calbk+102)) (accessed 2/16/2009).

11. Ibid.

12. Jane Alison Knight, *An Examination of the Lowthorpe School of Landscape Architecture for Women, Groton, Massachusetts, 1901–1945* (Ithaca: Cornell University Press, 1986).

13. Haines, "Gardening Schools for Women," 23.

14. Valencia Libby, "Jane Haines' Vision: The Pennsylvania School of Horticulture for Women," *New England Garden History Society Journal* 10 (2002): 44–52; Nicole Juday, personal interview with the author, January 24, 2010; "The Trained Hand with the Trained Mind," docent notes from Wyck Gardens tour, author and date unknown, from Wyck ephemera files, provided by Nicole Juday.

15. Nolan, *A Chronicle*, 1–2. According to Martha Nolan, "one day was devoted to the topic of work for women in agriculture and horticulture." The "Women's Agricultural and Horticultural Union of England" was renamed the "Women's Farm and Garden Association."

16. Haines, "Gardening Schools for Women," 24.

17. See Louisa Yeoman King, *The Well-Considered Garden* (New York: Scribner, 1915).

18. Laura Lawson, *City Bountiful: A Century of Community Gardening in America* (Berkeley: University of California Press, 2005).

19. Wendy Lebing. "The Pennsylvania School of Horticulture for Women," no date, Wyck Library Collection, Ambler file.

20. Temple University, 1 March 2005, www.temple.edu/flowershow.

21. Rodgers, *Atlantic Crossings*, 106.

22. Haines, "Gardening Schools for Women."

23. Pennsylvania School of Horticulture for Women, Spring Course, 1913; School of Horticulture for Women, Prospectus, 1919; Pennsylvania School of Horticulture for Women, Prospectus 1929–30.

24. Haines, "Gardening Schools for Women."

25. Ibid.

26. Pennsylvania School of Horticulture for Women, fundraising brochure.

27. Ibid.

28. For more information about the application of technology in rural life and its impact on women, read Katherine Jellison, *Entitled to Power: Farm Women and Technology, 1913–1963* (Chapel Hill: University of North Carolina Press, 1993). For information about how mechanization affected rural life, see Williams, *Fordson, Farmall, and Poppin' Johnny*.

29. P.D. Relf, "Human Issues in Horticulture," *HortTechnology* 2, no. 2, 159–287. See *Cyclopedia of American Horticulture*, 5th ed. (1906), vol. 1 A–D, vol. 2 E–M, vol. 3 N–Q, vol. 4 R–Z (1900); Allan C. Carlson, *The New Agrarian Mind: The Movement Toward Decentralist Thought in Twentieth Century America* (New Brunswick: Transaction, 2004), Chapter 1, "Toward a New Rural Civilization: Liberty Hyde Bailey"; A. D. Rodgers, *Liberty Hyde Bailey: A Story of American Plant Sciences* (Princeton: Princeton University Press, 1949).

30. For more information on the experiences of rural women, see Paula Baker, *The Moral Framework of Public Life: Gender, Politics, and the State in Rural New York, 1870–1930* (Oxford: Oxford University Press, 1991). Baker's work explores the connections between gender and public life, and how the growing role of government in American life changed those connections. Baker also explores the decline of domestic ideology. Jeanne Boydston, *Home and Work: Housework, Wages, and the Ideology of Labor in the Early Republic* (New York: Oxford University Press, 1990) provides enhanced understanding of the declining recognition of the value of domestic work as being of economic importance during the colonial period through the Civil War. See also Deborah Fink, *Agrarian Women: Wives and Mothers in Rural Nebraska, 1880–1940* (Chapel Hill: University of North Carolina Press, 1992); Deborah Fink, *Open Country, Iowa: Rural Women, Tradition, and Change* (Albany: State University of

New York Press, 1986); Katherine Jellison, *Entitled to Power: Farm Women and Technology, 1913–1963* (Chapel Hill: University of North Carolina Press, 1993); Joan Jensen, *Loosening the Bonds: Mid-Atlantic Farm Women, 1750–1850* (New Haven: Yale University Press, 1986); Joan Jensen, *With These Hands: Women Working on the Land* (Old Westbury, NY: The Feminist Press, 1981); Lu Ann Jones, *Mama Learned Us to Work: Farm Women in the New South* (Chapel Hill: University of North Carolina, Press 2001); Lu Ann Jones, "'God Giveth the Increase': Lurline Stokes Murray's Narrative of Farming and Faith," *Southern Cultures* (Fall 2002); Donald B. Marti, *Women of the Grange: Mutuality and Sisterhood in Rural America, 1866–1920* (New York: Greenwood Press, 1991); Martha A. Nolan, *A Chronicle: The History of Woman's National Farm and Garden Association* (Fremont, OH: Lesher, 1986); Mary Neth, *Preserving the Family Farm: Women, Community and the Foundations of Agribusiness in the Midwest, 1900–1940* (Baltimore: Johns Hopkins University Press, 1998); Rebecca Sharpless, *Fertile Ground, Narrow Choices: Women on Cotton Farms of the Texas Blackland Prairie, 1900–1940* (Chapel Hill: University of North Carolina Press, 1999); D. Schwieder, "Education and Change in the Lives of Iowa Farm Women, 1900–1940," *Agricultural History* 60, no. 2 (Spring 1986): 200–215; Melissa Walker, *All We Knew Was to Farm: Rural Women in the Upcountry South, 1919–1941* (Baltimore: Johns Hopkins University Press, 2002). Numerous female historians, including Lu Ann Jones, Mary Neth, Rebecca Sharpless, Melissa Walker and Katherine Jellison, to name a few, have built on the work of a previous generation of what I would call agri-feminist scholars, including Joan Jensen. Many of their works incorporate oral history. The field is dynamic. There is also more attention being paid to the history of women in horticulture, a sub-field of agricultural study, and it is less peripheral than previous work. For example, Witold Rybczynski's biography on Frederick Law Olmsted features a great deal of information about female horticulturists. Melanie Simo, Heath Schenker and Laura Lawson all examine some aspects of women in horticulture; Schenker in particular explores feminist aspects of their professional work in this field. For more information on the experiences of women in horticulture, see Laura Lawson, *City Bountiful: A Century of Community Gardening in America* (Berkeley: University of California Press, 2005); Witold Rybczynski, *A Clearing in the Distance: Frederick Law Olmsted and America in the 19th Century* (New York: Simon & Schuster, 1999); Heath Schenker and Suzanne Oullette, "The Garden as Women's Place: Celia Thaxter and Mariana Van Rensselaer," *Gendered Landscapes*, the Pennsylvania State University Center for Studies in Landscape History, 2000; Heath Schenker, "Feminist Interventions in the Histories of Landscape Architecture," *Landscape Journal*, xiii–2 (Fall 1994); Melanie Simo, *Forest and Garden: Traces of Wildness in a Modernizing Land, 1897–1949* (Charlottesville: University of Virginia Press, 2003); Elizabeth Stevenson, *Park Maker: A Life of Frederick Law Olmsted* (New Brunswick: Transaction, 1999).

31. There is a great deal of overlap between landscape architecture and horticulture. The history of women in landscape architecture is becoming increasingly well known through histories written by female landscape architects. See Valencia Libby, "Cultivating Mind, Body & Spirit: Educating the New Woman for Careers in Landscape Architecture," Beatrix Farrand Conference: A Century of Women: Evaluating Gender in Landscape Architecture, 2 March 2004, http://www.ced.berkeley.edu/events/farrand/Abstracts/Libby; Laura Lawson, "A Woman Has a Feeling About Dirt Which Men Only Pretend to Have: Women and the Civic Garden Campaigns of the Progressive Era," Beatrix Farrand Conference: A Century of Women: Evaluating Gender in Landscape Architecture, 2 March 2004, http://www.ced.berkeley.edu/events/farrand/Abstracts/Laura.htm 2 Feb 2005.

32. Haines, "Gardening Schools for Women."

33. See also Ernest B. Babcock, "Suggestions for Garden Work in California Schools," Circular No. 46 (Berkeley: University of California Press, 1909); Ernest B. Babcock and Cyril A. Stebbins, *Elementary School Agriculture: A Teacher's Manual to Accompany Hilgard and Osterhout's "Agriculture for Schools of the Pacific Slope"* (New York: Macmillan, 1911); Liberty Hyde Bailey, *The Nature Study Idea* (New York: Macmillan, 1909); John Dewey, *Schools of Tomorrow* (New York: E. P. Dutton, 1915); Aarti Subramaniam, "Garden-Based Learning in Basic Education: A Historical Review," University of California, 4-H Youth Development Center, Monograph Series, 2002, http://cyd.ucdavis.edu/publications/pubs/focus/pdf/MO02V8N1.pdf (accessed 4/5/2009); C.M. Weed and P. Emerson, *School Garden Book* (New York: Charles Scribner and Sons, 1909).

34. Haines, "Gardening Schools for Women," 1–2.

35. Ibid.

36. Edith Bradley letter to Jane Haines, 1905, Wyck Library Collection, ephemera files.

37. Hugh Spender, "Lady Warwick's Farming College for Girls," unknown journal, August 1905,

548–553, Wyck Library Collection, ephemera files.

38. Ibid., 2; Valencia Libby, "Jane Haines' Vision: The Pennsylvania School of Horticulture for Women," 45.

39. School brochure, p. 19, Wyck Library Collection, ephemera file. One of Haines' European correspondents insisted that three years training was "essentials." Haines, "Garden Schools for Women," 21.

40. Ibid.

41. Pennsylvania School of Horticulture for Women, Spring Course, 1913; Pennsylvania School of Horticulture for Women, Prospectus.

42. For an important and thoughtful discussion of rural-urban synthesis in American history, see James L. Machor, *Pastoral Cities: Urban Ideals and the Symbolic Landscape of America* (Madison: University of Wisconsin Press, 1987).

43. Machor, *Pastoral Cities*, 13.

44. Julia Chandler Mane, "Horticulture as vocation for women offers escape from devitalizing occupations," *The Washington Herald*, September 22, 1912; Haines, "Gardening Schools for Women," 24.

45. Simo, *Forest and Garden*, 11.

46. Ibid.

47. Robyn Muncy, *Creating a Female Dominion in American Reform, 1890–1935* (New York: Oxford University Press, 1991).

48. Margaret Rossiter, *Women Scientists in America: Struggles and Strategies to 1940* (Baltimore: Johns Hopkins University Press, 1982).

49. Simo, *Forest and Garden*, 13. In particular, landscape "expert" Charles Eliot had misgivings about her work.

50. Rose Hayden-Smith, "Sisters of the Soil: The Work of the Woman's Land Army in World War I," University of California Santa Barbara, 2004.

51. Winifred Starr Dobyns, *California Gardens* (1931; Santa Barbara: Allen A. Knoll, 1996).

52. Lebing, "The Pennsylvania School of Horticulture for Women," 2. In fact, Ambler became a fad among the social elite in Philadelphia.

53. Ibid., 2. Lebing tells of "the lady ... who asked for something to amuse the chauffeur."

54. Fundraising letter, 1919, Wyck Library Collection, ephemera file.

55. Board of Directors Luncheon Invitation, 1919, Wyck Library Collection, ephemera file.

56. See Marina Moskowitz, "'Qualities Adapted to the Country': The Place of Horticulture in the Nineteenth Century," paper presented at the annual meeting of the American Studies Association, http://www.allacademic.com/meta/p114102_index.html (accessed 5/24/2009); Julie S. Higginbotham, "Four Centuries of Planting and Progress: A History of the U.S. Nursery Industry," *American Nurseryman* 171, no. 12 (1990): 36–59.

57. Theodosia Burr Shepherd Papers, Collection 123, Department of Special Collections, Charles E. Young Research Library, University of California, Los Angeles. See also Buckner Hollingsworth, *Theodosia Burr Shepherd, 1845–1906: Her Garden Was Her Delight* (New York: Macmillan, 1962). This is a biography largely taken from an unpublished biography by Shepherd's daughter. See also Marca L. Woodhams, Smithsonian Institution Libraries, Horticultural Branch, "History of the American Seed and Nursery Industry and Their Trade Catalogs," online bibliography, 1999, http://www.sil.si.edu/SIL Publications/seeds/bibseednur.html.

58. Elizabeth MacPhail, *Kate Sessions: Pioneer Horticulturist* (San Diego: San Diego Historical Society, 1976).

59. Lawson, *City Bountiful*; Simo, *Forest and Garden*.

60. Margaret W. Rossiter, *Women Scientists in America*; Sally Gregory Kohlstedt, "In from the Periphery: American Women in Science, 1830–1880," *Signs* 4, no. 1 (1978): 81–96; Witold Rybcsynski, *A Clearing in the Distance: Fredrick Law Olmsted and America in the 19th Century* (New York: Scribner, 1999).

61. Nancy F. Cott, *The Bonds of Womanhood: "Woman's Sphere" in New England, 1780–1835* (New Haven: Yale University Press, 1977). The WLAA provides an example of this. For an understanding of "Republican Motherhood," see Gordon S. Wood, *The Creation of the American Republic 1776–1787* (New York: Norton, 1972).

62. Laurel Thatcher Ulrich, *Good Wives: Image and Reality in the Lives of Women in Northern New England 1650–1750* (New York: Vintage, 1980), 70. Ulrich discusses how "themes of gentility intermeshed with industrious housekeeping."

63. Catharine E. Beecher and Harriet Beecher Stowe, *An American Woman's Home*, 1869. See also Valerie Gill, "Catharine Beecher and Charlotte Perkins Gilman: Architects of Female Power," *Journal of American Culture* 21, no. 2 (1998): 17–24.

64. Ibid., 40.

65. "Appendix E: Properties Associated with the Women's Rights Movement," 3 March 2004, www.nps.gov/wori/Appendix E.pdf.

66. Board of Directors Luncheon Invitation, 1919, Wyck Library Collection, ephemera file.

67. The 1918 commencement program, Wyck Library Collection, ephemera file.

68. Pennsylvania School of Horticulture for Women, Prospectus, 1919.

69. Temple University, 1 March 2005, http://www.temple.edu/flowershow; Martha Nolan, *A Chronicle: The History of Woman's National Farm and Garden Association* (Fremont, OH: Lesher, 1986), 3.
70. W.E. Huffman and R.E. Evenson, *Science for Agriculture* (Ames: Iowa State University Press, 1993), 23–24.
71. Roth, "The Country Life Movement"; Danbom, *The Resisted Revolution*.
72. For more information, See Sarah Stage and Virginia Bramble Vincente, *Rethinking Home Economics: Women and the History of a Profession* (Ithaca: Cornell University Press, 1997).
73. Nolan, *A Chronicle*, 3.
74. Beatrice Williams, "A Practical Gardening School," August 7, 1925, 2, from Wyck Library Collection.
75. Kenyon L. Butterfield Papers, 1889–1945, held by Special Collections and University Archives, W.E.B. Du Bois Library, University of Massachusetts Amherst, Collection number RG 3/1.
76. Ibid.
77. Pennsylvania School of Horticulture for Women, Prospectus, 1929–30.
78. Ibid., 21.
79. Williams, "A Practical Gardening School"; Pennsylvania School of Horticulture for Women, Prospectus, 1929–30.
80. School of Horticulture for Women. Prospectus, 1929–30, PA: Ambler, 1930.

Chapter Six

1. Helen Kennedy Stevens, "City Girl as Farm Worker—Her Own Story. How Nursing the Crops in Westchester County Furnished a Healthful Vacation, a Little Fun Now and Then, Much Valuable Experience, and Cash Wages," *The New York Times*, February 24, 1918, 71.
2. *The New York Times*, July 28, 1918.
3. Stevens, "City Girl as Farm Worker."
4. It is difficult to identify the first usage of the term "farmerette." The Merriam-Webster Online Dictionary dates the first usage to 1902. http://www.merriam-webster.com/dictionary/farmerette January 24, 2009. Some sources identify first usage between 1915–1920. The term was used by America's European allies prior to America's entry into World War I. By the end of World War I, the term was in common use.
5. Stevens, "City Girl as Farm Worker."
6. Ibid.
7. Christopher Joseph Capozzola. "Uncle Sam Wants You: Political Obligations in World War I America." Ph.D. Dissertation, Columbia University, 2002): 150.
8. Ibid. See also William J. Breen, "Foundations, Statistics, and State-Building: Leonard P. Ayres, the Russell Sage Foundation, and U.S. Government Statistics in the First World War," *Business History Review*, 68, no.4 (1994): 451–482; William J. Breen, "Mobilization and Cooperation Federalism: The Connecticut State Council of Defense, 1917–1919," *Historian* 42, no.1 (November 1979): 58–84; William J. Breen, "The Mobilization of Skilled Labor in World War I: 'Voluntarism,' the U.S. Public Service Reserve, and the Department of Labor, 1917–1918," *Labor History* 32, no.2 (1991): 253–272; Robert D. Cuff, "Herbert Hoover, The Ideology of Voluntarism and War Organization During the Great War," *Journal of American History* 64, no.2 (September 1977): 358–372.
9. Ibid. For a particularly rich discussion of women's wartime work through voluntary associations during World War I, refer to Chapter Three of Capozzola's dissertation, "Uncle Sam Wants You: Political Obligations in World War I America."
10. Ibid., 133–134.
11. Capozzola, "Uncle Sam Wants You," 136–137.
12. Martha Nolan, *A Chronicle: The History of Woman's National Farm and Garden Association* (Fremont, OH: Lesher, 1986).
13. Melanie Simo, *Forest and Garden: Traces of Wilderness in a Modernizing Land, 1897–1949* (Charlottesville: University of Virginia Press, 2003). Several women enjoyed notable success in the emerging field of landscape architecture, which was originally called landscape art. Lacking formal training, many of these women first carved out a professional place on the periphery of the field. These women included writer, historian, and critic Mariana Griswold Van Rensselaer, who wrote the first biography of Fredrick Law Olmsted. Her book *Art Out-of-Doors*, was standard reading in Harvard's landscape architecture program for decades. (As referenced in Melanie Simo's book, *Forest and Garden*, 13–14, early landscape architect Charles Elliot chided Van Rensselaer for ignoring the "essentially virile and practical nature" of the profession, although he praised the style and tone of the book.) Kate Sessions was a University of California graduate, largely self-trained, who created the landscape at San Diego's Balboa Park; see Elizabeth McPhail, *Kate Sessions: Pioneer Horticulturist* (San Diego: San Diego Historical Society, 1976). At Harvard, Theodora Kimball, a librarian, was busy co-writing what would become the standard textbook for landscape ar-

chitecture programs with the Harvard professor who was later to become her husband (Simo, 113–114). See also *Henry Vincent Hubbard and Hubbard, Theodora Kimball, An Introduction to the Study of Landscape Design* (New York: Macmillan, 1917); *Henry Vincent Hubbard and Theodora Kimball, Landscape Architecture: A Comprehensive Classification Scheme for Books, Plans, Photographs, Notes and Other Collected Material, with Combined Alphabetic Topic Index and List of Subject Headings* (Cambridge: Harvard University Press, 1920). See also "Theodora Kimball Hubbard: A Biographical Minute," *Landscape Architecture* 26, 2 (January 1936): 53–55. By the time of Beatrix Farrand, landscape architecture was a field with a strong female presence; see Eleanor M. McPeck, "Beatrix Jones Farrand," in *Pioneers of American Landscape Design*, Charles A. Birnbaum, Robin Karson, eds. (New York: McGraw-Hill, 2000), 117–119.

14. Elaine F. Weiss, *Fruits of Victory: The Woman's Land Army of America in the Great War* (Washington, DC: Potomac Books, 2009), 21–22.

15. Nolan, *A Chronicle*, 22–23.

16. Weiss, *Fruits of Victory*, 21–22. See also Nolan, *A Chronicle*, 21–24. For primary source documents, see Minutes of the Council Meeting, March 12, 1917, Records of the WNFGA, B-4, Box 6, Folder 35, Schlesinger Library.

17. Nolan, *A Chronicle*, 21–24.

18. Ibid. See also Weiss, *Fruits of Victory*.

19. Ibid.

20. Helen Fraser, *Women and War Work* (New York: G. Arnold Shaw, 1918), foreword by H.N. MacCracken.

21. Weiss, Fruits of Victory, 21.

22. Ibid. See also Nolan, *A Chronicle*, 23–24.

23. Ibid. Also Harriet Stanton Blatch, *Mobilizing Woman-Power* (New York: Womans Press, 1918). Commissioned by the National Board of the Young Women's Christian Association. This book appeared after the WLAA began, but the appeal by Roosevelt must have been somewhat affirming for WLAA members.

24. It is commonly accepted that between 15,000 and 20,000 women from between twenty-one and thirty states were formally registered through the WLAA in America. This is documented in numerous sources. States with the highest number of participants were California, Illinois, New York, Pennsylvania, and Washington, D.C. For additional information, refer to Elaine F. Weiss, *Fruits of Victory: The Woman's Land Army of America in the Great War* (Washington, DC: Potomac Books, 2009); Stephanie Carpenter, *On the Farm Front: The Women's Land Army in World War II* (DeKalb: Northern Illinois University Press, 2002); Esther M. Colvin, "Another Women's Land Army?" *Independent Woman* 21 (April 1942); and Judy Barrett and David Smith Litoff, "To the Rescue of the Crops: The Woman's Land Army During World War II," *Prologue: The Journal of the National Archives* 25, no. 4 (1993).

25. Middle class women did work during this period. There is an extensive literature regarding "shop girl" culture. See Nan Enstad, *Ladies of Labor, Girls of Adventure: Working Women, Popular Culture, and Labor Politics at the Turn of the Century* (New York: Columbia University Press, 1999); John F. Kasson, *Amusing the Million: Coney Island at the Turn of the Century* (New York: Hill & Wang, 1978); Alison M. Kibler, *Rank Ladies: Gender and Cultural Hierarchy in American Vaudeville* (Chapel Hill: University of North Carolina Press, 1999). Other middle class women worked in reform movements. See Robyn Muncy, *Creating a Female Dominion in American Reform 1890–1935* (New York: Oxford University Press, 1991). Women also worked in agriculture during this period. However, the participation of largely urban, middle and upper-middle class women in hard, physical labor was contrary to "modern" as well as Victorian domestic expectations.

26. Cora Call Whitely, Private Collection, *Cora Call Whitely Papers, 1862–1937*, Iowa Women's Archives, University of Iowa Libraries, Iowa City, 1917–1919, Ref Box 1, Council of National Defense Women's Committee, National and State Organization; Ref Box 2, Woman's Land Army of America.

27. Ibid. See also Nolan, A Chronicle: History of the WNF&GA; Weiss, *Fruits of Victory: The Woman's Land Army of America in the Great War*; Capozzola, *Uncle Sam Wants You: Political Obligations in World War I America*.

28. Cora Call Whitely, Private Collection, *Cora Call Whitely Papers, 1862–1937.*

29. Ibid.

30. Ibid. Also Nolan, *A Chronicle*, 23; Weiss, *Fruits of Victory*.

31. There is a rich and large body of historical literature exploring the history of club women. See Capozzola, *Uncle Sam Wants You*, 124–178; Paula Baker, "The Domestication of Politics: Women and American Political Society, 1780–1920," *American Historical Review* 89 (June 1984): 620–47; Karen J. Blair, *The Clubwoman as Feminist: True Womanhood Redefined, 1868–1914* (New York: Holmes and Meier, 1980); Elisabeth S. Clemens, "Securing Political Returns to Social Capital: Women's Association sin the United States, 1880s–1920s," *Journal of Interdisciplinary History* 29 (Spring 1999): 613–38; Nancy F. Cott,

The Grounding of Modern Feminism (New Haven: Yale University Press, 1987); Robyn Muncy, *Creating a Female Dominion in American Reform, 1890–1935* (New York: Oxford University Press, 1991); Theda Skocpol, *Protecting Soldiers and Mothers: The Political Origins of Social Policy in the United States* (Cambridge: Belknap Press of Harvard University Press, 1992). Primary sources are Harriet Stanton Blatch, *Mobilizing Woman-Power* (New York: Womans Press, 1918); Ida B. Clark, *American Women and the World War* (New York: D. Appleton, 1918); Mrs. Josiah Evans Cowles, "A Call to Club Women," *Ladies Home Journal* 34 (June 1917): 72; Carolyn Ruutz-Rees, "The Mobilization of American Women," *Yale Review* 7 (July 1918): 801–18; Martha E.D. White, "Women's Clubs and Patriotism," *The Nation* 105 (October 4, 1917): 367–68; "Editorial: Her Chance for Service," *Ladies Home Journal* 34 (June 1917): 7; "Editorial: The Woman Slacker," *Ladies Home Journal* 34 (June 1917): 7.

32. Cora Call Whitely, Private Collection, *Cora Call Whitely Papers, 1862–1937*.

33. R. L. Adams and T.R. Kelly, "A Study of Farm Labor in California," Circular No. 193, March 1918, published by the California Agricultural Experiment Station, Berkeley.

34. Ibid., 13.

35. Ibid., 14.

36. Catherine Gabriel Kipp, "Women on the Land: The Woman's Land Army, Northern California Division, 1918–1920," MA thesis, California State University, 1960, 38. Students were mentored in this project by Mrs. Sydney Joseph, who would later become chair of the Northern California Division. University of California, *Digital History Archives*, 9 October 2006, http://sunsite.berkeley.edu/uchistory/archives_exhibits/collections/president_reports.html (accessed 1/28/2010).

37. Kipp, "Women on the Land: The Woman's Land Army, Northern California Division, 1918–1920," 39.

38. Ibid.

39. Ibid., 38. The survey's national sponsor was the National League for Women's Service. See also *Report of the Women's Committee*, June 1, 1917–January 1, 1919, California State Council of Defense, Los Angeles, 1920, 77.

40. See Douglas Sackman, "'Nature's Workshop': The Work Environment and Workers' Bodies in California's Citrus Industry, 1900–1940," *Environmental History* 5, no. 1 (2000): 27–53; Harrington Emerson and William F. Muhs, "Worker Participation in the Progressive Era: An Assessment," *The Academy of Management Review* 7, no. 1 (1982): 99–102; Sharon Corwin, "Picturing Efficiency: Precisionism, Scientific Management, and the Effacement of Labor," *Representations* 84 (2003): 139–165.

41. Theodore Roosevelt. On January 22, 1909, President Theodore Roosevelt delivered a "Special Message" to the United States Senate and the United States House of Representatives. In this message, Roosevelt discussed the report of the National Conservation Commission (Charles Lathrop Pack was involved in this effort) and mentioned "national efficiency" several times. The quote is from *A Compilation of the Messages and Papers of the Presidents* (New York, 1897–1922), 10: 7640–41. This information also appeared in Frederick Winslow Taylor's *The Principles of Scientific Management* (New York: Harper and Brothers, 1911) and also is quoted in Sharon Corwin's article, "Picturing Efficiency: Precisionism, Scientific Management, and the Effacement of Labor."

42. Taylor, The Principles of Scientific Management.

43. Corwin, "Picturing Efficiency," 141.

44. Samuel P. Hays, *Conservation and the Gospel of Efficiency: The Progressive Conservation Movement, 1890–1920* (Cambridge: Harvard University Press, 1959). While Hays does not specifically talk about wartime gardening programs, the competing political processes he describes apply to wartime gardening programs.

45. Prospectus of the Woman's Land Army, 6 March 1918, New York, No. 1A-1918-5,000.

46. For additional information about shop girl life, gender and consumer culture, see Elaine S. Abelson, *When Ladies Go A-Thieving: Middle-Class Shoplifters in the Victorian Department Store* (New York: Oxford University Press, 1989); Victoria De Grazia, ed., *The Sex of Things: Gender and Consumption in Historical Perspective* (Berkeley: University of California Press, 1996); Ellen Gruber Garvey, *The Adman in the Parlor: Magazines and the Gendering of Consumer Culture, 1880's to 1910's* (Oxford: Oxford University Press, 1996).

47. Women on the Land, 1918, Advisory Council of the Woman's Land Army of American, New York, January 1918, 1–6.

48. Mildred E. Buller Smith Papers, photo album, Schlesinger Library, Radcliffe Institute for Advanced Study, Harvard University, http://nrs.harvard.edu/urn-3:RAD.SCHL:sch0.

49. "The Duties of American Citizenship, " speech delivered by Theodore Roosevelt on January 26, 1883, http://www.theodoreroosevelt.org/life/quotes.htm (accessed 2/15/2009). See also Theodore Roosevelt, *Theodore Roosevelt. An Autobiography* (New York: Macmillan, 1913).

50. Ibid.

51. Matthew Frye Jacobson, *Barbarian Virtues: The United States Encounters Foreign Peoples at Home and Abroad, 1876–1917* (New York: Hill & Wang, 2000).

52. Women on the Land, 1918, Advisory Council of the Woman's Land Army of America, New York City, January 1918, 1–6.

53. Ida Ogilvie, "The Spirit of the Land Army," *The Farmerette* (December 1918): 1.

54. Sharon Ouditt, *Fighting Forces, Writing Women: Identity and Ideology in the First World War* (London: Routledge, 1994); Nancy Cott, *The Bonds of Womanhood: "Woman's Sphere" in New England, 1780–1835* (New Haven: Yale University Press, 1977); Robyn Muncy, *Creating a Female Dominion in American Reform 1890–1935* (New York: Oxford University Press, 1991); Paula Baker, *The Moral Frameworks of Public Life: Gender, Politics, and the State in Rural New York, 1870–1930* (New York: Oxford University Press, 1991).

55. See Ernest Lutz, ed., *Agriculture and the Environment: Perspectives on Sustainable Rural Development* (Washington, DC: World Bank, 1998); Janice Peterson and Margaret Lewis, eds., *The Elgar Companion to Feminist Economics* (North Hampton, MA: Edward Elgar, 2001); Julie A. Matthaei, *An Economic History of Women in America: Women's Work, the Sexual Division of Labor, and the Development of Capitalism* (New York: Shocken, 1981).

56. See Laurel Thatcher Ulrich, *Good Wives: Image and Reality in the Lives of Women in Northern New England, 1650–1750* (New York: Alfred A. Knopf, 1982); John Mack Faragher, *Women and Men on the Overland Trail*, 2d ed. (New Haven: Yale University Press, 2001).

57. For an excellent discussion of voluntarism in World War I, refer to William J. Breen, "Foundations, Statistics, and State-Building: Leonard P. Ayres, the Russell Sage Foundation, and U.S. Government Statistics in the First World War," *Business History Review* 68, no. 4 (1994): 451–482; William J. Breen, "Mobilization and Cooperation Federalism: The Connecticut State Council of Defense, 1917–1919," *Historian* 42, no.1 (November 1979): 58–84; William J. Breen, "The Mobilization of Skilled Labor in World War I: 'Voluntarism,' the U.S. Public Service Reserve, and the Department of Labor, 1917–1918," *Labor History* 32, no. 2 (1991): 253–272; Robert D. Cuff, "Herbert Hoover, The Ideology of Voluntarism and War Organization during the Great War," *Journal of American History* 64, no. 2 (1977): 358–372; Robert D. Cuff, "The Dilemmas of Voluntarism: Hoover and the Pork-Packing Agreement of 1917–1919," *Agricultural History* 53, no. 4 (October 1979): 727–747; Daniel Pope, "The Advertising Industry and World War I," *Public Historian* 2, no. 3 (Spring 1980): 4–25; Theda Skocpol and Morris P. Fiorina, eds., *Civic Engagement in American Democracy* (Washington, DC: The Brookings Institute/Russell Sage Foundation, 1999); chapter two is of particular interest.

58. See in particular Capozolla, *Uncle Sam Wants You*, 4–9.

59. See Richard W. Amero, "The Making of the Panama-California Exposition, 1909–1915," *The Journal of San Diego History* 36 (1990).

60. Cuff, "Herbert Hoover, the Ideology of Voluntarism and War Organization," 358–372; William E. Leuchtenburg, *The Perils of Prosperity 1914–1932* (Chicago: University of Chicago Press, 1958), 35–36.

61. For an excellent discussion of the parastate model, highly relevant to the institutional forms of World War I, see Eldon Eisenach, *The Lost Promise of Progressivism* (Lawrence: University Press of Kansas, 1994).

62. There is a wonderful body of literature surrounding this topic. Consider David B. Danbom, *The Resisted Revolution: Urban America and the Industrialization of Agriculture, 1900–1930* (Ames: Iowa State University Press, 1979); David B. Danbom, *Born in the Country: A History of Rural America* (Baltimore: Johns Hopkins University Press, 1995); Dianne D. Glave, "A Garden So Brilliant with Colors, So Original in Its Design: Rural African American Women, Gardening, Progressive Reform, and the Foundation of an African American Environmental Perspective," *Environmental History* 8 (July 2003); Marilyn Irvin Holt, "From Better Babies to 4-H: A Look at Rural America, 1900–1930," *Prologue: The Journal of the National Archives* 24, no. 3 (Fall 1992); R. Douglas Hurt, *American Agriculture: A Brief History* (Ames: Iowa State University Press, 1994); James L. Machor, *Pastoral Cities: Urban Ideals and the Symbolic Landscape of America* (Madison: University of Wisconsin Press, 1987).

63. *The Farmerette* 1, no. 3 (January 1919): 1–2.

64. Women's National Land Service Corps, Annual Report October 1, 1916, to September 30, 1917, London.

65. Helen Fraser, *Women and War Work* (New York: G. Arnold Shaw, 1918), foreword, Chapter VIII.

66. "Women in Agriculture," *The Women's Industrial News* 20 (July 1916).

67. In a lecture delivered at Vassar College in 1917, Helen Fraser stated that 258,300 were then participating in the Land Army of Women in Great Britain. Fraser, *Women and War Work*, 155.

68. Ibid., 166.
69. Ibid., 167.
70. "Statistics," *The Farmerette* (January 1919): 3.
71. Ida H. Ogilvie, Women's Agricultural Camp, Bedford, New York, First Annual Report, New York, 1917.
72. Ida H. Ogilvie, *Women's Agricultural Camp, Bedford, New York, Second Annual Report*, Department of Agriculture, National Agricultural Library, New York, 1918.
73. Ogilvie, Women's Agricultural Camp, 1917; Ogilvie, Women's Agricultural Camp, 1918.
74. Woman's National and Service Corps, *Annual Report*, October 1, 1916, to September 30, 1917, London.
75. "Help for the Farmer," Advisory Council of the Woman's Land Army of America, January 1918, New York.
76. Fraser, Women and War Work, 261.
77. Ibid., 262. Other groups have used their wartime contributions to press claims for full citizenship, including African-Americans after the American Civil War.
78. Ibid., 267.
79. Ibid., 277.
80. Harriet Stanton Blatch, *Mobilizing Woman-Power* (New York: Woman's Press, 1918). Commissioned by the National Board of the Young Women's Christian Association.
81. Ibid., 173–74.
82. Ida H. Ogilvie, "Agriculture, Labor and Woman," *Columbia University Quarterly* (October 1918).
83. Edson was also a board member of the California Federation of Women's Clubs from 1910 to 1916. She also was appointed as a special agent to the California Bureau of Labor Statistics. She was an appointee on the California Industrial Welfare Commission, a position that enabled her to encourage changes in labor practices.
84. Ida Ogilvie, "The Spirit of the Land Army," *The Farmerette* (December 1918): 1.
85. Eisenach, *The Lost Promise of Progressivism*.
86. "Help for the Farmer," Advisory Council of the Woman's Land Army of American, New York, January 1918.
87. "Help for the Farmer," Advisory Council of the Woman's Land Army of America, New York, January 1918. In practice, a unit might exceed seventy members.
88. Woman's Land Army of America, brochure, Washington, DC, 1918.
89. Much wonderful information about this topic is found in the literature surrounding the history of rural women in America. For additional reading that touches on this topic, please see Katherine Jellison, *Entitled to Power: Farm Women and Technology, 1913–1963* (Chapel Hill: University of North Carolina Press, 1993). California and some parts of the west, which utilized foreign migrant labor may have been the exception to this general experience.
90. "The L.A. and the Farmer's Wife," *The Farmerette* (October 1919): 2.
91. Ibid.
92. Fighting Song of the Farmerettes" sung to "It's a Long, Long Way to Tipperary," Emma L. George Papers, Library of Congress.
93. *The Farmerette* (December 1918): 3.
94. Emma L. George, private collection, Emma L. George Papers, Library of Congress.
95. *New York Times*, December 16, 1917, X2.
96. Weiss, *Fruits of Victory*, 36.
97. Clarence Ousley, *Women on the Farm. Address before Woman's Committee, Council of National Defense* (Washington, DC: Department of Agriculture, 1918), 7, National Agricultural Library.
98. Ibid., 6.
99. Dudley Harmon, "Is the Woman Needed on the Farm? What the United States Government Has to Say About Farm Work for Women This Summer," *Ladies' Home Journal* 35 (May 1918): 105–106.
100. Ibid.
101. Ibid.
102. Ibid., 8.
103. "Help for the Farmer," 2d ed., *The Woman's Land Army of America, New York, 1918*.
104. Ibid.
105. Woman's National Farm and Garden Association, corporate collection, Records, 1913–1980, Schlesinger Library, Radcliffe College, Cambridge, MA, Ref Control MHVW85-A514, IV, no. 9, February1918.
106. Womans' Land Army of America, *What the Farmers Say about the Work of the Woman's Land Army of America in 1918*, New York, 1918.
107. Ibid.
108. *San Francisco Examiner*, August 4, 1918.
109. "Miss Ihlseng in the South," *The Farmerette* (January 1919): 3.
110. Weiss, *Fruits of Victory*, 185–188.
111. Ibid., 186–187.
112. "Miss Ihlseng in the South," *The Farmerette* (January 1919): 3.
113. See Margo McBane, "The Role of Women in Determining the California Farm Labor Structure: A Case Study of the Woman's Land Army During World War I," MA thesis, UC Davis; Catherine Gabriel Kipp, "Women on the Land: The Woman's Land Army, Northern Cali-

fornia Division, 1918–1920," MA thesis, California State University, 1960; Weiss, *Fruits of Victory*.

114. *New York Times*, February 13, 1918, 59.

115. Stevens, "City Girl as Farm Worker," *New York Times*.

116. Ibid.

117. Cornelia Throop Geer, "Out of the Kitchen—Into the Fields," *House Beautiful*, XLIV (September 1918): 84.

118. Richard Barry, "War as a Tonic for Jaded Feminine Nerves," *New York Times*, June 23, 1918.

119. Ibid.

120. *The Farmerette* 1, no. 5 (December 1919).

121. *The Farmerette* 1, no. 6 (May 1920).

122. Mary Van Kleeck, Report of the Women in Industry Service of the Department of Labor to June 30, 1919, Washington, DC, 1919.

123. Cornelia Throop Geer, "Out of the Kitchen—Into the Fields," *House Beautiful*, XLIV (September 1918): 84.

124. Marguerite Wilkinson, "My Experiences as a Farmerette," *Independent*, XCV (September 14, 1918): 364.

125. Stevens, "City Girl as Farm Worker," *New York Times*.

126. Opportunities for Women in Agriculture and Country Life," *M.A.C. Bulletin*, May 1920. Published by Massachusetts Agricultural College, University of Massachusetts, Amherst. Newspaper articles, pamphlets and other printed materials, 1917–1958, related to vocational training in agriculture for women at Massachusetts Agricultural College; also, programs, proceedings and other materials related to a conference on "Women in Agriculture and Country Life," held October 7–8, 1920, at M.A.C.

127. This belief is also shared by author Catherine Kipp. See Catherine Gabriel Kipp, "Women on the Land: The Woman's Land Army, Northern California Division, 1918–1920," MA thesis, California State University, 1960.

128. *The Farmerette* 1, no. 6 (May 1920).

129. This argument is presented by Catherine Kipp. See Catherine Gabriel Kipp, "Women on the Land."

130. Matt Garcia, *A World of Its Own: Race, Labor, and Citrus in the Making of Greater Los Angeles, 1900–1970* (Chapel Hill: University of North Carolina Press, 2001), 70–71.

131. Kipp, "Women on the Land," 55.

132. *The Farmerette* 1, no. 1 (December 1919).

133. Ogilvie, "Agriculture," 299.

134. Harriet Geithman, "Chronicles of Woodcock Farm," *Overland* LXXXI (June 1918), 483. Quote excerpted from a letter written by a Woman's Land Army of America member at the Bedford Unit, to her family, July 1917.

Chapter Seven

1. David Kennedy, *Over Here: The First World War and American Society* (New York: Oxford University Press, 1980), 16.

2. Ibid., 17; David B. Danbom, *The Resisted Revolution: Urban America and the Industrialization of Agriculture, 1900–1930* (Ames: Iowa State University Press, 1979).

3. Kennedy, *Over Here*, 17.

4. Ibid.; Theodore Saloutos, *The American Farmer and the New Deal* (Ames: Iowa State University Press, 1982), xviii, 327; Edward L. Schapsmeier and Frederick H. Schapsmeier, *Henry A. Wallace of Iowa: The Agrarian Years, 1910–1940* (Ames: Iowa State University Press, 1968), xiii, 327.

5. Harvey Levenstein, *Paradox of Plenty: A Social History of Eating in Modern America*, rev. ed. (Berkeley: University of California Press, 2003), 65.

6. Ibid., 66.

7. Proceedings of the National Defense Gardening Conference (United States Department of Agriculture, 1941).

8. Ibid.

9. Ibid 1826–41, 1. M-Day for Gardening.

10. Ibid., 2.

11. Ibid., 2. Vegetables, Vitality and Victory.

12. Ibid.

13. Ibid.

14. Ibid.

15. Amy Bentley, *Eating for Victory: Food Rationing and the Politics of Domesticity* (Urbana: University of Illinois Press, 1998); 1940 census; Letter from Andrew Wing, National Victory Garden Institute, to H. W. Hochbaum, November 14, 1944, RG 208, Entry 66, Box 8, File: Master File/Victory Gardens, NA.

16. Levenstein, *Paradox of Plenty*.

17. Ibid., 85; Bentley, *Eating for Victory*, 114.

18. Bentley's *Eating for Victory* provides more detailed information about World War II Victory Garden statistics. See Chapter 5.

Conclusion

1. Charles Lathrop Pack, *The War Garden Victorious: Its War Time Need and Its Economic Value in Peace* (Philadelphia: J.B. Lippincott, 1919).

2. See Chicago Botanic Gardens, "Urban Agriculture: Feeding the Movement," Proceedings of the Chicago Botanic Gardens urban agriculture symposium, June 2009, http://www.chicagobotanic.org/wed/documents/WED_Proceedings_0629.pdf.

3. State Land Settlement Board, "Introduction regarding progress under the land settlement act of the State of California and about the plans for soldier settlement in the future," California, 1919; State Land Settlement, Delhi, California, 1920–1922, BANC PIC 1966.033, Bancroft Library, University of California, Berkeley.

4. Lawson, *City Bountiful*, 145. The years 1931–1935 marked the peak of Depression Era gardening. During the early years of this Depression, there was less organized aid from the government; gardening may have been driven more by necessity during these years.

5. Laura Lawson, *City Bountiful: A Century of Community Gardening in America* (Berkeley: University of California Press, 2005), 145. Gardens were called by many names. Providing work for the unemployed and improving community access to food were two primary goals.

6. United States Department of Agriculture, "National Defense Gardening Conference."

7. Ibid., from section on Extension Service, 1844–41.

8. Ibid., 1841–41.

9. Ibid., Section 3, 2.

10. Ibid., Section I, 2.

11. http://www.jointhefarm.com.

12. United States Department of Agriculture, Map 07-M127, "Percent of farms with female principal operators: 2007," http://www.agcensus.usda.gov/Publications/2007/Online_Highlights/Ag_Atlas_Maps/Operators/index.asp.

Bibliography

Primary Sources

Manuscript Collections

American Forestry Association Records, Library and Archives, Forest History Society, Durham, NC.

Aurelia H. Reinhardt, private collection, Reinhardt (Aurelia H.) Papers. Held at Mills College, California. Ref Record Group II, Office of the President Files, 1916–1943. Series Bound Volumes, 73 Women's Land Army: correspondence, re: women agricultural workers during World War I and Mills volunteers.

Charles W. Eliot, letters to P. P. Claxton, April 18 and April 27, 1918, Historical File, 18701950, Office of the Commissioner of Education, Department of the Interior, U.S. National Archives.

Cora Call Whitely, private collection, Cora Call Whitely Papers, 1862–1937. Held at Iowa Women's Archives, University of Iowa Libraries, Iowa City, 1917–1919. Ref Box 1, Council of National Defense Women's Committee, National and State Organization; Ref Box 2, Woman's Land Army of America.

Emma L. George, private collection, Emma L. George Papers, Library of Congress.

Henry Churchill King, private collection, Henry Churchill King Papers, correspondence, 1897–1928. Held at Oberlin College. Ref 661.

Jane Bowne Haines, "Gardening Schools for Women." February 1907, personal document, Wyck Papers, collection of the Wyck Association, held by the American Philosophical Society, Philadelphia. Series 11, Box 296A, Folder 137.

Katherine P. Edson, private collection, Edson (Katherine P.) Papers, Held at University of California, Los Angeles, Department of Special Collections. Ref Woman's Land Army, Box 1, Folder 5, Folder 7; Box 2, Folder 13; Box 7, Folder 1.

Kenyon L. Butterfield, private collection, President Kenyon L. Butterfield Collection. Held at Five Colleges Archives and Manuscripts Collections, W.E.B. DuBois Library, University of Masschusetts, Amherst, 1917–1918. Ref Folder 75: Committee on Food Production—Women's Committee on Food Conservation, 1917–1918.

R.S. Trumbull and Isabella Ferguson, private collection, Woman's Land Army Letters. Held at Fray Angelico Chavez History Library, Palace of the Governors, Santa Fe, 1918.

Theodosia Burr Shepherd Papers, Collection 123, Department of Special Collections, Charles E. Young Research Library, University of California, Los Angeles.

Woman's National Farm and Garden Association, corporate collection, minutes of the Council Meeting, March 12, 1917, Records of the WNFGA, B-4, Box 6, Folder 35, Schlesinger Library, Radcliffe College, Cambridge, MA.

Woman's National Farm and Garden Association, corporate collection, Records, 1913–1980. Held at Schlesinger Library, Radcliffe College, Cambridge, MA. Ref Control MHVW85-A514.

Published Primary Sources

Included in this list are books and articles published during the World War I era, as well as edited document collections published after the war. General club histories are listed with secondary sources.

Adams, Emma H. *To and fro in Southern California*. Cincinnati: W.M.B.C. Press, 1887.

Adams, R. L., and T.R. Kelly. "A Study of Farm Labor in California." Circular No. 193. California Agricultural Experiment Station, Berkeley, March 1918.

Advisory Council of the Women's Land Army of America. *Help for the Farmer.* New York: Advisory Council of the Woman's Land Army of America, 1918.

———. *Women on the Land.* New York: Advisory Council of the Woman's Land Army of America, 1918.

"Ann Street School Doing Its Bit." *Ventura Star*, September 21, 1917.

"Appeals to Women to Train for War Work: Dr. Franklin H. Martin Says They Can Guard the Nation's Moral Standards." *New York Times*, September 17, 1917.

Babcock, Ernest. "Agriculture in California Schools." *Sierra Education News* 6, no. 1 (1910).

———. "Agriculture in Secondary Schools." *The Nature Study Review* 5, no. 8 (1910).

———. "Co-operation Between the Schools and the College of Agriculture." *University of California Chronicle* 13, no. 3 (1910): 1–10.

———. *Information for Students Concerning the School of Agriculture of the University of California*, Circular No. 52. Berkeley: University of California Agricultural Research and Experiment Station, 1906.

———. *Suggestions for Garden Work in California Schools*, Circular No. 46. Berkeley: University of California Press, College of Agriculture, 1909.

Babcock, Ernest B., and L.H. Miller. *Outline of Course in Nature Study.* Los Angeles: Los Angeles Normal School, 1906.

Babcock, Ernest B., and Cyril A. Stebbins. *Elementary School Agriculture: A Teacher's Manual to Accompany Hilgard and Osterhout's* "Agriculture for Schools of the Pacific Slope." New York: Macmillan, 1911.

Bailey, Liberty Hyde. *The Country-Life Movement in the United States.* New York: Macmillan, 1911.

———. *The Nature Study Idea*, 3d ed. New York: Macmillan, 1909.

———. *The Training of Farmers.* New York: The Century Company, 1909.

Barney, Maginel W. Poster. "Follow the Pied Piper: Join the United States School Garden Army." Washington, DC: The Graphic Company, 1919.

———. Poster. "War Gardens Over the Top: The Seeds of Victory Insure the Fruits of Peace." Washington, DC: National War Garden Commission, 1919.

Barrows, Sarah T. "Teaching English to Immigrants: Some Suggestions on Methods and Materials, Columbus, Ohio Branch." Council of National Defense, ca. 1918.

Barry, Richard. "War as a Tonic for Jaded Feminine Nerves." *New York Times*, June 23, 1918.

Beecher, Catharine E., and Harriet Beecher Stowe. *An American Woman's Home*, 1869.

"Best Years of Their Lives: Women's Land Army Has Final Reunion." *The Economist*, May 7, 1988.

Blatch, Harriot Stanton. *Mobilizing Woman-Power.* New York: Womans Press, 1918.

"Children Line Up to Defeat the Huns." *Los Angeles Times*, May 27, 1918.

Clapp, H.L. "School Gardens." *Education* 21 (May 1901): 522–30, 611–17.

———. "School Gardens." *Popular Science* 52 (February 1898): 445–56.

———. "School Gardens as an Educational Means." *Education* 21 (June 1901): 611–17.

Clark, Ida Clyde Gallagher. *American Women and the World War.* New York: D. Appleton, 1918.

Claxton, Philander P. "United States School Garden Army." *Review of Reviews* 7 (April 1918): 393–94.

———. United States Bureau of Education Commissioner. School Garden Association of America Annual Report. New York: School Garden Association of America, 1916.

Cockerell, T.D.A. "War Work of College Women in the West." *School and Society* 6 (15 December 1917): 669–705.

Colvin, Esther M. "Another Women's Land Army?" *Independent Woman* 21 (April 1942): 102–04, 126.

Cook, Catherine. "National Service and the Women's National Farm and Garden Association: Join the Land Army, A Call to the Women of America." *Women's National Farm and Garden Association Monthly Bulletin* 4 (October 1917): 1–2.

Council of the Woman's Land Army of America. *Women's National Farm and Garden Association Monthly Bulletin* 4 (February 1918): 6–8.

Cowles, Mrs. Josiah Evans. "A Call to Club Women." *Ladies' Home Journal* 34 (June 1917): 72.

Creel, George. *How We Advertised America.* New York: Harper and Brothers, 1920.

———. "The United States School Garden Army." *School Life* 1 (1918).

"Crop Prolific on Small Lot: Jack's Wonderful Beanstalk Has Little, if Anything, on Harriet's." *The Los Angeles Times*, September 2, 1917.

Department of the Interior, Bureau of Education. *The Fall Manual of the United States School Garden Army.* Washington, DC: Government Printing Office, 1918.

———. *The Spring Manual of the United States School Garden Army*. Washington, DC: Government Printing Office, 1919.

———. Record Group 12. Records of the Office of Education, Administrative History.

"Destroys War Garden, and Is Ordered Interned." *Los Angeles Times*, May 20, 1918.

Dewey, John. *Schools of Tomorrow*. New York: E.P. Dutton, 1915.

———. "What Are We Fighting For?" *The Independent*, June 22, 1918.

Diehl, Edith, dir. *Wellesley College Training Camp for Women, Women's Land Army of America*. Wellesley, MA: Wellesley College, 1919.

"Editorial: Her Chance for Service." *Ladies' Home Journal* 34 (June 1917).

"Editorial: The Women Slacker." *Ladies' Home Journal* 34 (July 1917).

"Enlist in School Farm Army. Government Tells of Big Results from the Work of Country's Boys and Girls. 60,000 Acres Are Tilled." *New York Times*, October 20, 1918.

Erskine, John. "Society as a University." *Educational Review* 58 (September 1918): 91–108.

Farmerette, December 1918–May 1920.

"Farmerette Need Seen By First Lady." *New York Times*, April 7, 1942.

Findlay, Hugh. "School Garden Army 6,000,000 Strong." *The Independent* May 4, 1918.

Flagg, James M. Poster. "Will You Have a Part in Victory?" Washington, DC: National War Garden Commission, 1918.

"Food Work Praised. Garden Movement Here Sets Nation an Example." *Los Angeles Times*, July 29, 1917.

"Fourteen Thousand Children Working War Gardens Here." *Los Angeles Times*, March 24, 1918.

Francis, John H. United States, Bureau of Education. Bulletin. *United States School Garden Army*. Washington, DC, 1919.

Fraser, Helen. *Women and War Work*. New York: G. Arnold Shaw, 1918.

Garden Army and the State Councils of Defense. *School and Society* 8 (October 19, 1918): 464–65.

"Garden Army Is Directed by Francis. Former Head of Los Angeles City Schools Is Mobilizing Boys and Girls to Increase Food Supply." *Los Angeles Times*, May 26, 1918.

"Garden for White House: Diana Hopkins Will Grow Vegetables in Flower Bed." *New York Times*, March 23, 1943.

"Garden for White House: First Lady Says Victory Planting Depends on Soil Test." *New York Times*, March 2, 1943.

Garden Schools. *The Independent* (September 26, 1901): 2312–14.

"Garden Teacher Going to Hollister." *Los Angeles Times*, May 17, 1918.

"Gardeners a National Asset." *New York Times*, November 10, 1918.

"Gardens in Europe." *Current Literature* 28 (May 1900): 188–90.

"Gardens in Sweden." *Scientific American Supplement* 52 (September 21, 1905).

Geer, Cornelia T. "Out of the Kitchen—Into the Fields." *House Beautiful* XLIV, September 1918.

Geithman, Harriet. "Chronicles of Woodcock Farm." *Overland* LXXXI, June 1918.

Geyer, O.R. "Gardens Add $100,000,000 to Nation's Wealth." *Garden Magazine* 26, no. 3 (1917): 93–95.

Gibson, Charles Dana. Print. "Help! The Woman's Land Army of America, New Jersey Division, State House, Trenton." New York: Greenwich Lithograph, 1918.

Gowans, Ethel. *Home Gardening for City Children of the Fifth, Sixth, and Seventh Grades, United States School Garden Army*. Washington, DC: Government Printing Office, Department of the Interior, Bureau of Education, 1919.

Greene, Louise M. *Among School Gardens*. New York: Russell Sage Foundation, 1910.

Guenther. "Get Behind the Girl He Left Behind Him, Join the Land Army." New York: American Lithographic, 1918. War poster commissioned by the New York State Land Army Membership Committee. Held in the Library of Congress (POS-World War I-US. No. 156).

Harmon, Dudley. "Is the Woman Needed on the Farm? What the United States Government Has to Say About Farm Work for Women This Summer." *Ladies Home Journal* 35 (May 1918): 105–06.

"Help for the Farmer." Advisory Council of the Woman's Land Army of America, New York, January 1918.

"Help the Woman's Land Army." War poster commissioned by the New Jersey Division of the Woman's Land Army Membership Committee, 1918. Held at the Museum of Ventura County.

Hubbard, Henry V., and Theodora Kimball Hubbard. *An Introduction to the Study of Landscape Design*. New York: Macmillan, 1917.

———, and ———. *Landscape Architecture: A Comprehensive Classification Scheme for Books, Plans, Photographs, Notes and Other Collected Material, with Combined Alphabetic Topic Index and List of Subject Headings*. Cambridge: Harvard University Press, 1920.

Hunt and Davis. "A Study of Farm Labor in California," Circular No. 193. Published by the California Agricultural Experiment Station, Berkeley, 1918.

Bibliography 237

Ivins, Lester S. "United States School Garden Army in 1919." *Industrial Arts Magazine* 7, December 1918.

Jewell, James Ralph. *Agricultural Education Including Nature Study and School Gardens*, Bulletin 2, Department of the Interior, Bureau of Education. Washington, DC: GPO, 1907.

Kleeck, Mary V. Report of the Women in Industry Service of the Department of Labor to June 30, 1919. Washington, DC, 1919.

Knapp, Seaman. "The cities of the United States have moved forward by leaps and bounds." *Proceedings of the Ninth Conference for Education in the South*. Chattanooga: Executive Committee of the Conference, 1906.

Knight, George H. "Plea for School Gardens." *Harper's Bazaar* (January 5, 1901): 44–8.

"Laborers on Small Farms at $2 a Day: Land Army of America Starts Its Spring Drive, Centralizing the Work Which Proved Successful Last Year Under the Direction of Scattered Agencies." *New York Times*, February 3, 1918.

Landman, M.V. "Women Farmers." *Cornell Countryman* (Spring 1918).

Lebing, Wendy. "The Pennsylvania School of Horticulture for Women." No date. Wyck Library Collection, Ambler file.

"Living Civics." *The New York Times*, August 10, 1920.

Lovewell, Reinette. "A Woman Who Needs You." *A City Woman Who Found Her War Job on a Farm*. Washington, DC: U.S. Department of Agriculture, 1918.

Mane, Julia C. "Horticulture as Vocation for Women Offers Escape from Devitalizing Occupations." *The Washington Herald*, September 22, 1912.

Merrill, Jenny B. "Children's Gardens." *National Education Association, Proceedings and Addresses* 37. National Education Association, 1898: 598–602.

Miller, Louise Klein. *Children's Gardens for School and Home, a Manual of Cooperative Learning*. New York: D. Appleton, 1904.

"Million Boys and Girls Wanted for the United States School Garden Army." *Touchstone* 3 (June 1918): 203–07.

Montessori, Maria. *The Absorbent Mind*. New York: Dell, 1912.

Murphy, Ethel A. *The Victory of the Gardens: A Pageant in Four Episodes, for the United States School Garden Army*. Washington, DC: Government Printing Office, 1918.

National Board of the Woman's Land Army of America with the Endorsement of the United States Employment Service. *Handbook of Standards, 1919*. Washington, DC, 1919.

Office of the President: Ernest O. Holland, Washington State University Libraries, Manuscripts, Archive and Special Collections, Records, 1890–1950.

Ogilvie, Ida H. "Agriculture, Labor and Woman." *Columbia University Quarterly* (October 1918): 293–300.

_____. "The Spirit of the Land Army." *The Farmerette* (1918): 1.

_____. *Women's Agricultural Camp, Bedford, New York, First Annual Report*. New York, National Agricultural Library. U.S. Department of Agriculture, 1917.

_____. *Women's Agricultural Camp, Bedford, New York, Second Annual Report*. New York, National Agricultural Library. U.S. Department of Agriculture, 1918.

Ousley, Clarence. *Women on the Farm. Address Before Woman's Committee, Council of National Defense*. New York, National Agricultural Library. U.S. Department of Agriculture, 1918.

Pack, Charles Lathrop. *The War Garden Victorious: Its Wartime Need and Its Economic Value in Peace*. Philadelphia: J. B. Lippincott, 1919.

Paus, Herbert Andrew. Print. "The Woman's Land Army of America— Training School at University of Virginia—Apply Woman's Land Army, U.S. Employment Service, Richmond, Va." Woman's Land Army of America, 1918.

Penfield, Edward. "The Girl on the Land Serves the Nation's Need Apply Y.W.C.A. Land Service Committee." New York: United States Printing & Lithograph, 1918. Held by the Library of Congress (POS—US.P452, no. 106 [C size]).

_____. Poster. "Join the United States School Garden Army. Enlist Now." Washington, DC: Bureau of Education, Department of the Interior, 1919.

Pennsylvania School of Horticulture for Women. Fundraising brochure. Ambler Campus History Folder, 1910, Ambler Archives, Temple University, Ambler, Pennsylvania.

_____. Spring Course, 1913.

"Placing Women on the Land: Experiments in the Eastern United States." *Women's National Farm and Garden Association Monthly Bulletin* 4 (February 1918): 1–6.

Proceedings of the National Defense Gardening Conference. Washington, DC: United States Department of Agriculture, 1941.

"Prolific on Small Lot, Jack's Wonderful Beanstalk Has Little, If Anything, on Harriet's." *Los Angeles Times*. September 2, 1917.

"Raised 'Em Myself in My U.S. School Garden." Washington, DC: Bureau of Education, Department of the Interior, 1918.

Report of the Commissioner of Education. Washington, DC: United States Department of the Interior, Bureau of Education, 1918: 183–186.

Report of the Women's Committee. Los Angeles, CA: California State Council of Defense, June 1, 1917–January 1, 1919 (1920): 77.

Riis, Jacob. "What Ails Our Boys." *The Craftsman* (1911).

Roosevelt, Theodore. *Theodore Roosevelt: An Autobiography*. New York: Macmillan, 1913.

Ruutz-Rees, Caroline. "The Mobilization of American Women." *Yale Review* 7 (July 1918): 801–18.

"Same Wage Scale for Women and Men." *New York Times*, December 16, 1917.

"She Makes Idle Acres Feed the Hungry." *Literary Digest* 8 (8 March 1919): 98–102.

Sherman, Mary B. "Gardening for Every Child, Through the Aid of the United States School Garden Army." *Touchstone* 4 (March 1919): 491–495.

Spender, Hugh. "Lady Warwick's Farming College for Girls." unknown journal (August 1905): 548–553.

Stebbins, C.A. *A Manual of School-Supervised Gardening for the Western States, United States School Garden Army*. Washington, DC: Department of the Interior, Bureau of Education, 1920.

_____. *The Principles of Agriculture through the School and the Home Garden*. New York: Macmillan, 1913.

_____. *School-Supervised Gardening for the Western States*. Department of the Interior, Bureau of Education, United States School Garden Army. Washington: Government Printing Office, 1918, 38–39.

Stevens, Helen K. "City Girl as Farm Worker—Her Own Story. How Nursing the Crops in Westchester County Furnished a Healthful Vacation, a Little Fun Now and Then, Much Valuable Experience, and Cash Wages." *New York Times*, February 24, 1918.

Taylor, Frederick W. *The Principles of Scientific Management*, New York: Harper and Brothers, 1911.

"Teach Agriculture." *Los Angeles Times*, May 4, 1919.

"Tell How to Plant War Gardens." *Los Angeles Times*, March 17, 1918.

"Tells Woman's Part in Winning the War: Council of Defense Report Reviews Their Contribution to the National Strength, Predicts Future Benefits, Wider Vision of Sex's Interests and Place in Government Expected to Result." *New York Times*, August 1, 1920.

"Uncle Sam Likes Farmerettes." *New York Times*, February 16, 1919, p. 48.

Waheenee and Gilbert L. Wilson. *Buffalo Bird Woman's Garden: Agriculture of the Hidatsa Indians*. 1917. St Paul: Minnesota Historical Society, 1987.

War Advertising Council. "Sound the Call to Farms! Helps for Recruiting Local Emergency Farm Workers in 1945." Washington, DC, 1945. 22 pieces in folder.

"War Gardens Town's Hobby. Armies of School Children Plant for Prizes." *Los Angeles Times*, April 29, 1917.

Weed, C.M., and P. Emerson. *School Garden Book*. New York: Charles Scribner's Sons, 1909.

Western College for Women. *Report of War Activities*. Miami, OH: Western College for Women, 1919.

_____. *Report on the War Service Training Courses of the Western College for Women*, Miami, OH: Western College for Women, 1918.

_____. *War Work at Western College for Women*, Miami, OH: Western College for Women, 1918.

Wetmore, Edith. *Report of the Newport Farmerette Unit, 1918, First Annual Report*. National Agricultural Library, U.S. Department of Agriculture, 1918.

White, Martha E.D. "Women's Clubs and Patriotism." *The Nation* 105 (October 4, 1917): 367–68.

Wilkinson, Marguerite. "My Experiences as a Farmerette." *Independent* XCV, September 14, 1918.

"Wilson Cheers Children. Hopes Every School will Have a Regiment in the Garden Army." *New York Times*, March 10, 1918.

"Win the War, Mass Nation's Forces to Grow More Food. School Children are to Play a Huge Part in the Campaign for Greater Production." *Los Angeles Times*, May 31, 1918.

Woman's Land Army of America, Inc. *What the Farmers Say About the Work of the Woman's Land Army of America in 1918*. New York, 1918.

"Women Aid War: Britain's 300,000 Land Army Felicitates American Workers." *New York Times*, August 12, 1918.

"Women Disband Land Army: Organization Which Furnished War Helpers to Farmers Is Dissolved." *New York Times*, February 3, 1925.

"Women in Agriculture." *The Women's Industrial News* (London), 20 July 1916.

Women on the Land, 1918, Advisory Council of the Woman's Land Army of America. New York, 1918.

"Women Unite for Service: Committee of Defense Council to Open Quarters at Astor." *New York Times*, May 27, 1917.

Women's National Land Service Corps, Annual Report October 1, 1916, to September 30, 1917. London, England.
"Work for Local Woman to Organize School Children in Western Cities." *Los Angeles Times*, September 19, 1918.
"The World's News in Today's Times Covering the Globe." *Los Angeles Times*, July 7, 1917.
Wyatt, Edith Franklin. "The Illinois Training Farm for Women." *Kimball's Dairy Farmer*, 15 April 1918.
"Young Gardeners—United States School Garden Army." *Review of Reviews* 58 (December 1918): 651-52.
Y.W.C.A. Land Service Division. Print. "Y.W.C.A. Land Service Committee Poster." *The Girl on the Land Serves the Nation's Need*. 1918. Library of Congress, American Memory, Prints and Photographs Division, LC-USZC4-10322.

Secondary Sources

Anderson, Clifford. "The Metamorphosis of American Agrarian Idealism in the 1920s and 1930s." *Agricultural History* 35 (October 1961): 182-188.
Anderson, S.A. "Core Indicators of Nutritional State for Difficult to Sample Populations." *The Journal of Nutrition* 120 (1990): 1557S-1600S.
Archibald, Robert R. *A Place to Remember: Using History to Build Community*. Walnut Creek, CA: Altamira Press, 1999.
Aubitz, Shawn, and Gail F. Stern. "Ethnic Images in World War I Posters.". *Journal of American Culture* 9, no. 4 (1986).
Autobee, Robert. "Every Child in a Garden: George H. Maxwell and the American Homecroft Society." *Prologue: The Journal of the National Archives* 28, no. 3 (1996): 194-206.
Baker, Paula. "The Domestication of Politics: Women and American Political Society, 1780-1920." *American Historical Review* 89 (1984): 620-47.
Barrett, Judy, and David Smith Litoff. "'To the Rescue of the Crops': The Woman's Land Army During World War II." *Prologue: The Journal of the National Archives* 25, no. 4 (1993).
Barry, John M. *The Great Influenza: The Epic Story of the Deadliest Plague in History*. New York: Viking, 2004.
Beeman, Cynthia. "Farmerettes: The Woman's Land Army of World War I." *Agricultural History* 67, no. 2 (1993).
Belasco, Warren J. *Appetite for Change: How the Counterculture Took on the Food Industry*. New York: Pantheon, 1989.
Belasco, Warren, and Philip Scranton, eds. *Food Nations: Selling Taste in Consumer Societies*. New York: Routledge, 2002.
Bender, Thomas. *Toward an Urban Vision: Ideas and Institutions in Nineteenth Century America*. New York: Oxford University Press, 1980.
Bentley, Amy. *Eating for Victory: Food Rationing and the Politics of Domesticity*. Urbana: University of Illinois Press, 1998.
Berry, Wendell. *The Unsettling of America: Culture and Agriculture*. Berkeley: University of California Press, 1996.
Bird, William, Henry R. Rubenstein, and William L. Bird. *Design for Victory: World War II Posters on the American Homefront*. Princeton: Princeton Architectural Press, 1998.
Blair, Karen J. *The Clubwoman as Feminist: True Womanhood Redefined, 1868-1914*. New York: Holmes and Meier, 1980.
Bodnar, John. *Remaking America: Public Memory, Commemoration and Patriotism in the 20th Century*. Princeton: Princeton University Press, 1992.
Borkan, Gary. *World War I Posters*. Atglen, PA: Schiffer, 2002.
Breen, William J. "Foundations, Statistics, and State-Building: Leonard P. Ayres, the Russell Sage Foundation, and U.S. Government Statistics in the First World War." *Business History Review* 68, no. 4 (1994): 451-482.
———. "Mobilization and Cooperation Federalism: The Connecticut State Council of Defense, 1917-1919." *Historian* 42, no. 1 (1979): 58-84.
———. "The Mobilization of Skilled Labor in World War I : 'Voluntarism,' the U.S. Public Service Reserve, and the Department of Labor, 1917-1918." *Labor History* 32, no. 2 (1991): 253-272.
———. *Uncle Sam at Home: Civilian Mobilization, Wartime Federalism, and the Council of National Defense, 1917-1919*. Westport, CT: Greenwood Press, 1984.
Buder, Stanley. *Visionaries and Planners: The Garden City Movement and the Modern Community*. New York: Oxford University Press, 1990.
Campbell, D'Ann. *Women at War in America: Private Lives in a Patriotic Era*. Cambridge: Harvard University Press, 1984.
Capozzola, Christopher. "The Only Badge Needed Is Your Patriotic Fervor: Vigilance, Coercion, and the Law in World War I Americanization." *Journal of American History* 88, no. 4 (2002): 1354-1382.
Carpenter, Stephanie. *On the Farm Front: The Women's Land Army in World War II*. DeKalb: Northern Illinois University Press, 2002.

———. "Regular Farm Girl: the Women's Land Army in World War II." *Agricultural History* 71, no. 2 (1997): 163–185.

Clemens, Elisabeth S. "Securing Political Returns to Social Capital: Women's Associations in the United States, 1880s–1920s." *Journal of Interdisciplinary History* 29 (1999): 613–38.

Cohen, Lizabeth. *A Consumers' Republic: The Politics of Mass Consumption in Postwar America*. New York: Alfred A. Knopf, 2003.

Coleman-Jensen, Alisha, Mark Nord, Margaret Andrews, and Steven Carlson. *Statistical Supplement to Household Food Security in the United States in 2010*, AP-057, U.S. Department of Agriculture, Economic Research Service, September 2011.

Cott, Nancy. *The Bonds of Womanhood: "Woman's Sphere" in New England, 1780–1835*. New Haven: Yale University Press, 1977.

Cremin, Lawrence. *The Transformation of the School: Progressivism in American Education, 1870–1957*. New York: Vintage, 1994.

Cronon, William. "A Place for Stories: Nature, History and Narrative." *Journal of American History* 78, no. 4 (1992): 1347–1376.

Cuff, Robert D. "The Dilemmas of Voluntarism: Hoover and the Pork-Packing Agreement of 1917–1919." *Agricultural History* 53, no. 4 (1979): 727–747.

———. "Herbert Hoover, the Ideology of Voluntarism and War Organization During the Great War." *Journal of American History* 642 (1977): 358–372.

———. *The War Industries Board: Business-Government Relations During World War I*. Baltimore: Johns Hopkins University Press, 1973.

Danbom, David B. *Born in the Country: A History of Rural America*. Baltimore: Johns Hopkins University Press, 1995.

———. *The Resisted Revolution: Urban America and the Industrialization of Agriculture, 1900–1930*. Ames: Iowa State University Press, 1979.

———. *"The World of Hope": Progressives and the Search for an Ethical Public Life*. Philadelphia: Temple University Press, 1987.

Darracott, Joseph. *First World War Posters*. London: Imperial War Museum, 1972.

Davis, Benjamin M. *Agricultural Education in the Public Schools*. Bibliolife, 2009.

Davis, O.L. "School Gardens and National Purpose During World War I." *The Journal of the Midwest History of Education Society* 22 (1995): 115–126.

Desmond, Daniel, James Grieshop, and Aarti Subramaniam, "Revisiting Garden-Based Learning in Basic Education." published by the *United Nations Food and Agriculture Organization and the International Institute for Educational Planning* (2004): 25–36.

Dobyns, Winifred S. *California Gardens*. Santa Barbara, CA: Allen A. Knoll Publishers, 1996. Original published in 1931.

Dumenil, Lynn. "American Women and the Great War." *OAH Magazine of History* 17, no. 1 (2002): 35–38.

Effland, Anne B., and Gold, Mary, comps. *Women in Agriculture and Rural Life: An International Bibliography*. Beltsville, MD: National Agricultural Library, U.S. Department of Agriculture, 1998.

Eighmey, Rae K. *Food Will Win the War: Minnesota Crops, Cooks, and Conservation During World War I*. St. Paul: Minnesota Historical Society Press, 2010.

Eisenach, Eldon. *The Lost Promise of Progressivism*. Kansas: University of Kansas Press, 1994.

Ellis. Edward Robb. *Echoes of Distant Thunder: Life in the United States, 1914–1918*. New York: Coward, McCann and Geoghegan, 1975.

Eyle, Alexandra. *Charles Lathrop Pack: Timberman, Forest Conservationist, and Pioneer in Forest Education* (Syracuse: State University of New York, 1992).

Faust, Drew Gilpin. *Mothers of Invention: Women of the Slaveholding South in the American Civil War*. New York: Vintage Books, 1996.

Fink, Deborah. *Agrarian Women: Wives and Mothers in Rural Nebraska, 1880–1940*. Chapel Hill: University of North Carolina Press, 1992.

Finnegan, Margaret Mary. *Selling Suffrage: Consumer Culture and Votes for Women*. New York: Columbia University Press, 1999.

Fitzgerald, Deborah. *Every Farm a Factory: The Industrial Ideal in American Agriculture*. New Haven: Yale University Press, 2003.

Frieberger, William. "War Prosperity and Hunger: New York Food Riots of 1917." *Labor History* 25, no. 2 (1984): 217–239.

Fussell, Paul. *The Great War and Modern Memory*. New York: Oxford University Press, 1975.

Garcia, Matt. *A World of Its Own: Race, Labor, and Citrus in the Making of Greater Los Angeles, 1900–1970*. Chapel Hill: University of North Carolina Press, 2001.

Gill, Valerie. "Catharine Beecher and Charlotte Perkins Gilman: Architects of Female Power." *Journal of American Culture* 21, no. 2 (1998): 17–24.

Glassberg, David. "Public History and the Study of Memory." *The Public Historian* 18, no. 2 (1996): 7–23.

———. *Sense of History: The Place of the Past in*

American Life. Amherst: University of Massachusetts Press, 2001.

Graham, Patricia Albjerg. *Community and Class in American Education, 1865–1918*. New York: Twayne Publishers, 1997.

Gregory, Adrian. *The Silence of Memory: Armistice Day, 1919–1946*. Providence, RI: Berg, 1994.

Gruber, Carol S. *Mars and Minerva: World War I and the Uses of Higher Learning in America*. Baton Rouge: Louisiana State University Press, 1975.

Gullace, Nicoletta. *The Blood of Our Sons: Men, Women, and the Renegotiation of British Citizenship During the Great War*. New York: Palgrave Macmillian, 2002.

Harris, Neil. "American Poster Collecting: A Fitful History." *American Art* 12, no. 1 (1998): 10–39.

Hawes, Joseph M. *Children Between the Wars: American Childhood, 1920–1940*. New York: Twayne Publishers, 1997.

Hawley, Ellis W. *The Great War and the Search for a Modern Order*. Prospects Heights, Il: Waveland Press, 1992.

Hayden, Dolores. *Building Suburbia: Green Fields and Urban Growth, 1820–2000*. New York: Vintage, 2004.

———. *The Grand Domestic Revolution: A History of Feminist Design for American Homes, Neighborhoods, and Cities*. Cambridge, MA: MIT Press, 1981.

———. The Power of Place: Urban Landscapes as Public History. Cambridge, MA: MIT Press, 1997.

Hayden-Smith, Rose. "Sisters of the Soil: The Work of the Woman's Land Army in World War I." Santa Barbara: University of California Santa Barbara, 2004.

———. "Soldiers of the Soil": The Work of the United States School Garden Army in World War I." *Applied Environmental Education and Communication*, 6, no. 1 (2007).

Hays, Samuel P. "Conservation and the Gospel of Efficiency; the Progressive Conservation Movement, 1890–1920." Cambridge: Harvard University Press, 1959.

Helphand, Kenneth I. *Defiant Gardens: Making Gardens in Wartime*. San Antonio: Trinity University Press, 2006.

Hise, Greg. *Magnetic Los Angeles: Planning the Twentieth-Century Metropolis*. Baltimore: Johns Hopkins University Press, 1999.

Hise, Greg, and William Deverell. *Eden by Design: The 1930 Omsted-Bartholomew Plan for the Los Angeles Region*. Berkeley and Los Angeles: University of California Press, 2000.

Hochschild, Adam. *To End All Wars: A Story of Loyalty and Rebellion, 1914–1918*. Boston: Houghton Mifflin Harcourt, 2011.

Holli, Melvin G., *Reform in Detroit: Hazen S. Pingree and Urban Politics*. New York: Oxford University Press, 1969.

Hollingsworth, Buckner. *Theodosia Burr Shepherd, 1845–1906: Her Garden was Her Delight*. New York: Macmillan, 1962.

Holt, Marilyn Irvin. "From Better Babies to 4-H: A Look at Rural America, 1900–1930." *Prologue: The Journal of the National Archives* 24, no. 3 (1992): 244–255.

———. *Linoleum, Better Babies and the Modern Farm Woman, 1890–1930*. Albuquerque: University of New Mexico Press, 1995.

Huffman, W.E., and R.E. Evenson, *Science for Agriculture*. Ames: Iowa State University Press, 1993.

Hurt, R. Douglas. *American Agriculture: A Brief History*. Ames: Iowa State University Press, 1994.

———. *American Farms: Exploring Their History*. Malabar, FL: Kreiger, 1996.

Hynes, H. Patricia, *A Patch of Eden: America's Inner City Gardens*. White River Junction, VT: Chelsea Green, 1996.

Illick, Joseph E. *American Childhoods*. Philadelphia: University of Pennsylvania Press, 2002.

Jellison, Katherine. *Entitled to Power: Farm Women and Technology, 1913–1963*. Chapel Hill: University of North Carolina Press, 1993.

———. "Farm Women in American History: A Note on Sources Available in Washington, D.C." *Annals of Iowa* 51, no. 2 (1991): 168–77.

Jensen, Joan M. "Crossing Ethnic Barriers in the Southwest: Women's Agricultural Extension Education, 1914–1940." *Agricultural History* 60, no. 2 (1986): 169–181.

Jensen, Joan M. *Loosening the Bonds: Mid-Atlantic Farm Women 1750–1850*. New Haven: Yale University Press, 1986.

———. *With These Hands: Women Working on the Land*. Old Westbury, NY: The Feminist Press, 1981.

Jones, Calvin, and Rachel Rosenfeld. "Facing the Bureaucracy: Farm Women and the U.S. Department of Agriculture Programs, Policies." *American Farm Women: Findings from a National Survey*. National Opinion Research Center. 1981.

Jones, Lu Ann. "God Giveth the Increase": Lurline Stokes Murray's Narrative of Farming and Faith." *Southern Cultures* (2002): 106–121.

———. *Mama Learned Us to Work: Farm Women in the New South*. Chapel Hill: University of North Carolina Press, 2002.

Jones, Lu Ann, and Osterud, Nancy Grey. "Breaking New Ground: Oral History and Agricultural History." *Journal of American History* 76 (1989): 551–564.

Kennedy, David M. *Freedom from Fear: The American People in Depression and War, 1929–1945*. New York: Oxford University Press, 1999.

———. *Over Here: The First World War and American Society*. Oxford: Oxford University Press, 1980.

Kennedy, Kathleen. "Declaring War on War: Gender and the American Socialist Attack on Militarism, 1914–1918." *Journal of Women's History* 7 (1995): 27–51.

Kliebard, Herbert M. *Forging the American Curriculum: Essays in Curriculum History and Theory*. Boston: Routledge, 1992.

———. *Schooled to Work: Vocationalism and the American Curriculum, 1876–1946*. New York: Teacher's College Press, 1999.

———. *The Struggle for the American Curriculum, 1893–1958*. Boston: Routledge, 1986.

Labrie, J.M. "The Depiction of Women's Field Work in Rural Fiction." *Agricultural History* 67, no. 2 (1993): 119–133.

Laird, Pamela Walker. *Advertising Progress: American Business and the Rise of Consumer Marketing*. Baltimore: Johns Hopkins University Press, 1998.

Laswell, Harold, Daniel Lerner, and Hans Speier. *Propaganda and Communication in World History*. Honolulu: University Press of Hawaii, 1979.

Lawson, Laura. *City Bountiful: A Century of Community Gardening in America*. Berkeley: University of California Press, 2005.

Leach, William R. *Land of Desire: Merchants, Power and the Rise of a New American Culture*. New York: Vintage Books, 1994.

Lears, Jackson. *Fables of Abundance: A Cultural History of Advertising in America*. New York: BasicBooks, 1994.

Leuchtenburg, William E., *The Perils of Prosperity 1914–1932*. Chicago: University of Chicago Press, 1958.

Levenstein, Harvey. *Paradox of Plenty: A Social History of Eating in Modern America*. Berkeley: University of California Press, 1993.

———. *Revolution at the Table: The Transformation of the American Diet*. Berkeley: University of California Press, 2003.

Libby, Valencia. "Jane Haines' Vision: The Pennsylvania School of Horticulture for Women." *New England Garden History Society Journal* 10 (2002): 44–52.

Lindenmeyer, Kriste. *"A Right to Childhood": The U.S. Children's Bureau and Child Welfare, 1912–1946*. Urbana: University of Illinois Press, 1997.

Linenthal, Edward. "Struggling with History and Memory." *The Journal of American History* 82, no. 3 (1995): 1094–1101.

Litoff, Judy Barrett, and David Smith. "To the Rescue of the Crops": The Woman's Land Army During World War II." *Prologue: The Journal of the National Archives* 25, no. 4 (1993): 31–53.

Lopez, Steve. "In the Weeds of Bureaucratic Insanity There Sprouts a Small Reprieve." *Los Angeles Times*, August 20, 2011.

Lutz, Ralph Haswell. "Studies of World War Propaganda, 1914–33." *The Journal of Modern History* 5, no. 4 (1933): 496–516.

Machor, James L. *Pastoral Cities: Urban Ideals and the Symbolic Landscape of America*. Madison: The University of Wisconsin Press, 1987.

MacLeod, David I. *The Age of the Child: Children in America, 1890–1920*. London: Twayne Publishers, 1998.

———. *Building Character in the American Boy: The Boy Scouts, YMCA, and Their Forerunners, 1870–1920*. Madison: University of Wisconsin Press, 1983.

Maniace, Len. "Edith Diehl." *The Journal News*, June 16, 2003.

Marchand, Roland. *Advertising the American Dream: Making Way for Modernity, 1920–1940*. Berkeley: University of California Press, 1985.

Martelet, Penny. "The Women's Land Army, World War I" in *Clio Was a Woman: Studies in the History of American Women*, 136–146. Washington, DC: Howard University Press, 1980.

Marti, Donald B. *Women of the Grange: Mutuality and Sisterhood in Rural America, 1866–1920*. Westport, CT: Greenwood Press, 1991.

Matthaei, Julie A. *An Economic History of Women in America: Women's Work, the Sexual Division of Labor, and the Development of Capitalism*. New York: Shocken Books, 1981.

Maurer, Donna, and Jeffrey Sobal, eds., *Eating Agendas: Food and Nutrition as Social Problems*. New York: Adline de Gruyter, 1995.

McLoughlin, Virginia. "Hoeing Smokes": A New Milford Connecticut Unit of the Woman's Land Army, World War I." *Connecticut History* 40 (2001): 32–60.

McPeck, Eleanor M. "Beatrix Jones Farrand" in *Pioneers of American Landscape Design*, Charles A. Birnbaum, Robin Karson, eds. New York: McGraw-Hill, 2000.

McPhail, Elizabeth. *Kate Sessions: Pioneer Horti-*

culturist, San Diego, CA: San Diego Historical Society, 1976.
Meyer, G.J., *A World Undone: The Story of the Great War, 1914–1918*. New York: Bantam Dell, 2006.
Milkman, Ruth. *Gender at Work: The Dynamics of Job Segregation by Sex During World War II*. Urbana: University of Illinois Press, 1987.
Mintz, Sidney. *Tasting Food, Tasting Freedom: Excursions into Eating, Culture, and the Past*. Boston: Beacon Press, 1996.
Mintz, Steven. *Huck's Raft: A History of American Childhood*. Cambridge: Belknap Press/Harvard University Press, 2004.
Mintz, Steven, and Susan Kellog, eds. *Domestic Revolutions: A Social History of American Family Life*. New York: The Free Press, 1988.
Mitchell, Reid. *The Vacant Chair*. New York: Oxford University Press, 1995.
Mock, James R., and Cedric Larson. *Words That Won the War: The Story of the Committee on Public Information*. Princeton: Princeton University Press, 1939.
Mosher, Anne E. *Capital's Utopia: Vandergrift, Pennsylvania, 1855–1916*. Baltimore: Johns Hopkins University Press, 2004.
Mullendore, William C. *History of the United States Food Administration, 1917–1919*. Stanford, CA: Stanford University Press, 1941.
Mumford, Kevin J. *Interzones: Black/White Sex Districts in Chicago and New York in the Early Twentieth Century*. New York: Columbia University Press, 1985.
Muncy, Robyn. *Creating a Female Dominion in American Reform 1890–1935*. New York: Oxford University Press, 1991.
Murolo, Priscilla. *The Common Ground of Womanhood: Class, Gender, and Working Girls Clubs, 1884–1928*. Urbana: University of Illinois Press, 1997.
Nasaw, David. *Children of the City: At Work and at Play*. Garden City, NY: Anchor Press, 1985.
____. *Schooled to Order*. New York: Oxford University Press, 1981.
Nash, George H. *The Life of Herbert Hoover: Master of Emergencies, 1917–1918*. New York: W.W. Norton, 1996.
Neth, Mary. *Preserving the Family Farm: Women, Community and the Foundations of Agribusiness in the Midwest, 1900–1940*. Baltimore: Johns Hopkins University Press, 1998.
Nolan, Martha A. *A Chronicle: The History of Woman's National Farm and Garden Association*. Fremont, OH: Lesher Printers, 1985.
Nord, David Paul. "The Uses of Memory: An Introduction." *The Journal of American History* 85, no. 2 (1998): 409–410.

Norwood, Margaret. *Made from this Earth: American Women and Nature*. Chapel Hill: University of North Carolina Press, 1993.
Opie, John. *Two Hundred Years of American Farmland Policy*. Lincoln: University of Nebraska Press, 1994.
Osterud, Nancy Grey. *Bonds of Community: The Lives of Farm Women in the Nineteenth Century*. Ithaca: Cornell University Press, 1991.
Ouditt, Sharon. *Fighting Forces, Writing Women: Identity and Ideology in the First World War*. London: Routledge, 1994.
Parker, Alison M. *Purifying America: Women, Cultural Reform, and Pro-Censorship Activism, 1873–1933*. Urbana: University of Illinois Press, 1997.
Parson, Kermit C., and David Schuyler. *From Garden City to Green City: The Legacy of Ebenezer Howard*. Baltimore: Johns Hopkins University Press, 2002.
Peters, Scott J. "Every Farmer Should Be Awakened: Liberty Hyde Bailey's Vision of Agricultural Extension Work." *Agricultural History* 80, no. 2 (2006): 190–219.
Peters, Scott J., and Paul A. Morgan. "The Country Life Commission: Reconsidering a Milestone in American Agricultural History." *Agricultural History* 78 (2004): 289–316.
Pirog, Rich, and Andrew Benjamin. "Computing Food Miles for Local Versus Conventional Produce Sales to Iowa Institutions: Checking the Food Odometer." Leopold Center for Sustainable Agriculture. Iowa State University, 2003.
Pope, Daniel. "The Advertising Industry and World War I." *Public Historian* 2, no. 3 (1980): 4–25.
Potter, David M. *People of Plenty: Economic Abundance and the American Character*. Chicago: University of Chicago Press, 1954.
Proctor, Tammy. *Civilians in a World at War, 1914–1918*. New York: New York University Press, 2010.
Quinn, Patrick J. *The Conning of America: The Great War and American Popular Literature*. Amsterdam-Atlanta, GA: Rodopi, 2001.
Rasmussen, Wayne D. *Taking the University to the People: Seventy-Five Years of Cooperative Extension*. Ames: Iowa State University, 1989.
____, ed. *Agriculture in the United States: A Documentary History*. New York: Random House, 1975.
Reese, William J. *Power and the Promise of School Reform: Grassroots Movements During the Progressive Era*. Boston: Routledge and Kegan Paul, 1986.
Reiser, Andrew. *The Chautauqua Moment: Protestants, Progressives, and the Culture of Modern*

Liberalism. New York: Columbia University Press, 2003.
Rochester. Stuart I. *American Liberal Disillusionment in the Wake of World War I.* University Park: Pennsylvania State University Press, 1977.
Rodgers, Daniel T. *Atlantic Crossings: Social Politics in a Progressive Age.* Cambridge: Belknap Press/Harvard University Press, 1998.
———. "In Search of Progressivism." *Reviews in American History* 10 (1982): 113–32.
Roeder, George. *The Censored War: American Visual Experience During World War II.* New Haven: Yale University Press, 1993.
Rossiter, Margaret W. *Women Scientists in America: Struggles and Strategies to 1940.* Baltimore: Johns Hopkins University Press, 1982.
Rosenzweig, Roy, and David Thelen. *The Presence of the Past: Popular Uses of History in American Life.* New York: Columbia University Press, 1998.
Rutherford, Janice Williams. *Selling Mrs. Consumer: Christine Frederick and the Rise of Household Efficiency.* Athens: University of Georgia Press, 2003.
Rybczynski, Witold. *A Clearing in the Distance: Frederick Law Olmsted and America in the 19th Century.* New York: Simon and Schuster, 1999.
Sachs, Carolyn E. *Gendered Fields: Rural Women, Agriculture, and Environment.* New York: Westview Press, 1996.
Sackman, Douglas. "'Nature's Workshop': The Work Environment and Workers' Bodies in California's Citrus Industry, 1900–1940." *Environmental History* 5, no. 1 (2000): 27–53.
Saloutos, Theodore. *The American Farmer and the New Deal.* Ames: Iowa State University Press, 1982.
Sanders, Elizabeth. *Roots of Reform: Farmers, Workers, and the American State, 1877–1917.* Chicago: University of Chicago Press, 1999.
Schapsmeier, Edward L., and Frederick H. Schapsmeier. *Henry A. Wallace of Iowa: The Agrarian Years, 1910–1940.* Ames: Iowa State University Press, 1968.
Schenker, Heath. "Feminist Interventions in the Histories of Landscape Architecture." *Landscape Journal* 13, no. 2 (1994): 107–112.
———. "The Garden as Women's Place: Celia Thaxter and Mariana Van Rensselaer, co-authored with Suzanne Ouellette. *Gendered Landscapes*, the Pennsylvania State University Center for Studies in Landscape History, 2000.
Schmitt, Peter. *Back to Nature: The Arcadian Myth in Urban America.* New York: Oxford University Press, 1969.

Schudson, Michael. *Advertising, the Uneasy Persuasion.* New York: Basic Books, 1984.
Schwartz, J. "American Women and Their Gardens: A Study in Health, Happiness, and Power, 1600–1900." *Journal Home and Consumer Horticulture* 1, no. 2/3 (1994): 9–31.
Scott, Roy C. *The Reluctant Farmer: The Rise of Agricultural Extension to 1914.* Urbana: University of Illinois Press, 1971.
Sharpless, Rebecca. *Fertile Ground, Narrow Choices: Women on Cotton Farms of the Texas Blackland Prairie, 1900–1940.* Chapel Hill: University of North Carolina Press, 1999.
Shideler, James H. *Farm Crisis, 1919–1923.* Berkeley: University of California Press, 1957.
Simo, Melanie. *Forest and Garden: Traces of Wildness in a Modernizing Land, 1897–1949.* Charlottesville: University of Virginia Press, 2003.
Skocpol, Theda. *Protecting Soldiers and Mothers: The Political Origins of Social Policy in the United States.* Cambridge: Belknap Press of Harvard University Press, 1992.
Skocpol, Theda, and Morris P. Fiorna, eds. *Civic Engagement in American Democracy.* Washington: Brookings Institution Press, 1999.
Skowronek, Stephen. *Building a New American State: The Expansion of National Administrative Capacities, 1877–1920.* New York: Cambridge University Press, 1982.
Slosson. Preston Williams. *The Great Crusade and After, 1914–1928.* New York: Macmillan, 1930.
Smith, Jane. *The Garden of Invention: Luther Burbank and the Business of Breeding Plants.* New York: Penguin Books, 2009.
Smith, L.M. "The California School of Gardening for Women: a History." *California Horticultural Society Journal* 31, no. 4 (1970): 132–134.
Stage, Sarah, and Virginia Bramble Vincente. *Rethinking Home Economics: Women and the History of a Profession.* Ithaca: Cornell University Press, 1997.
Stebbins, Leybard G. *Ernest Brown Babcock: A Bibliographic Memoir.* Washington, DC: National Academy of the Sciences, 1958.
Steinson. Barbara J. *American Women's Activism in World War I.* New York: Garland Publishing, 1982.
Stevenson, Elizabeth. *Park Maker: A Life of Frederick Law Olmsted.* Edison, NJ: Transaction Publishers, 1999.
Studebaker, John W. "The American School System and War Gardens." United States Department of Agriculture, National Defense Gardening Conference Proceedings. Washington, DC, 1941.

Subramaniam, Aarti. "Garden-Based Learning in Basic Education: An Historical Review." *University of California 4-H Center for Youth Development Monograph Series*, 2002.

Sullivan, Joan L. "The Pursuit of Legitimacy: Home Economists and the Hoover Apron of World War I." *Dress* 26 (1999): 31–46.

Tashjian, Dickran. "Art, World War II, and the Home Front." *American Literary History* 8, no. 4 (1996): 715–727.

"Theodora Kimball Hubbard: A Biographical Minute." *Landscape Architecture* 26, no. 2 (1936): 53–55.

Thompson. John A. *Reformers and War: American Progressive Publicists and the First World War*. New York: Cambridge University Press, 1987.

Tice, Patricia. *Gardening in America 1830–1910*. Rochester, NY: The Strong Museum, 1984.

Trask, David F., ed. *World War I at Home: Readings on American Life, 1914–1920*. New York: John Wiley & Sons, 1970.

True, Alfred Charles. *A History of Agricultural Experimentation in the United States, 1607–1925*. Washington, DC: U.S. Department of Agriculture, 1937.

Turner, Frederick Jackson. *The Frontier in American History*. 1920.

Turner, Victor, ed. *Celebrations: Studies in Festivity and Ritual*. Washington, DC: Smithsonian Institution Press, 1982.

Walker, Melissa. *All We Knew Was to Farm: Rural Women in the Upcountry South, 1919–1941*. Baltimore: Johns Hopkins University Press, 2000.

Walsh, Jeffrey. *American War Literature 1914 to Vietnam*. New York: St. Martin's Press, 1982.

Ward, Barbara McLean, ed., *Produce and Conserve, Share and Play Square: The Grocer and the Consumer on the Home-Front Battlefield During World War II*. Portsmouth, NH: Strawberry Banke Museum, 1994.

Warner, Sam Bass. *To Dwell Is to Garden: A History of Boston's Community Gardens*. Holliston, MA: Northeastern, 1987.

Weiss, Elaine F. *Fruits of Victory: The Woman's Land Army of America in the Great War*. Washington, DC: Potomac Books, 2009.

Wiebe, Robert. *The Search for Order, 1877–1920*. New York: Hill and Wang, 1967.

———. *Self-Rule: A Cultural History of American Democracy*. Chicago: University of Chicago Press, 1996.

Williams, Robert C. *Fordson, Farmall, and Poppin' Johnny: A History of the Farm Tractor and Its Impact on America*. Urbana: University of Illinois Press, 1987.

Winker, Allan M. *The Politics of Propaganda: The Office of War Information, 1942–1945*. New Haven: Yale University Press, 1978.

Wynn, Neil A. *World War I and American Society*. New York: Holmes & Meier, 1986.

Zelizer, Viviana A. *Pricing the Priceless Child: The Changing Social Value of Children*. New York: Basic Books, 1985.

DISSERTATIONS AND UNPUBLISHED WORKS

Bassett, Thomas. "Vacant Lot Cultivation: Community Gardening in America, 1893–1978." Dissertation, University of California, Davis, 1979.

Capozzola, Christopher Joseph. "Uncle Sam Wants You: Political Obligations in World War I America." Dissertation, Columbia University, 2002.

Fraser, Bruce. "Yankees at War: Social Mobilization on the Connecticut Homefront, 1917–1918." Dissertation, Columbia University, 1984.

Jensen. Kimberly S. "Minerva on the Field of Mars: American Women, Citizenship, and Military Service in the First World War." Dissertation, University of Iowa, 1992.

Kipp, Catherine Gabriel. "Women on the Land: The Woman's Land Army, Northern California Division, 1918–1920." MA thesis, California State University. 1960.

McBane, Margo. "The Role of Women in Determining the California Farm Labor Structure: A Case Study of the Women's Land Army of America During World War 1." MA thesis, University of California, Davis. 1983.

INTERNET SOURCES

Child Nutrition Services. "Healthy Schools Project." http://www.venturausd.org/childnutrition/healthyschoolsproject.htm (accessed February 20, 2010).

Environmental Protection Agency. Ag 101. http://www.epa.gov/oecaagct/ag101/demographics.html.

Five Colleges. "Student Affairs: Women in Agriculture, 1917–1958." http://clio.fivecolleges.edu/umass/30-24student-affairs/women-in-agriculture.

The Food Project. http://thefoodproject.org (accessed February 28, 2010).

Hayden-Smith, Rose. "Soldiers of the Soil: A Historical Review of the United States School Garden Army." University of California, 4-H Center for Youth Development, Monograph Series,

2006. http://ceventura.ucdavis.edu/files/255 58.pdf.

Libby, Valencia. "Cultivating Mind, Body & Spirit: Educating the New Woman for Careers in Landscape Architecture." Beatrix Farrand Conference: A Century of Women: Evaluating Gender in Landscape Architecture. http://www.ced.berkeley.edu/events/farrand/Abstracts/Libby.html (accessed March 2, 2004).

Michigan State University Libraries. School Gardening in the Early 1900s. http://libguides.lib.msu.edu/content.php?pid=46894&sid=446374.

Subramaniam, Aarti. "Garden-Based Learning in Basic Education: A Historical Review." University of California, 4-H Youth Development Center, Monograph Series, 2002. http://cyd.ucdavis.edu/publications/pubs/focus/pdf/MO02V8N1.pdf (accessed February 5, 2009).

Temple University. www.temple.edu/flowershow/ (accessed March 1, 2005).

http://www.theodoreroosevelt.org/life/quotes.htm (accessed February 15, 2009).

University of California. Digital History Archives. http://sunsite.berkeley.edu/uchistory/archives_exhibits/collections/president_reports.html (accessed January 28, 2010).

University of California, Sustainable Agriculture Research and Education Program. What is a sustainable community food system? http://www.sarep.ucdavis.edu/cdpp/cfsdefinition.htm.

University of Wisconsin. "Bibliography on Women and Agriculture." www.library.wisc.edu/libraries/WomensStudies/core/cragri.htm.

Woodhams, Marca L. Smithsonian Institution Libraries, Horticultural Branch. "History of the American Seed and Nursery Industry and Their Trade Catalogs." Online bibliography, 1999. http://www.sil.si.edu/SILPublications/seeds/bibseednur.html.

Index

abundance 23, 35, 55, 90, 116, 119, 183
The Abundant Table 201–202
Adams, Emma 123, 151
Adams Act 135
advertising 37, 54, 84, 91, 99, 106–107
agricultural education 7, 47, 49, 70, 72, 74–75, 77–79, 82–83, 85–87, 91, 93–94, 157, 178, 186; *see also* Babcock, Ernest; Bailey, Liberty Hyde; experiential learning; nature study; scientific agriculture; Stebbins, Cyril
Agricultural Experiment Station 46, 71–73, 75–80, 82, 85–86, 118, 125, 135, 189, 192; *see also* University of California–Berkeley
agricultural production/productivity 1, 17, 20, 29, 38, 40, 42, 44, 47, 51, 65, 71, 80, 159, 181, 194, 196, 199; *see also* scientific agriculture
Agriculture Marketing Act 183
Allen, Will 44
Ambler 121–141, 145, 147, 157, 201–203; *see also* Land Army; Pennsylvania School of Horticulture for Women; Philadelphia; Woman's Land Army of America
American Civil War 18, 26, 40
American Core Historical Literature of Agriculture 48
American Farm Bureau 181; *see also* Farm Bureau
American Forestry Association 46–47
Among School Gardens 20; *see also* Greene, Louise
Anathoth Community Garden 211
Arab Spring 43
Archibald, Robert 104
architecture 105–106
Armistice 26, 70–71, 87, 96, 157, 176–177, 195
Art Noveau 107
Assembly Bill 1535 (California) 86, 199
Australia 16
Austria 18, 75, 125

Babcock, Ernest 74–75, 78–79, 86, 150
Bahnson, Fred 211

Bailey, Liberty Hyde 42, 71, 73, 79–80, 82, 86, 127, 135, 189; *see also* Cornell; Country Life Movement; experiential learning; nature study
Baker, Newton 48
Barnard College 161–162, 164, 167, 177, 180; *see also* Bedford Camp; Olgivie, Ida
Barney, Maginel Wright 63, 69, 109–111
Bartram, John 122, 203
Bedford Camp 147, 161, 164, 167, 177; *see also* Barnard College; Olgivie, Ida
Beecher, Catharine E. 134
Belgium 59, 76, 125
La Belle Epoque 106
Bentley, Amy 67–68
Berlin Airlift 35, 120
biofuels 20–21
Blatch, Harriet Stanton 164
Boas, Franz 103
Boer War 18
Boston Common 15, 45, 51, 66
botanical 122, 157, 203
Boy Scouts 51
Bradley, Edith 129
Brazil 21
Britain *see* United Kingdom
Brown (university) 162
Bryn Mawr 123, 125–126, 136, 147
Burbank, Luther 49, 83, 186
Bureau of Education 11, 21, 38, 48, 71, 77, 79, 81, 83, 85, 87–89, 90–91, 93, 95, 98, 146, 149, 181, 185–186; *see also* Department of Education
Bureau of the Interior 83, 85; *see also* Department of the Interior
Bush-Brown, Louise 139–140
Butterfield, Kenyon 80, 139

California 1, 27, 53, 72–74, 79, 85–86, 95, 98, 123, 132, 149–151, 157, 162, 164–166, 168–171, 173, 175, 177, 179, 182, 190, 194–195, 198–202

247

California Junior Gardener Program 74, 86; *see also* Babcock, Ernest; Stebbins, Cyril; University of California
Canada 15, 81, 145, 147, 159
Capozzola, Christopher 145
census 29, 181
Census of Agriculture 29, 201–202; *see also* United States Department of Agriculture
Cheret, Jules 106–107
childhood nutrition 25, 74, 183, 188, 207; *see also* FoodCorps; National School Lunch Act/Program
Children's Gardens for School and Home, a Manual of Cooperative Learning see Miller, Louise Klein
China 17, 21, 72, 139, 190
Circular No. 46 73–75, 79; *see also* University of California, Berkeley Agricultural Experiment Station
Circular 193 150–151 *See also* University of California, Berkeley Agricultural Experiment Station
citizenship: obligations 35–36, 42, 88–90, 94, 98, 208; women and 9, 111, 154–156, 163, 177–178
civic virtue 13, 42, 67, 153
Civil Rights Movement 105, 205
Civilian Conservation Corps 183
class (social) 19, 22, 42, 52, 57, 64, 67, 80, 82, 90, 125, 129, 132–134, 141, 145–146, 148, 152, 154, 158, 161–163, 168, 174–175
Claxton, P.P. 50, 81, 83, 89, 93, 146, 185
Clean Air Act 190
Clean Water Act 190
Cold War 35, 188–189
Columbia, depictions of 32, 64, 98, 108–110, 114, 116–119, 193
Comenius, John Amos 75
Committee for Public Information 99, 155; *see also* Creel, George; propaganda
common core curriculum 12, 211
community-based food security 7, 21, 44, 51, 93, 203, 205, 208; *see also* food access; food insecurity; food security; local and regional food systems; urban agriculture
Confino, Alon 101
consumer culture 19, 91
Consumer Product Safety Act 190
Cooperative Extension Service 40, 70, 78, 87, 94–95, 135, 148–149, 151, 166, 181, 199, 206
Cornell 79–80, 131–132, 134–136; *see also* Bailey, Liberty Hyde; experiential learning; nature study
Cott, Nancy 133
Country Life Commission/Movement 42, 80, 82, 125, 131–132, 139, 158; *see also* Bailey, Liberty Hyde; Butterfield, Kenyon; Roosevelt, Theodore
Creel, George 37, 99; *see also* Committee for Public Information; propaganda

Cultivate Iowa 23, 204–205; *see also* Tagtow, Angie

D–Town Farm 44; *see also* Detroit
Danbom, David 36, 40
DDT 190
DeBusschere, Paul 201–202
Densmore, John 148
Department of Defense 11; *see also* War Department
Department of Education 11–12, 86, 200; *see also* Bureau of Education
Department of the Interior 83, 85; *see also* Bureau of the Interior
Detroit, Michigan 40, 43–45; *see also* D–Town Farm; Hantz Farm; Panic of 1893; Pingree, Hazen; Potato Patch; vacant lot cultivation
Dewey, John 6–8, 71, 75
DeWitt Clinton Farm School 76, 78
diabetes 23, 208
Diehl, Mary "Edith" 132, 138; *see also* Ambler; Pennsylvania School of Horticulture for Women
Dock, Mira Lloyd 134, 137, 203
Doiron, Roger 198, 200
domestic sphere/separate spheres 77, 85–87, 116, 121, 126–128, 132–136, 141, 144–146, 155, 157, 173–174, 177, 180
draft 17, 55, 57–58, 67, 111, 144, 150, 152, 173, 175, 179, 183, 188; *see also* Selective Service
Drake University 29

Easements 50, 52, 66
Eastin, Delaine 86
Economic Research Service 21; *see also* United States Department of Agriculture
The Edible Schoolyard 200, 208; *see also* Waters, Alice
Edson, Katherine 151, 164, 168
Egypt 20
Eighmey, Rae 54
Eisenach, Eldon 166
Eisenhower, Dwight 24, 188–189
Eliot, Charles 50, 88
Ellis, Curt 200; *see also* Food Corps
Endangered Species Act 190
England *see* United Kingdom
Environmental Protection Act/Agency 55, 190
Episcopal Diocese of Los Angeles 201–202
Eschmeyer, Debra 200; *see also* Food Corps
exceptionalism 36, 98, 119–120
experiential learning 68, 71, 79, 86; *see also* agricultural education; Bailey, Liberty Hyde; Cornell; 4-H; nature study; school gardens
expositions 157

Farm Bill 30, 207, 210
Farm Bureau 148–149, 151, 181; *see also* American Farm Bureau
farm crisis 182–183

Farm Security Administration 183
farm-to-school 198, 200, 202, 206–209
The Farmerette 159, 161, 170–171, 177, 179
Farmerettes 123, 141, 143–144, 153, 156, 169, 173–176, 178
farmers markets 28–29, 76, 106, 123, 201, 209
Federal Farm Loan Act 181
Federal Highway Act 181
Federal Security Administration 196
Federal Water Pollution Act 190
Feeding America 23
Fernow, Bernhard 131
FFA 96–97
Finland 119, 123
Finley, Ron 21, 103
Fisher, Andy 205
Flagg, James Montgomery 64, 107–108
food access 21–23, 27–28, 38, 44, 55, 60, 105, 157, 171, 188, 202–205, 207–209; *see also* community-based food security; food insecurity; food security; hunger
Food Administration 6, 37–39, 56–58, 60, 62, 64–65, 67, 70, 100, 111, 115–116, 204, 209; *see also* Hoover, Herbert
Food and Nutrition Service 190
food conservation 47, 53–56, 60, 63, 67–68, 95, 100, 116, 171, 206, 209
Food Corps 71, 93, 200, 211; *see also* Ellis, Curt; Eschmeyer, Debra
Food for Freedom 185–186; *see also* Victory Gardens; World War II
Food for Peace 189
Food, Inc. 2
food insecurity 22, 187, 203; *see also* community-based food security; food access; food security; hunger
food mile 13, 29
food preservation 40, 48, 71, 116, 146–147, 157, 206
The Food Project 76
food riots 20, 40, 60
food safety 190, 208
food security 7, 20–22, 30, 44, 51, 93, 184, 189, 203, 205–206
food systems 2, 5, 9, 12, 14, 21, 23–24, 27–30, 93, 101, 105, 122, 187, 189, 198–199, 203–205, 207, 210; *see also* sustainable food systems
food waste 55, 116, 206
Food Waste Challenge 55
forestry 46–49, 83, 131, 134, 137–138
4-H 7, 71, 75, 81, 86–87, 96–97, 182, 197, 200; *see also* Bailey, Liberty Hyde; Cornell; experiential learning; nature study; United States Department of Agriculture
France 17, 19, 34, 43, 50, 76, 88, 106
Francis, John 83, 89, 93–95
Fraser, Helen 147, 160–164; *see also* Vassar
Froebel, Friedrich 75
Future Homemakers of America 97

The Garden 103
garden cities 26, 36, 41, 45, 76, 135, 193; movement 45–46, 86, 140
Garden Club of America 124, 130, 135, 147
Gardening Schools for Women 121, 123, 125, 128, 154; *see also* Ambler; Haines, Jane Bowne; Pennsylvania School of Horticulture for Women
George Putnam School 76
GI 35, 189
Gilded Age 76, 106, 136
Gingrich, Newt 43
Girl Scouts 64
Glassberg, David 102, 104, 117
good food, good food movement 23, 27–29, 127, 184, 196, 198, 211
Grasset, Eugene 107
Great Britain *see* United Kingdom
Great Depression 29, 182, 196
Great Society 25, 207
Greene, Louise 76–77; *see also Among School Gardens*
Growing Power 44

Haines, Jane Bowne 121–126, 128–130, 136–137, 139, 141–142, 147, 154, 202–203; *see also* Ambler; Pennsylvania School of Horticulture for Women
Halbwachs, Maurice 101–102
Hamilton, Alissa 11
Hantz Farm 44; *see also* Detroit
Harvard 50, 88, 131, 139
Hatch Act 38, 78, 85, 135
Hayden, Delores 105
Hemmelgarn, Melinda 210
home economics 70, 92, 131, 134, 157, 167, 182, 185–186; *see also* food conservation and preservation
Homeland Security 21, 85
Hoover, Herbert 5–6, 38, 59–61, 64, 89, 100, 209; *see also* Food Administration
Hoover, Lou Henry 64
Houston, David 146, 172
hunger 19–23, 26, 55, 76, 91, 183, 187–188, 202–208; *see also* community-based food security; food insecurity; food security

immigrants 8, 43, 46, 50, 53, 66, 85, 91, 100, 154
India 16–21

Jacobs, Leonebel 116, 193
Jefferson, Thomas 24, 41–42, 127, 158
Jewell, James Ralph 79, 81
Johns, Harriet 72
Johnson, Lady Bird 25
Johnson, Lyndon 25, 182, 207
Junior Master Gardener Program 86, 197; *see also* 4-H; Texas A&M

Kennedy, Jackie 25

Kent Horticultural College 129
King, Louisa Yeoman 124, 203
kitchen gardens 26, 42, 67, 133
Kivirist, Lisa 201

labor children 68, 82, 91, 94, 113, 119; farmers as percentage of labor force 181–183, 188, 190, 201–202; forced 18; organization 152, 165–167, 175; production 27; shortages 18–19, 22, 38, 147, 19, 151, 156, 159–160, 168; women 35, 123, 125, 127, 132, 138, 141, 142–145, 148, 153–155, 157, 160, 164, 169–170, 172–174, 176–178, 180; unrest 72, 150, 168, 171, 179
Ladies' Home Journal 116, 172
Lady Liberty 64, 116
Lady Warwick College 129
land: and abundance 23, 35, 55, 90, 116, 119, 183; and liberty 23, 26, 37, 42, 52, 63, 143
land army 2, 5, 17, 52, 82, 121, 129, 135, 137–138, 141, 143–145, 147–149, 154, 156, 159–162, 164–165, 170, 172–173, 175–177, 180; *see also* Ambler; Pennsylvania School of Horticulture for Women; Woman's Land Army
Landscape art and architecture 9, 45, 65, 91, 100–101, 104, 109–110, 128–133, 137–140, 146, 180, 197
landscape, symbolic 64, 100–101, 104, 109, 128
Lappe, Anna 2
Lawson, Laura 53, 76
Lee, Elizabeth Leighton 130, 137–139, 203; *see also* Ambler; Pennsylvania School of Horticulture for Women
Leopold Institute 29
Liberty Gardens 5, 9, 12, 35–36, 51, 53, 67, 82, 101–102, 105, 134; *see also* Victory Gardens, War Gardens
Lincoln, Abraham 24–25, 52, 79, 197, 199, 216
Lippincott, C.H. 132–133
local and regional food systems 28–30; *see also* urban agriculture
Loines, Hilda 146–147
Los Angeles Times 72, 194
Low, Judith 123; *see also* Lowthorpe School
Lowthorpe School 123, 132; *see also* Low, Judith
Lubin, David 52

Marshall Plan 35, 120
Master Gardeners 70, 86, 103, 195, 197, 211
McNutt, Paul 184
Mead, Elwood 195–196; *see also* University of California
military gardens 15, 32, 66, 118
Miller, Louise Klein 77; *see also* *Children's Gardens for School and Home, a Manual of Cooperative Learning*
Mills College 162, 168
Montessori, Maria 75, 86

moon farming 84
Morrill Land Grant Act 25, 78–80, 135, 199; *see also* Lincoln, Abraham
Morris, Julie 201–202
MOSES 201
Muncy, Robyn 131, 155
Murphy, Ethel Allen 117–118; *see also* *The Victory of the Gardens: A Pageant in Four Episodes*
Mwendo, Jenga 205

National Defense Gardening Conference 184–185, 196
National Gardening Association 14
National Institute for Food and Agriculture 1
National Interstate and Defense Highways Act 24–25, 181, 188–189
National Mall 15, 25, 197–198
National Nutrition Conference for Defense 184
National School Lunch Program 24, 187, 207; *see also* childhood nutrition; Food Corps; nutrition
national security (food and) 2, 7, 12–13, 21, 23, 26, 29, 36, 80, 82, 89, 93, 96, 111, 116, 183, 188–189, 192, 207–208
National War Garden Commission 5, 88, 107–108, 110, 192
nature study 46, 71–73, 75–80, 82, 85–86, 118, 125, 135, 189, 192; *see also* agricultural education; Bailey, Liberty Hyde; experiential learning; school gardens
New Deal 24, 60, 209
New Nutrition 57
New York 28, 45, 49, 51–52, 64–66, 76, 78–79, 88, 99, 123, 131, 129, 143, 146–147, 149, 163–164, 166–167, 171, 173–177
New York Times 28, 65, 88, 143, 174, 176
New Zealand 16, 139
9/11 7
Nora, Pierre 100–102
nutrition 21–22, 25, 55, 57, 63, 73–74, 86, 183–185, 188–190, 192, 196, 198, 200, 203–204, 208, 210; *see also* childhood nutrition
nutritional defense 196; *see also* childhood nutrition; nutrition

Obama, Barack 1, 207
Obama, Michelle 2, 25, 198
obesity 2, 19, 26, 198, 207–208; *see also* childhood nutrition; diabetes; nutrition
Occupy 43
Ogilvie, Ida 154, 164–165, 167, 177, 180; *see also* Barnard College; Bedford Camp
oil 20, 190
Oldenburg, Roy 104
Olmsted, Frederick Law 46, 88, 131
Ousley, Clarence 171–174

Pack, Charles Lathrop 32, 35–36, 46–50, 52, 64, 66, 68–71, 83, 116, 147, 159

pageants 37, 116–119
Paine, Thomas 2
Panama-California Exposition 157
Panic of 1893 40, 43, 53; *see also* Detroit, Michigan; Pingree, Hazen; Potato Patch; vacant lot cultivation
Patel, Raj 2, 210
Pearl Harbor 70, 184, 196; *see also* World War II
Penfield, Edward 111–112
Pennsylvania School of Horticulture for Women 9, 47, 145; *see also* Ambler; land army; Philadelphia; Woman's Land Army of America
People's Garden 197–198; *see also* United States Department of Agriculture
Perkins, Frances 183
Pestalozzi, Johann 75
Philadelphia 125, 130, 132, 138, 141, 201, 203; *see also* Ambler; Pennsylvania School of Horticulture for Women
Pinchot, Gifford 49, 131, 137
Pingree, Hazen 40, 43–45; *see also* Detroit, Michigan; Panic of 1893; vacant lot cultivation
Pollan, Michael 2
Portland, Oregon 28–29, 72, 206, 209
posters 9, 37, 48, 54, 61, 63, 64, 68, 70, 96, 169; *see also* propaganda
Potato Patch 40, 43–45, 66, 195
Prince Charles 2
Prior, Jessie R. 132–133
professionalization/specialization 9, 46, 70, 90, 124, 131, 133, 135, 137, 140, 157
Progressive Era (including leadership, characteristics, impulses) 8, 24, 29, 36–38, 41, 46, 50, 54, 65–66, 71–73, 76, 78, 80, 82, 85, 88–92, 94–95, 97, 102, 124, 127–128, 130, 132, 134–136, 140, 144, 149, 151–152, 154, 147–160, 168, 180–181, 189, 195
Propaganda 15, 36, 169; *see also* Committee for Public Information; Creel, George
public policy (food systems) 3, 8, 12, 24, 27, 65, 80, 86, 192, 197, 206–207
Pure Food and Drug Act 24

Recommended Daily Allowances 184
Red Cross 65
reform (including gardens as site of) 8–9, 13, 19, 36–37, 45–46, 50, 63, 77–78, 80, 82, 85, 88, 91–92, 94, 121–122, 124, 128, 133–135, 138, 140, 142, 151, 155, 157–158, 164, 168, 179, 192, 194–195, 201
Reinhardt, Aurelia 168
Relf, P.D. 127
Richmond, California 195
Riis, Jacob 77
Risdale, P.S. 47, 52, 116
Robinson, Mary 203
Rogers, Zilda 73; *see also* University of California–Berkeley Agricultural Experiment Station; Ventura Unified School District
Roosevelt, Eleanor 25
Roosevelt, Franklin Delano 24, 183
Roosevelt, Theodore 24, 48, 80, 152–154, 164
Rosseau, Jacques 75
Rossiter, Margaret 131
Roudebush, Marc 100–101
Rural Electrification Administration 183
Russia 16–18, 38, 72, 76, 119, 189

San Francisco 51, 99, 116, 143, 188, 194–195
school gardens 65, 72–77, 79, 81–82, 85, 100, 128, 135, 140, 150, 186, 200, 207
scientific agriculture 40, 78, 84, 92, 96, 124, 133, 158, 195, 199
Second Morrill Act 135
Selective Service 183
Shepherd, Theodosia Burr 132–133
Sheridan, John 115
Shipman, Ellen 133
Silent Spring 189
slacker 15, 53, 64, 100
Smith-Lever 40, 60, 78, 80, 135–136, 181
Snieckus, Bob 197
social technologies 54, 66, 105, 209
State Councils of Defense 67, 149, 165
Stebbins, Cyril 74–75, 78, 83, 86, 150
Stevens, Helen Kennedy 143–144, 176
Stevenson, Adlai 21
Stowe, Harriet Beecher 134
Studebaker, John 185–186
suffrage 15, 121, 138, 155, 157, 162–164, 168, 171; *see also* woman's rights
sustainable food systems (definitions, conditions) 27–31
Sweden 43, 119
synthesis (rural-urban) 8, 46, 71, 83, 90, 96, 130, 158

Tagtow, Angie 204–205; *see also* Cultivate Iowa
Temple University 121, 140, 203; *see also* Ambler; Pennsylvania School of Horticulture for Women
Texas A&M 86, 200; *see also* 4-H; Junior Master Gardener Program
third places 104–106
The Touchstone 65–66, 101
tractors 40, 182
Truman, Harry 24, 187, 207

Uncle Sam 37, 65, 72, 109–110, 114–115
United Kingdom (includes Britain, England and Great Britain) 17, 19, 20, 103, 119, 128, 129, 145, 147, 159–163, 167, 176, 187, 190
United Nations 20, 187, 190
United States Department of Agriculture: Beginning Farmers and Ranchers 199; census 29, 201–202; Cooperative Extension Service 40, 87, 95, 136, 151, 173, 182; Economic

Research Service 43; food conservation and preservation 57, 60, 62, 100; food programs 25, 187–188; Food Waste Challenge 55; Foreign Agriculture Service 120; 4-H 75, 86–87, 96–97; history 24, 90, 114, 116, 131, 181, 183, 189; hunger 21–22, 203; Know Your Farmer, Know Your Food 30, 41; Master Gardeners 70, 86, 103, 195, 197, 211; National War Garden Commission 47, 70, 81, 86; NIFA 1; People's Garden 197; policy recommendations 190, 209; statistics 28–30, 202; Wallace, Henry 183–184; women 148, 151, 173; World War II 183–185, 196
United States Grain Standard Act 181
United States School Garden Army (USSGA) 5, 7, 11–12, 48, 50, 53, 111–112, 144, 146, 150, 153, 159, 181, 185–187, 192, 195, 197, 199, 201
United States State Department: Feed the Future 203
University of California: agricultural settlement colonies at Durham and Delhi 195; Agriculture and Natural Resources (ANR) 27, 199, 202; Berkeley Agriculture Experiment Station 73–74, 79, 86; Berkeley Food Institute 199; Davis 199; farm at Davisville 150; Junior Gardener Program 74, 86; Riverside 150; Santa Cruz 199; UC work in World War I 149–151, 162, 169; *see also* Babcock, Ernest; Circular No. 46; Mead; Elwood; Stebbins, Cyril
urban agriculture 14, 30, 42–44, 93, 141–142, 194–195, 199, 202, 205–206; *see also* local and regional food systems

vacant lot cultivation 41, 45–46, 52–53, 66, 103, 192
Vacaville, California 179
Van Rensselaer, Marianna Griswold 131
Van Rensselaer, Martha 134, 136
Vassar 147, 160, 162, 164; *see also* Fraser, Helen
Ventura Unified School District 73–74, 200, 202; *see also* Rogers, Zilda
Victory Gardens 5, 9, 12, 14, 19, 25, 32, 35–37, 51, 53, 65, 67, 71, 82, 101–102, 105, 134, 152–153, 186–187, 192, 196–197, 206, 213; *see also* Liberty Gardens; war gardens
Victory Grower 11, 211
The Victory of the Gardens: A Pageant in Four Episodes 117–120; *see also* Murphy, Ethel Allen
Vilsack, Tom 25, 187; *see also* United States Department of Agriculture
voluntarism/voluntary 5, 43, 47, 60, 63, 70–71, 96, 145, 149, 152, 154, 156, 159–160, 168, 171, 194
Vrooman, Carl 50, 83

Wallace, Henry Aagard 24, 183–184, 211
Wallace, Henry Cantwell 183
War Department 7, 11, 12
The War Garden Victorious 48, 69
War Gardens 32, 36–37, 51, 62–63, 67–72, 99, 110; *see also* Liberty Gardens; Victory Gardens
Warburg, Aby 102–103
Ward, Artemas 107
Washington, George 24
Waters, Alice 200; *see also* The Edible Schoolyard
White, Emma V. 133
White House 2, 14, 25, 28, 48
White House Garden 2, 15, 26, 195, 198
Whitely, Cora Call 148
Whitten Building 25, 197
Wickard, Claude 184–185
Wiebe, Robert 91, 117
Wilson, Edith 25
Wilson, M.L. 184
Wilson, Woodrow 11–12, 19, 32, 48, 50, 85, 89, 93, 99, 146, 149
W.K. Kellogg Foundation 27; Food and Society Policy Fellows 198, 200, 205
Woman's Land Army of America 121, 126–127, 129, 134, 136, 138–139, 141, 195, 201; *see also* Ambler; land army; Pennsylvania School of Horticulture for Women
Woman's National Farm and Garden Association (WNFGA) 67, 124, 137–138, 145–147, 149, 159, 165, 177, 180
woman's rights 8, 124, 126, 133, 134, 137, 140–141, 147, 154, 158, 160, 165; *see also* suffrage
women's club 50, 65–66, 71, 124, 130, 135–136, 145, 147, 149, 151
workplace gardens 12, 14, 36, 51–53, 65–66, 196
World War II 5, 16, 25, 35, 67–68, 70–71, 103, 120, 162, 180, 184–187, 192, 195, 196–198, 206, 208, 211
Wyck 122, 141–142, 202–203

Yale 49–50, 131, 168
YWCA/Y.W.C.A. 147, 165

www.ingramcontent.com/pod-product-compliance
Lightning Source LLC
Chambersburg PA
CBHW051216300426
44116CB00006B/596